FREEDOM OF ENVIRONMENTAL INFORMATION

FREEDOM OF ENVIRONMENTAL INFORMATION

Aspirations and Practice

Sean WHITTAKER
Colin T. REID
Jonathan MENDEL

Cambridge – Antwerp – Chicago

Intersentia Ltd
8 Wellington Mews
Wellington Street | Cambridge
CB1 1HW | United Kingdom
Tel: +44 1223 736 170
Email: mail@intersentia.co.uk
www.intersentia.com | www.intersentia.co.uk

Distribution for the UK and
Rest of the World (incl. Eastern Europe)
NBN International
1 Deltic Avenue, Rooksley
Milton Keynes MK13 8LD
United Kingdom
Tel: +44 1752 202 301 | Fax: +44 1752 202 331
Email: orders@nbninternational.com

Distribution for Europe
Lefebvre Sarrut Belgium NV
Hoogstraat 139/6
1000 Brussels
Belgium
Tel: +32 (0)800 39 067
Email: mail@intersentia.be

Distribution for the USA and Canada
Independent Publishers Group
Order Department
814 North Franklin Street
Chicago, IL 60610
USA
Tel: +1 800 888 4741 (toll free) | Fax: +1 312 337 5985
Email: orders@ipgbook.com

Freedom of Environmental Information. Aspirations and Practice
© Sean Whittaker, Colin T. Reid and Jonathan Mendel 2023

The authors have asserted the right under the Copyright, Designs and Patents Act 1988, to be identified as authors of this work.

No part of this book may be reproduced, stored in a retrieval system, or transmitted, in any form, or by any means, without prior written permission from Intersentia, or as expressly permitted by law or under the terms agreed with the appropriate reprographic rights organisation. Enquiries concerning reproduction which may not be covered by the above should be addressed to Intersentia at the address above.

Artwork on cover: Peter King - Autumn Valley, oil on canvas 40 x 40 cm

ISBN 978-1-83970-285-3
D/2023/7849/11
NUR 823

British Library Cataloguing in Publication Data. A catalogue record for this book is available from the British Library.

PREFACE

In recent decades, the introduction of a right of public access to environmental information has been acclaimed as a major achievement in improving environmental governance across the world and it is frequently asserted that this right "will improve environmental protection".[1] Yet remarkably little work has been undertaken to examine how the right is being used in practice and whether it is in fact making a difference. This book will provide some answers to those vital questions, building on empirical work in Scotland to identify lessons that are of general application. It offers insights into the workings of the processes for accessing environmental information – who is using them, what information is being sought and for what purposes? – and into whether what is happening in practice lives up to the aspirations that underpin the introduction of the right. The findings reveal a significant mismatch between aspirations and practice that requires consideration of what is currently being achieved and how the position might be improved.

The research behind this book was carried out at the University of Dundee and was supported by a grant from the Economic and Social Research Council (ref. ES/P010067/1), running from January 2018 to June 2020. The investigators who submitted the proposal, Professor Colin Reid in Law and Dr Jonathan Mendel in Geography, were joined by Dr Sean Whittaker as a research assistant until he was appointed Lecturer in Law in late 2019. For the final months of the funded project, this research assistant post was filled by Dr Petya Dragneva who – despite the disruptions caused by the COVID-19 pandemic – was able to do excellent work in preparing interview material for archiving, working on interview transcripts, and other parts of the project. A project website was established and is available at: https://sites.dundee.ac.uk/envinfo.

The project was assisted by an Advisory Board, and we are most grateful for their support and their helpful comments and suggestions

---

[1] Council Directive 90/313/EEC of 7 June 1990 on the freedom of access to information on the environment [1990] OJ L158/56, recital 8.

Preface

as the work progressed, especially in relation to the publications that were produced:

- Rhoda Davidson – Scottish Natural Heritage (NatureScot).
- Carole Ewart – Campaign for Freedom of Information in Scotland.
- Professor Elizabeth Fisher – University of Oxford.
- Daren Fitzhenry – Scottish Information Commissioner.
- Alison Mackinnon – Scottish Environment Protection Agency.
- Bridget Marshall – Scottish Environment Protection Agency.
- Professor Áine Ryall – University College Cork.

We also wish to thank the many people who enabled the project to succeed by generously participating in our surveys and interviews. Participants were engaged with environmental information in many ways, as occasional or regular users in a personal or professional capacity and as staff employed in handling environmental information and requests for access. Further assistance was provided by staff of Scottish Natural Heritage (now NatureScot) and the Scottish Environment Protection Agency, whose role as holders of large quantities of environmental information gives them particular insights into the topic. We are also deeply indebted to the support and assistance provide by the Office of the Scottish Information Commissioner and the Commissioner, Daren Fitzhenry. Their interest, support and the data they were able to provide were of great value; indeed, without the data routinely collected and published by them, it would not be possible to gain a clear picture of this area. We benefited greatly from the requests for environmental information that have been made public by mySociety's WhatDoTheyKnow project and are grateful to them for helping to publicise our project. Many other people – involved as users of information, within public authorities holding it, or as academics interested in the topic – also provided useful information and insights in informal conversations before, during and after the core period of the project, for example, at the conferences held by the Centre for Freedom of Information at the University of Dundee. We are grateful to them as well, not least for the interest shown in the work which reassured us that there was something of value to be discovered.

The COVID-19 pandemic has affected the emergence of the book in two ways. Fortunately, all of the fieldwork had been completed just before the first lockdown in the spring of 2020, but the restrictions that were introduced ruled out what was planned to be a significant programme of activity disseminating our initial findings and discussing them with various stakeholders. Participation in these events, which we had hoped would be mutually beneficial, proved not to be possible. Second, the demands of converting all of our teaching activity into an online format and making all the adjustments arising from an unexpected, and unexpectedly prolonged, transition to remote learning meant that the authors' attention had to be diverted away from this and other research.

At a personal level, we would like to thank Dr Dragneva for her invaluable help in completing some necessary work at the end of the project, which proved to be difficult due to the COVID-19 pandemic. The encouragement from other colleagues at Dundee and elsewhere, notably the Environmental Law Section of the Society of Legal Scholars, the Royal Geographical Society annual conference, and the Social Futures Research Group and the MSc Social Research seminars at Dundee University, is something that should never pass without saying – so much is missing from online business meetings compared to what emerges from the casual discussions of our work with colleagues and around the edges of meetings and events in person, whether that is new suggestions, supportive interest or puzzlement that prompts a rethink on how to explain things.

Finally, we would also like to thank our respective families, who have provided so much in more ways than we can count.

Dr Sean Whittaker
Professor Colin T. Reid
Dr Jonathan Mendel
University of Dundee, October 2022

CONTENTS

Preface v

Chapter 1. Introduction 1

1. Development of the Right of Access to Environmental Information 3
2. Freedom of Information and the Right to Environmental Information: Similarities and Differences 7
3. Assumptions and Mismatches 10
4. Methodology and Theoretical Framework 14
5. The Structure of the Book 18

Chapter 2. Theoretical and Legal Frameworks 23

1. Actor-Network Theory 25
   1.1. Actors 26
   1.2. Networks 28
   1.3. The Environment as an Actor and Environmental Politics 30
2. The Legal Framework: The Context and Development of the Right of Access to Environmental Information 32
   2.1. The Rio Declaration 33
   2.2. The Aarhus Convention 36
   2.3. Law in the European Union and Scotland 42
3. The Legal Framework: Content 44
   3.1. Definitions and Scope of the Right of Access to Environmental Information 45
   3.2. The Proactive Duty to Provide Information 48
   3.3. Requests for Information 49
   3.4. Exceptions 51
   3.5. Review Procedures 53
4. Conclusion 55

Contents

Chapter 3. Professional Users 57

1. Introduction 57
2. Professional Users and the Right of Access to Environmental
   Information 60
   2.1. Journalists 61
   2.2. Professionals Representing Clients 71
   2.3. Academics and Students 77
   2.4. Non-Governmental Organisations (NGOs). 81
   2.5. Users from within the Public Sector 85
3. Conclusion. 89

Chapter 4. Personal Users 93

1. Introduction 93
2. Motive. 95
   2.1. Personal Users, Motives and the Ideals of the Aarhus
        Convention 97
   2.2. Personal Users, Motives and Trust. 100
3. Seeking Access to Environmental Information 103
   3.1. Proactive Disclosure 104
   3.2. Disclosure on Request 108
4. Advice. 111
   4.1. Advice Provided by Public Authorities. 113
   4.2. Advice Provided by Other Users 115
5. Receiving and Understanding Environmental Information. 118
   5.1. Non-Disclosure of Environmental Information 119
   5.2. Understanding Disclosed Environmental Information 124
6. Conclusion. 127

Chapter 5. Information and Participation 131

1. Introduction 131
2. Theories of Public Participation 134
   2.1. The Rationale Behind Public Participation. 135
   2.2. Public Participation and Arnstein's Ladder
        of Participation. 137
3. Public Participation, Environmental Information and the Aarhus
   Convention. 141

4.	Using Environmental Information: Theory and Practice	145
	4.1. Rationales of Public Participation: Do they Influence Actors' Opinions?	145
	4.1.1. Users	146
	4.1.2. Public Authorities	149
	4.2. Identified Uses of Environmental Information	151
	4.3. Translating Rationales into Reality: Opinions on how Environmental Information is Used	158
5.	Conclusion	166

Chapter 6. Non-Human Actors 169

1. Introduction 169
2. Non-Human Actors Constructed by Humans 171
   2.1. Organisations 172
        2.1.1. Public Authorities 172
        2.1.2. Regulators of the Right to Environmental Information 176
   2.2. Law 181
   2.3. Technologies 186
3. The Environment 191
   3.1. The Environment as an Actor 192
   3.2. Anthropocentrism and the "Environment" in Environmental Information 196
   3.3. Putting the "Environment" in the Right of Access to Environmental Information 200
4. Conclusions 204

Chapter 7. Reflections and Lessons 207

1. Awareness 208
2. Aspirations and Practice 209
3. The Range of Actors 213
4. Lessons 216
   4.1. Refining the Rules 217
   4.2. Is a Distinct Right to Environmental Information Needed? 218
5. Conclusion 221

Index 223

CHAPTER 1

INTRODUCTION

In recent decades, the introduction of a public right to access environmental information has been acclaimed as a major achievement in improving environmental governance across the world and it is frequently asserted that this right "will improve environmental protection".[2] This book critically assesses that assertion, examining the operation and impact of the right in practice to see how far what happens in real life matches the assumptions and aspirations that surround the right. Ultimately this leads to an examination of the value of a distinct right to environmental information operating separately from wider rules on transparency and freedom of information.

There can be no doubt that the environment needs greater protection, not least from the overarching issue of climate change[3] and its negative impacts on both humanity and the wider environment.[4] Such global concerns are also felt locally in relation to climate adaptation and mitigation measures, but local concerns also focus on other issues, such as land use and urban planning matters, waste disposal, water quality, noise and smells. An increased interest in environmental matters has led to a more intense desire from the public for greater transparency and involvement in environmental governance. While this interest is seen in non-environmental issues as well,[5] there has been a particular emphasis on

---

[2] Council Directive 90/313/EEC of 7 June 1990 on the freedom of access to information on the environment [1990] OJ L158/56, recital 8.

[3] As recognised in the Paris Agreement (13 December 2015), in UNFCCC, COP Report No. 21, Addendum, UN Doc. FCCC/CP/2015/10/Add, 1 (13 December 2015).

[4] See, for example, *Climate Change 2022: Impacts, Adaptation and Vulnerability*, the Working Group II contribution to the Sixth Assessment Report of the Intergovernmental Panel on Climate Change, available at <https://www.ipcc.ch/report/sixth-assessment-report-working-group-ii/> accessed 18 April 2022.

[5] R. HAZELL, B. WORTHY and M. GLOVER, *The Impact of the Freedom of Information Act on Central Government in the UK: Does FOI Work?*, Palgrave Macmillan, Basingstoke 2010.

transparency, accountability and public participation in the environmental context due to the increased recognition of our shared vulnerability to, and responsibility for, the Earth's environmental degradation. It is from this recognition that the right of access to environmental information was born.

This right was created as a means of promoting the flow of environmental information between the state and the public, either through proactively publishing environmental information or disclosing environmental information on request. At the core of the right is the assumption that the disclosure of such environmental information will contribute to humanity's efforts to slow, or even reverse, the degradation of the environment. This will be achieved by promoting the transparency and accountability of public bodies in environmental matters, but even more so by encouraging and enabling public participation in decision-making on environmental issues.[6]

These aims of the right of access to environmental information, and the achievement of these aims, are based on a particular understanding of the right and its operation. It is assumed that users of the right are motivated to seek out environmental information for altruistic, environmentally driven reasons, in turn fulfilling the environmental moral duty to "protect and improve the environment for the benefit of present and future generations".[7] Further, it is also assumed that these users are using the right to facilitate participation in environmental decision-making procedures. These assumptions are fundamental to the right, but the research here shows that they are often not matched in practice.

This divergence between theory and practice is created by the way in which the roles of the "key players" who engage with the right of access to environmental information are conceptualised. Users of the right are largely treated as a singular category acting in line with the proclaimed aspirational motives, despite the variety of individuals that exist within society and of the ways in which they behave. The public authorities that are obliged to make information available are also characterised as singular entities, simplifying the complex interactions between and within these authorities. Perhaps more significantly, the impact of non-human "players", such as the environment and normative legal instruments such as

---

[6] Convention on Access to Information, Public Participation in Decision-Making and Access to Justice in Environmental Matters (hereinafter Aarhus Convention), 25 June 1998, UNTS, vol. 2161, p. 447, Preamble.
[7] Ibid., Preamble, para. 7.

the Aarhus Convention, is often excluded or set aside. As a result, the true picture of how the right is operating in practice is obfuscated and distorted by a range of assumptions and misunderstandings. This is not to say that the right does not bring about benefits, but with a better appreciation of how the right is being used and perceived, and why this is the case, there is a chance of greater satisfaction for all those who can benefit from the right being recognised and a greater potential to achieve its environmental benefits.

Through empirical work carried out in Scotland, this book challenges the assumptions and misunderstandings about the actors who engage with the right. The application of Actor-Network Theory allows the book to unpick the assumed categories of users and public authorities to better reflect how these actors are engaging with the right in practice and how the right itself is being utilised. This enables the book to identify that, despite some users engaging with the right for its intended purpose, the vast majority of users deviate from the right's intended use as a means of promoting environmental protection and public participation. Further, the book also identifies that current environmental information regimes underplay the significance of non-human actors. In particular, the significance of the environment itself is often not considered by users, public authorities or the relevant environmental information regimes themselves. Ultimately, these mismatches, and the assumptions which underlie them, act to hinder the achievement of the right's environmental and participative aims. By addressing these issues, it is possible to gain a clearer understanding of how the right is being used and how it is viewed, enabling some assessment of how far it is contributing to the realisation of the environmental benefits that it seeks to achieve.

1. DEVELOPMENT OF THE RIGHT OF ACCESS TO ENVIRONMENTAL INFORMATION

The history behind the right of access to environmental information is one strand in the broader development of information rights.[8] Central to any consideration of information rights is the position of the state in society and the power it wields through its capacity to gather, store and

---

[8] An in-depth exploration of these various information rights can be found in texts such as P. COPPELL, *A Practitioner's Guide to Data Protection, Freedom of Information and Other Information Rights*, 5th edn, Hart Publishing, Oxford 2020.

control access to information. This is not the sole focus of these rights,[9] but the extent to which the state is free to determine when to disclose or withhold information is of significant concern to this area of law.[10] The recognition of the power and responsibilities of the state has driven two strands of what can be broadly defined as "freedom of information laws" across the globe.

The first, and better known, of these strands is the wider movement towards freedom of information that affects all aspects of government. First implemented by Sweden in 1776[11] and recognised in international law since the 1940s,[12] this strand of the right is characterised by the prioritisation of promoting transparency in, and ensuring the accountability of, public authorities. The right has since become a mainstay in political and legal discourse, with freedom of information legislation being adopted in numerous countries[13] and at the international level.[14] This is manifested in the UK with the implementation of the Freedom of Information Act 2000 (along with the Freedom of Information (Scotland) Act 2002),[15] which reflected this strand's priorities of transparency and accountability.[16] As a marked departure from a tradition of secrecy for all official information,

---

[9] Indeed, a large strand of law in this area is concerned with privacy and the rights and obligations of private companies and entities in relation to storing and processing personal data: see Regulation (EU) 2016/679 of the European Parliament and of the Council of 27 April 2016 on the protection of natural persons with regard to the processing of personal data and on the free movement of such data, and repealing Directive 95/46/EC (General Data Protection Regulation) [2016] OJ L119/1.

[10] The extent to which public access obligations should be extended to environmental information held outwith public authorities is a question that is beyond the scope of this book.

[11] Freedom of the Press Act 1776.

[12] Universal Declaration of Human Rights (adopted 10 December 1948) UNGA Res 217 A(III), art. 19.

[13] See, for example, France under the Law of 17 July 1978 (Loi No. 78-753 du Juillet 17, 1978 de la liberté d'access aux documents adminstratifs); and Bulgaria under the Constitution of Bulgaria of 1991, art. 41.

[14] See American Convention on Human Rights O.A.S. Treaty Series No. 36 (adopted 22 November 1969, entered into force 18 July 1978), art. 13(1); and UNCHR, *Report of the Special Rapporteur on the Right to Seek and Receive Information, the Media in Countries of Transition and in Election, the Impact of New Information Technologies, National Security, and Women and Freedom of Expression* (1998) UN Doc E/CN.4/1998/40.

[15] The Freedom of Information (Scotland) Act 2002 covers information held by authorities which are governed by devolved responsibilities in Scotland and, although broadly parallel to the Freedom of Information Act 2000, does have some differences in its provisions on both substance and procedures.

[16] HAZELL et al., above n. 5, p. 18.

the introduction of the 2000 Act was announced as a "fundamental and vital change in the relationship between government and governed".[17]

The second strand is much narrower and constitutes the primary focus of this book: the right of access to *environmental* information. While the importance of accessing environmental information was recognised to some degree prior to 1992,[18] it was the Rio Declaration that clearly asserted its role in environmental governance:

> Environmental issues are best handled with the participation of all concerned citizens, at the relevant level. At the national level, each individual shall have appropriate access to information concerning the environment that is held by public authorities, including information on hazardous materials and activities in their communities, and the opportunity to participate in decision-making processes. States shall facilitate and encourage public awareness and participation by making information widely available. Effective access to judicial and administrative proceedings, including redress and remedy, shall be provided.[19]

This assertion explicitly highlights the emphasis placed on environmental information as a prerequisite for public participation in environmental decision-making procedures, which has long been recognised as a desirable element of environmental governance.[20] The intended benefits of such participation can be summarised as: improving the quality of decisions; environmental problem-solving; promoting environmental citizenship; improving procedural legitimacy and eliciting the values that influence environmental choices.[21]

The Rio Declaration and the right to environmental information more generally do not discard the objectives of promoting transparency and accountability that underlie the wider freedom of information laws.[22]

---

[17] Prime Minister's Preface to *Your Right to Know: The Government's Proposals for a Freedom of Information Act* (Cm 3818, 1997).

[18] Stockholm Declaration on the Human Environment (1972) (Report of the United Nations Conference on the Human Environment, UN Doc. A/CONF.48/14), Principle 19; Directive 90/313/EEC, above n. 2.

[19] Rio Declaration on Environment and Development (1992) (Report of the United Nations Conference on Environment and Development, UN Doc. A/CONF.151/26 (Vol. I)), Principle 10.

[20] S. BELL et al, *Environmental Law*, 9th ed., Oxford University Press, Oxford 2017, chap. 9.

[21] See generally E. BARRITT, *The Foundations of the Aarhus Convention: Environmental Democracy, Rights and Stewardship*, Hart Publishing, Oxford 2020.

[22] O. MARCOS, "Governance and the Sustainable Development Goals: The Increasing Relevance of Access Rights in Principle 10 of the Rio Declaration" (2016) 25(1) *Review of European, Comparative and International Environmental Law* 50, 53.

At the broadest level, such transparency is seen as enabling individuals to monitor and assist in the effective implementation of environmental regulation.[23] Yet the Rio Declaration reduces the dominance of these aims by promoting public participation as a means of securing its overall objective of a more sustainable environment. There is thus a clear contrast between the right to environmental information that the Declaration embodies and the general right to information.

The approach adopted by the Rio Declaration is notable because subsequent legal instruments have followed its example. This underlying rationale for the right has been adopted by the Convention on Access to Information, Public Participation in Decision-Making and Access to Justice in Environmental Matters, known as the Aarhus Convention. The Aarhus Convention is important because it is broadly considered to be a normative legal instrument which establishes the standards that operate in this area of law.[24] At the procedural level, the Aarhus Convention establishes a range of normative procedural rights relating to accessing environmental information and participating in environmental decision-making processes. These procedural rights, and their associated obligations, are often held as the benchmark by which domestic implementations of the right are judged, regardless of whether the state in question has ratified the Convention.[25] Additionally, the Aarhus Convention has further emphasised the environmental and participative aims of the right by declaring a shared responsibility to protect the environment and through its structure, which frames the right to information as a precursor to public participation.[26]

---

23   For example, by enabling breaches of permit conditions to be reported.
24   The influence on other international agreements is very clear: Regional Agreement on Access to Information, Public Participation and Justice in Environmental Matters in Latin America and the Caribbean (Escazú Agreement), 4 March 2018, C.N.195.2018.TREATIES-XXVII.18 of 9 April 2018; Guidelines for Development of National Legislation on Access to Information, Public Participation and Access to Justice in Environmental Matters (the Bali Guidelines), adopted by the Governing Council of UNEP, UNEPGCSS.XI/11, Decision SS.XI/5 pt A, 26 February 2010. See S. WHITTAKER, *The Right of Access to Environmental Information*, Cambridge University Press, Cambridge 2021.
25   See generally W. WILCOX, "Access to Environmental Information in the United States and the United Kingdom" (2001) *Loyola of Los Angeles International and Comparative Review* 121; and S. LAMDAN, "Beyond the FOIA: Improving Environmental Information Access in the U.S." (2016–2017) 29 *Georgetown Environmental Law Review* 481.
26   See Chapter 2, section 2.2.

The normative impact of the Aarhus Convention is clearly identifiable in the UK, and hence in Scotland, due to the ratification of the Convention by the UK on 23 February 2005.[27] Legally obliged to comply with the procedural obligations enshrined in the Convention, the UK guarantees the right of access to environmental information through the Environmental Information Regulations 2004[28] and the Environmental Information (Scotland) Regulations 2004.[29] In this way, the Aarhus Convention acts as one of the primary legal instruments that has advanced the development of the environmental strand of information rights in the UK.

2. FREEDOM OF INFORMATION AND THE RIGHT TO ENVIRONMENTAL INFORMATION: SIMILARITIES AND DIFFERENCES

The parallel development of both strands of information rights, as well as their areas of overlap, is important to this book's analysis of the right of access to environmental information. The two strands of information rights are conceptually very different: this can be evidenced from the aims and ultimate goals of the Aarhus Convention when compared against the aims of the legal regimes which guarantee the general right to information. Yet despite this stark difference, there is also a degree of overlap between the aims of both strands that intertwines the two rights together. Further, how these two rights are implemented and how they conceptualise the interactions between users and public authorities are also very similar. Clarifying these similarities and differences acts as a foundational starting point for the book and needs to be discussed before moving forward.

As previously noted, the general right of access to information is primarily concerned with the promotion of transparency and accountability. From the UK[30] to other jurisdictions such as Sri Lanka[31] and New Zealand,[32] there is an explicit or implicit focus on these goals as

---

[27] Details of the parties and ratifications can found in the United Nations Treaty Series at <https://treaties.un.org/Pages/ViewDetails.aspx?src=IND&mtdsg_no=XXVII-13&chapter=27&clang=_en> accessed 18 April 2022.
[28] SI 2004/3391.
[29] SSI 2004/520.
[30] HAZELL et al., above n. 5, p. 18.
[31] M. GOMEZ, "The Right to Information and Transformative Development Outcomes" (2019) 12(3) *Law and Development Review* 837.
[32] M. MCDONAGH, "The Right to Information in International Human Rights Law" (2013) 13(1) *Human Rights Law Review* 25, 54.

the primary objective.[33] Yet the aims of the general right are often broader than this focus implies. In the UK, for example, Hazell, Worthy and Glover identified 12 possible objectives for the general right, with the six aims predominantly mentioned in government documents being:[34]

- increasing the openness and transparency of government;
- increasing the accountability of government;
- improving the quality of government decision-making;
- improving public understanding of government;
- increasing public trust in government;
- increasing public participation in government.

While these six aims were those that featured most often, it was the first two that garnered the most attention.[35] This is worth noting because it is primarily concerned with procedural matters: specifically, ensuring that the decision-making process is transparent and that decision-makers can be held to account.

On the other hand, the right of access to environmental information has adopted a different perspective on the values of disclosing environmental information. Against the backdrop of a global decline of the natural environment, the right of access to environmental information is seeking to halt and reverse that decline.[36] There is an obvious contrast with the general right to information in that the general right does not incorporate environmental, or any other substantive, concerns into its internal logic.

This substantive, environmental aim marks a deep contrast with the more general right to information, which has its focus on the procedure by which a decision is reached rather than the result and the quality of the decision. The focus on the substantive outcome can be further evidenced in the environmental right's primary aim of promoting public participation in environmental decision-making procedures,[37] which is

---

[33] For a general overview, see R. PELED and Y. RABIM, "The Constitutional Right to Information" (2011) 42(2) *Columbia Human Rights Law Review* 357, 360–363 and 366–370.
[34] HAZELL et al., above n. 5, p. 18.
[35] Ibid., p. 19.
[36] At the broader level, this also connects to the right to live in a healthy environment: United Nations General Assembly resolution on the human right to a clean, healthy and sustainable environment (28 July 2022) A/RES/76/300.
[37] Aarhus Convention, Preamble, paras 8, 9, 11, 12.

viewed as improving the quality of environmental decisions.[38] This is not to suggest the right to environmental information discards transparency and accountability concerns; indeed, the right views these as useful tools to promote good governance in environmental matters.[39] However, whereas these goals are at the centre of the more general right, they are not the underlying objective of the environmental right which seeks public participation and environmental protection.

In this way, there is a fundamental difference at the core of the two rights to information in terms of how the disclosed information is intended to be used and in the divergent focus between procedural and substantive outcomes. Yet, despite this divergence in the primary objectives of the two strands of information rights, both are often characterised by users and academic literature[40] as being one and the same. One reason for this is that, notwithstanding their divergent primary aims, there is an overlap between each strand's objectives. As noted above, the environmental right recognises the value of transparency similarly to the general right to information, and one of the secondary objectives of the general right is to "increase public participation in government",[41] which matches the participative aims of the right to environmental information.

A second reason lies in the mechanics behind the disclosure of information, whether environmental or otherwise. Despite the divergent primary objectives of both strands, the procedure by which information is disclosed is often identical between the two. For proactive disclosure, public authorities will often use the same dissemination channels regardless of the nature of the information. Further, the procedures used for disclosing information on request are also broadly similar despite, in the UK, being conducted under different legislative instruments. In this way, from the perspective of the public, both strands of rights are essentially interchangeable in practice, despite their contrasting objectives.

The assumed interchangeability of the two strands of information rights plays a critical role in setting the scene for the analysis given in this book. Given its explicit, substantive objectives, a key indicator of the success of the right of access to environmental information is whether it has achieved

---

[38] Ibid., para 16.
[39] Ibid., paras 10 and 11.
[40] For some discussion on this, see S. WHITTAKER, J. MENDEL and C.T. REID, "Back to Square One: Revisiting How We Analyse the Right of Access to Environmental Information" (2019) 31 *Journal of Environmental Law* 465, 476–477.
[41] HAZELL et al., above n. 5, p. 18.

its aims of protecting the environment and promoting public participation. Yet, from the perspective of those using the right and those guaranteeing it, these aims can be diluted through its association with the general right to information. This is true even within international and domestic legal instruments guaranteeing the right: despite public participation being the primary aim, the underpinning rationale for promoting such participation is sometimes unclear and ambiguous. This in turn leads to competing interpretations of the right's primary aim and a failure to look beyond the simple disclosure of information as an end in itself.

There is also a broader theoretical point relating to the similarities in terms of how both strands of the right conceptualise the interactions which occur under it. Both strands are broadly anthropocentric; they are focused on the interactions between humans and the human-designed bodies that govern them, and exclude the influence and agency of non-human actors. For the general right to information, this is expected. Indeed, it explicitly positions itself as a right focused on procedural issues, which exist only in relation to relationships between humans. Yet, for the right of access to environmental information, the omission of the environment as an element is significant.[42] The environment is the intended beneficiary of the right, but is not considered to be an entity in and of itself. By denying the environment any agency as an entity independent of humanity, there is a question as to how far the right will be able to effectively achieve its environmental aims.

3. ASSUMPTIONS AND MISMATCHES

The theoretical aspects discussed above shape the way in which the right of access to environmental information is perceived. Practice, however, does not always match theory and there is a need to understand more about how the right is actually used, and how this use impacts on environmental governance. Despite the longstanding history of the right, there is remarkably little contemporary research about its use and effectiveness in practice. As a result, there are a range of assumptions which underpin how the right is believed to operate. These assumptions are critical, because any

---

[42] M. PETERSMANN, "Narcissus' Reflection in the Lake: Untold Narratives in Environmental Law beyond the Anthropocentric Frame" (2018) 30 *Journal of Environmental Law* 235, 247.

Chapter 1. Introduction

mismatch between them and how the right is actually used in practice can detrimentally affect how the right is utilised and achieves its aims.

The first of these assumptions is about the role of proactively disclosed environmental information. The right of access to environmental information is primarily conceptualised as a method by which interested individuals can directly request access to environmental information from public authorities.[43] This is partly due to the nature of the legal regimes guaranteeing the right. The procedures for requesting information are self-contained, with the requirements to submit, process and respond to requests enshrined in a single legal instrument. Conversely, the right to have environmental information proactively disclosed is implemented through a fragmented set of provisions which expressly identifies only some of the relevant categories of information and rules for their public availability. This leads to a skewed focus on the right to request access to environmental information, a focus further emphasised by the fact that the right to access on request information is the primary focus of the general law on freedom of information which is intertwined with the right to environmental information.

Yet to focus on information disclosed on request is deceptive. While the majority of provisions regarding the right focus on disclosure on request, the majority of environmental information which is accessed is proactively disclosed. A consequence of this misalignment is that there is a misunderstanding regarding the primary method by which environmental information is accessed. This not only influences how public authorities design their internal structures to respond to their obligations under to right, but it also underplays the role of technology in terms of how environmental information is proactively disclosed.[44]

A second assumption which leads to a gap between how the right of access to environmental information is expected to operate and how it actually operates in practice is the conceptualisation of those who use the right. Individuals seeking access to environmental information are broadly categorised as a singular category of users, who are believed to be uniformly knowledgeable in environmental matters and seeking to utilise environmental information to meet their moral duty enshrined in the Aarhus Convention "to protect and improve the environment for the benefit of present and future generations".[45] However, the reality is

---

[43] WHITTAKER et al., above n. 40.
[44] This is discussed throughout Chapter 3 and also in Chapter 6.
[45] Aarhus Convention, Preamble, para. 7.

Intersentia

that users are not uniform, and how they engage with the right will differ depending on a wide range of factors and circumstances. There is thus a considerable mismatch between the ideal on which the right is established and the reality in practice.

In addressing the diversity among users, this book groups them into two categories: professional users and personal users.[46] These broad categories, which require further internal differentiation and are far from water-tight, are based on two factors which have a significant impact on how users engage with the right of access to environmental information. The first of these factors is the motive of the user. Each user has a unique motive for seeking access to environmental information. For some, they wish to access environmental information in order to argue against a decision affecting them made by a local authority, or for other personal reasons. Others use the right as part of their job, such as investigating stories for publication or to advise clients. Those in either group may also be driven by environmental concerns, acting to fulfil the moral duty imposed by the Aarhus Convention. These motives are diverse, but do not always align with the environmental expectations embedded within the right and have a significant impact on how users actually engage with the right.

The second factor which influences how users engage with the right is their level of expertise and knowledge, where again a broad but far from water-tight distinction can be made. In many discussions there is no consideration of the user's degree of expertise in seeking access to environmental information, a concept that encapsulates a wide range of matters from environmental knowledge to make sense of materials provided to the ability to effectively submit a request for information. There is a clear difference between the abilities of a typical member of the public and of an experienced investigative journalist in terms of how they engage with public authorities and exercise their legal right to information. Such differences are critical, and they can influence how successful users are in obtaining access to environmental information and how efficiently the legal processes operate. However, categories of users can be blurred; for example, a retired public sector worker may be able to deploy great expertise similar to a professional user while pursuing a personal motive, emphasising the permeability of the divide between the two groups that is used to shape the further discussion here. Taken together, these factors create a multitude of different users, a diversity which is not reflected in the

---

[46] These particular categories of users are discussed in Chapters 3 and 4 respectively.

Chapter 1. Introduction

unitary conceptualisation of users within the right to access environmental information or the procedures which guarantee the right.

Assumptions about the nature of the users also fail to take into account how far the operation of the right is affected not only by the diversity of human actors but also by the role of non-human actors that influence and impact how the right of access to environmental information is utilised.[47] Although the environment is stated as being the ultimate beneficiary, the detailed provisions offer little recognition of the environment as an entity at any stage in the creation, handling or disclosure of information. Beyond the environment, technology also plays a significant role in shaping how users engage with public authorities and merits recognition as a significant non-human actor. Since the date of the drafting of the Aarhus Convention, technology has transformed the scale and formats in which environmental information is proactively disclosed and how users submit requests for environmental information.[48] In turn, this has changed how users and public authorities interact with each other and how the right itself operates.

Moreover, the law itself exerts a clear influence over how all actors under the right interact with each other. This is notable in itself because it is an influence which is too often simply taken for granted. The law, at both the international and domestic levels, is viewed as enshrining the legal obligations that authorities must adhere to and the legal rights individuals can enjoy. Yet the law does much more than just establish these rights and obligations. It contains normative elements that influence the design of the procedures through which interactions occur, while simple compliance with the law becomes an end in itself. Additionally, where there are conflicts and ambiguities within the law, these fuel mismatches that detrimentally affect how the right operates in practice.

A final assumption that leads to mismatches between expectations and reality is that the right of access to environmental information will necessarily lead to users contributing to, and having a beneficial impact on, environmental decision-making procedures. The right of access to environmental information is explicitly conceptualised within the Aarhus

---

[47] See Chapter 6, section 2.
[48] Such as through websites like WhatDoTheyKnow, a website which individuals can use to submit their requests to public authorities (<https://www.whatdotheyknow.com/> accessed 18 April 2022). Acting as an alternative to directly submitting the request to the authority, WhatDoTheyKnow offers support for individuals seeking to request access to environmental information in exchange of publishing the request and any further correspondence online. This is more fully discussed in Chapter 6, section 2.3.

Convention as a part of a series of rights, one of which is participation in decision-making procedures with a view to securing environmental benefits. However, users may wish to use environmental information in a different way, or to participate in environmental decision-making procedures in a way that protects other interests and actually undermines the right's environmental aims. Even if a user does align with the environmental expectations of the right, there is an underlying question as to the extent to which participation by users should be able to influence such decisions. The legal provisions guaranteeing the rights to access information and to participate do not address this in sufficient detail, leading to a divergence of views over how important the facts and opinions expressed through public participation should be in determining the outcome of formal decision-making procedures. However, perhaps more importantly, because of the lack of clarity regarding the justification of public participation in the Aarhus Convention and in domestic environmental information regimes, differing views can be considered as valid interpretations of the right's participative aims. The mismatches caused by these contrasting interpretations have the potential to leave individuals dissatisfied when their views have less impact than expected, potentially dissuading them from future participation and in turn hindering the achievement of the right's environmental and participative aims.[49]

The overall result of these assumptions, and the research gaps that enable them, is that very little is known about the use of the right of access to environmental information. It is not known who is seeking information, why they are doing so, what information is being sought, what they are doing with it once it is obtained and whether providing public access to environmental information is actually achieving any of the intended goals. This book addresses these gaps, identifying the aims that lie behind the legal rules and drawing on empirical research to analyse the use and effectiveness of the right.

4. METHODOLOGY AND THEORETICAL FRAMEWORK

In addressing these research gaps, this book closely examines the operation of the right to environmental information in Scotland from the

---

[49] This is discussed in more detail in Chapter 5.

Chapter 1. Introduction

perspectives of both users and holders of information. For primary data collection, both a survey of and interviews with users of environmental information and public authorities that hold this information were used to build a broad picture of how the right to environmental information is working in Scotland.

Participants for interviews and surveys were recruited through a combination of: social media advertising (in particular, on the co-authors' and relevant policy actors' Twitter accounts); asking contacts working in the field to advertise the project; contacting identified requesters whose details were publicly available through the WhatDoTheyKnow site and discussing the project at the Freedom of Information Practitioners' Conference hosted by the University of Dundee's Centre for Freedom of Information. Detailed semi-structured interviews were conducted with 15 users of the right to access environmental information and with 16 Scottish public authorities, including the Scottish Information Commissioner.[50] Interviews were carried out by one, two or all three of the co-authors of this book, depending on availability, expertise and on what was thought most likely to build rapport with participants. Interviews were carried out in-person, by telephone or using video conferencing software depending on the preferences of participants. Interviews were transcribed and, along with free text survey responses, they were coded to identify themes using NVivo software. The target number of interviewees was successfully met and interview saturation was reached; the fact that later interviews were bringing up the same themes as earlier ones indicates that the identified themes cover the range of views on this topic well. Conversely, recruitment for surveys was less successful and – despite promoting them extensively, over a number of months and through multiple channels – the response rate was too low to productively use these data for quantitative work.[51]

---

[50] Anonymised survey and interview data have been shared with the UK Data Archive for archiving and are publicly available: https://reshare.ukdataservice.ac.uk/855226/.

[51] The project received 13 responses from Public Authority staff and 52 responses from members of the public. While the project team appreciates the help of those who did respond – and these data are useful for background information – there are too few responses to claim representativeness or to allow significant quantitative work. For future work on this topic in Scotland, it would be worth noting that there seemed to be greater willingness to participate in interviews than to complete a survey on this topic; participants often seemed to find interviews quite engaging. An issue in approaching individuals known to have accessed proactively disclosed information was that since they had not been making specific requests, they did not think of themselves as having been exercising any legal right to information and therefore did not consider themselves eligible to participate, an attitude that highlights the difference between the two aspects of the right as discussed throughout this book.

Intersentia

Readers will therefore see that the work with primary data here is informed largely by the interviews and some free text responses in the surveys (from which key themes were identified); the additional information in the surveys provided helpful background information.

This primary evidence was supplemented with an extensive range of secondary data that is available about the requests submitted under the right to access environmental information and other aspects of the request process in Scotland. The Scottish Information Commissioner collects and publishes data gathered by Scottish public authorities[52] on how they guarantee the right of access to environmental information under the Environmental Information (Scotland) Regulations 2004.[53] Alongside reviewing these data, key themes related to the right and its use were drawn from the analysis of 625 requests for environmental information submitted to Scottish public authorities via the WhatDoTheyKnow website covering requests from 5 June 2017 to 31 December 2018.[54] By drawing on these primary and secondary sources, the book is able to build upon strong empirical evidence to provide a fuller picture of key actors' experiences of and motivations for using the right and to examine the impact of the right.

Scotland provides an appropriate focus for this book for several reasons. With its own legislative framework for guaranteeing the right of access to environmental information and its own Information Commissioner with responsibility for overseeing this area, Scotland offers a well-bounded case study. The research team already had extensive connections within Scotland, and the collegial nature of the field allowed excellent access to and interviews with key actors, providing a degree of confidence that the data collection had covered the key policy actors. A wide knowledge of environmental matters in Scotland enabled the findings to be put in context (e.g. linking patterns of requests with issues known to be attracting wide interest).

Notwithstanding the collegial nature of the Scottish information law landscape, there are tensions and conflicts on substantive matters and on how authorities are dealing with them, offering extensive activity in relation

---

[52] Examples of such data include the number of requests received by an authority and the number of requests which led to full or partial disclosure of the requested information. Statistics are available at <https://www.itspublicknowledge.info/statistics> accessed 19 April 2022.
[53] The legal framework for the right is discussed in Chapter 2.
[54] These requests can be read at <https://www.whatdotheyknow.com> accessed 18 April 2022.

Chapter 1. Introduction

to the right. Such activity sits within the broader context of international law and practice. Scotland's environmental governance arrangements fit a widely adopted pattern, with governance responsibilities being split between central and local government bodies and specialist agencies. For example, the Scottish Ministers set national planning policy, local authorities grant planning permission for individual developments and the Scottish Environment Protection Agency issues permits under the pollution control legislation.[55] In this context there is nothing unusual about Scotland that limits the drawing of wider lessons, whilst the environmental information regime itself is firmly based on international models derived from the Aarhus Convention.[56] This allows the impacts of trends to be considered with wider application – for example, the move towards requests for information being mediated by digital technology. A robust discussion of the use of the right in Scotland can be offered that will allow generalisation to how the right is working elsewhere, and will thus help to inform an understanding of how the right works in other jurisdictions.

The book's analysis of access to environmental information is informed by Actor-Network Theory and, in particular, Latour's approach to this.[57] Actor-Network Theory seeks to "trace the associations" between different things, which are described as "actors".[58] These associations and relationships between different actors, both human and non-human, are key to the value of applying Actor-Network Theory to the right of access to environmental information. Through identifying how actors exert influence over each other in the context of the right, it is possible to clarify and understand how the users engage with the right and interact (or fail to interact) with its environmental and participative aims.

In introducing Actor-Network Theory, it is important to note that an actor is defined as "something which acts or to which activity is granted".[59] This is a broad definition, encapsulating a range of different things which are associated with each other within the actor-network. Both humans and human-designed entities, such as companies and public authorities, are

---

[55] For an overview, see F. McManus, *Environmental Law in Scotland: An Introduction and Guide*, Edinburgh University Press, Edinburgh 2016.
[56] See Chapter 2, sections 2 and 3.
[57] See Chapter 2, section 1.
[58] B. Latour, *Reassembling the Social: An Introduction to Actor-Network Theory*, Oxford University Press, Oxford 2005, p. 5.
[59] B. Doolin and A. Lowe, "To Reveal is to Critique: Actor-Network Theory and Critical Information Systems Research" (2002) 17(2) *Journal of Information Technology* 69, 72.

Intersentia 17

encapsulated within the concept of an actor. Perhaps more significantly, Actor-Network Theory does not prioritise human and human-designed actors.[60] Unlike traditional social research, elements such as intentionality, purpose and freedom are not considered to be essential elements of what constitutes an actor.[61] In this way, non-human things, such as technology or the environment, can also be considered to be actors due to the influence they can exert in the context of the right.

Actor-Network Theory helps to unpick the traditional assumptions that underpin the right. At the broadest level, the right of access to environmental information is often envisioned as involving just two sets of actors who interact with each other: those who are seeking to access environmental information, often defined as "users", and those who hold the sought-after information, often defined as "public authorities". There is frequently no distinction drawn between different types of users or of public authorities, nor are interactions within these sets considered. Further, non-human actors, such as the law, the environment and technology, and the influence they exert, are often not considered. Through applying Actor-Network Theory, this book is able to look beyond current assumptions which underpin the right and more effectively identify and analyse the human and non-human actors which interact under the right.

5. THE STRUCTURE OF THE BOOK

This section sets out the structure of the book and its approach to examining how the right of access to environmental information is utilised in practice. This first introductory chapter has provided a brief account of the development of the right of access to environmental information in international law and its relationship with the general right to access information. It has also set out the methodology of the text, in particular highlighting the qualitative techniques used to gather the empirical evidence that underpins the text's findings and the basis of the Actor-Network Theory which is used as a tool for analysis.

---

[60] B. LATOUR, "On Actor-Network Theory: A Few Clarifications Plus More Than a Few Complications" (1996) 47 *Soziale Welt* 369, 373. See also the version of this paper on Latour's website, with a little more detail on some aspects of this, at <http://www.bruno-latour.fr/sites/default/files/P-67%20ACTOR-NETWORK.pdf> accessed 19 April 2022.
[61] M. EMIRBAYER and A. MISCHE, "What is Agency?" (1988) 103(4) *American Journal of Sociology* 962.

Chapter 2 further explores the theoretical and legal frameworks which underpin this text's analysis. It begins by explaining Actor-Network Theory in more detail, highlighting how the theory defines actors and the actor-network. It establishes the value of the theory for identifying and analysing the impact of different actors, both human and non-human, and how their relationships shape how the right to environmental information operates in practice. Analysis then turns to the development of the legal framework. The Aarhus Convention acts as the normative legal instrument for the right of access to environmental information internationally, and its aims are considered, before tracing how it came to provide the basis for the law in Scotland. The provisions of that law, the Environmental Information (Scotland) Regulations 2004, are then set out, establishing the legal framework within which those seeking and holding environmental information must operate.

Chapter 3 begins by viewing users of the right through the theoretical lens of Actor-Network Theory and distinguishing between two types of users: "professional" users and "personal" users. Since the presence of professional users marks the most obvious divergence from the vision of information rights as a tool for environmentally engaged citizens seeking to participate in environmental decision-making, their role is examined first, with personal users being considered in Chapter 4. The chapter clarifies what constitutes a professional user by identifying a number of key groups of professional actors and how they engage with the right in Scotland in practice. The text's distinction between "professional" and "personal" users, as well as the identification of individual categories of professional users, emphasises the importance of the variety of individual actors, their varied motives for seeking information and their uses of what they have accessed. This contributes to the text's core findings about how the right is used in practice and the divergence from the vision of the right as serving a single group of citizens with largely uniform characteristics.

Chapter 3's analysis considers the various professionals who use the right, including journalists and those employed by public authorities, a category of users which is often overlooked. The chapter examines the motivations that drive each group of professional users to seek access to environmental information and how they each use the information that is disclosed to them. After mapping these motives and uses, it then analyses them against the normative ideals of the Aarhus Convention and highlights their role as intermediaries between authorities holding information and the public, a role not fully reflected in the Convention. The chapter's analysis concludes by noting that professional users can have a positive impact on the right's environmental aims, an opinion shared by Scottish public authorities. However, it also highlights that there is a mismatch between these users and how the Convention expects users to engage with the right, at times getting in the way of the smooth operation of the relevant procedures.

Similar to Chapter 3, Chapter 4 builds on the distinction between professional and personal users by examining how personal users engage with the right to environmental information in Scotland. The chapter shows that personal users cannot readily be divided into categories as there is an infinite spectrum of potential personal users who may wish to access and use environmental information. Many do not match the vision of environmentally engaged citizens that is embedded within the Aarhus Convention, but are driven by a variety of more personal motives (or a combination of motives) linked more to impacts on their own lives than to environmental well-being. Further, even where users do hold altruistic environmental motives, the differences in their expertise in terms of dealing with public authorities or handling the information that is disclosed further distinguish different users of the right from each other. The chapter concludes by noting that the mismatch between the expectations of the Convention and the actual characteristics of personal users can act to undermine how these users engage with the right and its environmental motives.

Chapter 5 examines the uses that are made of the environmental information that is accessed. The creation of the right is intrinsically linked to the promotion of public participation in environmental matters and the chapter first considers the theoretical justifications for such participation, both generally and specifically in the context of environmental decision-making procedures. It then considers these justifications in relation to the understanding of public participation and its link to access to information as embodied by the Aarhus Convention. It then discusses the views of the public and of public authorities in terms of the success of public participation in Scotland, highlighting how far their understanding of what the right is seeking and actually managing to deliver aligns with or diverges from the Aarhus Convention's understanding of the concept. This analysis is significant because it highlights a disconnect between the views of those using the right, who are more concerned with substantive outcomes "on the ground", and the more procedural aims that are the focus of the operational provisions of the Convention, and hence the domestic law. This may lead to dissatisfied users being dissuaded from using the right in the future. The chapter concludes by highlighting the potential virtue of

Chapter 1. Introduction

recognising non-human actors within environmental information regimes as a means of narrowing this mismatch.

Chapter 6 focuses on the influence exerted by non-human actors over how the right of access to environmental information is guaranteed. The chapter first clarifies what is meant by non-human actors in the context of the right before identifying the non-human actors which influence on the operation of the right in practice. In particular, it identifies that technology, the law and the environment itself are non-human actors that play a significant role, but are not explicitly recognised by the Aarhus Convention or domestic environmental information regimes. It then continues by considering how this lack of recognition may hinder how the right is understood and guaranteed. One strand which is identified in the preceding chapters is the limited impact of the environmental dimension to the right, blurring the distinction with more general freedom of information laws. The chapter concludes by exploring the role of the environment as an actor and the potential of moving beyond anthropocentric understandings of the right.

The book concludes with Chapter 7, which brings together the core findings of the text and applies them to the mismatch discovered between experience in practice and the underpinning ideals that sit at the core of the right. The empirical nature of the work acts as a unique window through which the right can be examined. Using these findings, the chapter proposes various reforms which could help to better fulfil the goals the lie behind the creation of the right to environmental information, but also addresses a bigger question raised by the research here. Given that the environmental dimension has not played a significant role in most uses of the right, is there an adequate justification for the maintenance of a right to environmental information separate from the rights established under more general laws on freedom of information?

CHAPTER 2
THEORETICAL AND LEGAL FRAMEWORKS

Analysis of the right of access to environmental information is generally conducted through one of two legal perspectives. The work here offers insights beyond these typical approaches both by drawing more on social theory and through empirical study of how the right is operating in practice. The first conventional approach, relying on a widespread legal methodology, studies the legal framework and also the aims and aspirations that underpin the creation of the right, "grappling with the foundational concepts that inspire the ambitious vision" that lies behind it.[62] The second, narrower approach seeks to examine the right through the doctrinal method of analysis, an approach which focuses on the internal working and operation of "black-letter" law and its position within the legal hierarchy.[63] The latter perspective follows the legal origins of the right and the way it has been embodied.[64] From the Stockholm Declaration through the Rio Declaration and the Aarhus Convention to the measures ensuring its implementation in the EU and Scotland, the recognition and development of the right have been dominated by the law and the legal procedures which give it effect. The doctrinal methodology, with its basis in legal study, thus dominates discussion and analysis of the right of access to environmental information.

Both approaches bring numerous benefits in analysing the right of access to environmental information. The focus on the underlying concepts

---

[62] BARRITT, above n. 21, p.3.
[63] P. CHYNOWETH, "Legal Research" in A. KNIGHT and L. RUDDOCK (eds), *Advanced Research Methods in a Built Environment*, Wiley-Blackwell, Chichester 2008, pp. 29–30.
[64] J. PARADISSIS, *The Right to Access Environmental Information: An Analysis of UK Law in the Context of European, International and Human Rights Law*, VDM Verlag, Saarbrücken 2010; J. JENDROŚKA and M. BAR (eds), *Procedural Environmental Rights: Principle X in Theory and Practice*, Intersentia, Cambridge 2017.

and ambitions enables access to information to be considered in the wider context of analysing governance. The doctrinal approach, by adopting an internal perspective on the laws that govern the right, offers analysis that can consider the internal logic of these laws and whether they are aligned with the objectives that they are seeking to achieve. However, while both approaches provide valuable perspectives on the right, they do not consider whether the law operates in the "real world" as intended. Described as the gap between "the law in the books" and "the law in action", there is a risk that relying wholly on either methodology will result in a distorted understanding of the right that is based on how the law was intended to operate or is assumed to be operating rather than how it actually operates in practice.[65] Such a misunderstanding can lead to mismatches between the expectations of those who create and enforce the law, and of members of the public who actually use the rights enshrined in the law.

It is here that undertaking empirical work and drawing on social theory can help to fill in the gaps and clarify how the right operates in the "real world". To further its analysis, this book draws on Actor-Network Theory, which seeks to reconsider the assumed characteristics of and relationships between different actors (human and non-human) through examining how they operate and interact in practice. Through this approach, mismatches between the aspirations behind the law, the law as set out in the statute book and the law in action can be identified and understood. This understanding can then be used as the basis for proposing remedies that will help the right to achieve its environmental and participative aims.

This chapter examines the frameworks which underpin the analysis presented in this book. First, it begins by setting out some origins and key elements of Actor-Network Theory. It defines the terms "actor" and "network", two terms that are key to the theory, before moving on to discuss how this theory can be used to redefine humanity's relationship with the environment. The chapter then begins its analysis of the legal frameworks which underpin the right of access to environmental information. This section charts the development of the right of access to environmental information at the international level, through the Rio Declaration and the Aarhus Convention, as well as its development within the EU and Scotland. Following this, the discussion then sets out the content of the laws which govern how the right is implemented, focusing specifically

---

[65] CHYNOWETH, above n. 63, p. 30. Doctrinal work will consider the operation of the law in the circumstances leading to disputes that reach the higher courts, but these present an exceptionally limited and distorted view of what is happening in practice.

Chapter 2. Theoretical and Legal Frameworks

on the provisions of the Aarhus Convention and the Environmental Information (Scotland) Regulations 2004, and how they seek to fulfil the aims of environmental protection and public participation.

Intertwined throughout the chapter is a preliminary application of Actor-Network Theory, examining how these legal instruments conceptualise the right of access to environmental information and the actors which engage with it. Actor-Network Theory is used to critique some implicit, underpinning assumptions regarding the right and its use that are embedded within the legal instruments discussed in this chapter. These assumptions as to the motives behind seeking information and the uses made of it can lead to a mismatch of expectations where users of the right do not adhere to the expectations of the legal regimes guaranteeing the right. This mismatch of ambitions and practice generates a degree of tension, misunderstanding and dissatisfaction. Identifying this mismatch is necessary to address the source of these negative effects, an essential first step towards seeking greater fulfilment of the right's environmental and participative aims.

1. ACTOR-NETWORK THEORY

Bruno Latour played a key role in developing Actor-Network Theory, describing the theory as a move away from the idea that "the social" is a specific "kind of material or domain" that differs from other parts of the world.[66] Recognising the complexity in recontextualising "the social" in this way, Latour sought to address this through a particular idea of networks. Actor-Network Theory examines how networks of practice can build societies, seeking to "rebuild social theory out of networks".[67]

Looking at connections between things is clearly nothing novel in social or legal research. However, Actor-Network Theory offers a more significant shift in perspective away from viewing law or politics as having a domain distinct from the social.[68] It translates sociology into "the *tracing of associations*" and the social as "*a type of connection* between things that are not themselves social".[69] For Latour, Actor-Network Theory is a

---

[66] LATOUR, above n. 58, p. 1.
[67] LATOUR, above n. 60, p. 370.
[68] Ibid., p. 376.
[69] Ibid., p. 373.

Intersentia

project to change how we think of society and the world around us through making "association[s] between entities which are in no way recognizable as being social in the ordinary manner, except during the brief moment when they are reshuffled together".[70] This, in turn, provides a new perspective to analyse and construct the law governing the right of access to environmental information.

Actor-Network Theory drew from the engagement of Science Studies with a context where new discoveries and technologies were reshaping understandings of humanity and the wider world. As Latour puts it, Actor-Network Theory sought to engage with a world where "[m]icrobes, neutrinos [and] DNA are at the same time natural, social and discourse. They are real, human and semiotic entities in the same breath".[71] With this in mind, a starting point for Actor-Network Theory is the expansion of what constitutes an actor to include any "thing" which exerts influence over another. Such an approach challenges the traditional human-centric approach of research, encapsulating not just human or human-made entities which are perceived to have agency, but also non-human entities. Similar innovation is also applied in the construction of the network itself, which discards traditional hierarchical thinking and replaces it with a more localised perspective on how actors hold and exercise power. In part because of the complex and changing context from which it emerged, Actor-Network Theory can be a useful way to think about humanity and the environment in the current context of environmental change. By moving away from the conventional thinking that the law, and the actors within it, pre-exist as specific groups and that they are human-centric, it is possible to identify the invisible assumptions that underpin the operation of the right of access to environmental information. In turn, where there is evidence that these assumptions are not wholly reflective of how the right operates in practice, a study can reconstruct the network to better reflect the reality of the right.

1.1. ACTORS

A first question to ask is what constitutes an "actor"? This term is critical to how networks are constructed under the theory, as it is these actors

---

[70] LATOUR, above n. 58, p. 65.
[71] LATOUR, above n. 60.

Chapter 2. Theoretical and Legal Frameworks

which populate the networks through their associations with each other.[72] This term has a specific understanding external to Actor-Network Theory, generally requiring "actors" to embody elements such as intentionality, purpose and freedom,[73] in effect limiting them to human, or at least human-controlled, entities. However, actors can be understood more broadly in Actor-Network Theory. As a result, the delineation between what entities can or cannot be actors, both in the context of the theory itself and within specific networks, is significant.

The overarching definition given to "actors" under Actor-Network Theory is "something which acts or to which activity is granted".[74] This definition is intentionally broad and means that a wide range of things have the possibility of becoming an actor within a network, whether they be an individual or a group, human or non-human. Actor-Network Theory thus seeks to rethink what an actor is and recognise a broader range of entities that lack human-like intentionality yet have an impact on other human and non-human actors. Critically, it does not draw an absolute or binary distinction between human and non-human actors. Every entity is considered to have the potential to exert influence upon any identified network, regardless of their size or the agency attributed to them.[75] An example of this is how objects and technologies may exert agency – for example, the different type of influence that an official register might have if moved online rather than simply being present on paper in a single location.

The attention given to non-human actors is an aspect of Actor-Network Theory that can be applied to the right of access to environmental information. A key element of the right, as stated by the Aarhus Convention, is "to contribute to the protection of the right of every person of present and future generations to live in an environment adequate to his or her health and well-being".[76] This already blends nature, society and meaning in a way that, even when viewed from an anthropocentric perspective, emphasises the role of the "natural" environment in coping with environmental events such as global heating and pollution. In considering the environment

---

[72] J. MURDOCH, "The Spaces of Actor-Network Theory" (1998) 29(4) *Geoforum* 357, 359.
[73] M. EMIRBAYER and A. MISCHE, "What is Agency?" (1998) 103(4) *American Journal of Sociology* 962.
[74] DOOLIN and LOWE, above n. 59, p. 72.
[75] LATOUR, above n. 58, pp. 1–2. See also S. SISMONDO, *An Introduction to Science and Technology Studies*, 2nd ed, Wiley-Blackwell, Chichester 2009, p. 81.
[76] Aarhus Convention, art. 1.

and its needs, the right to environmental information distinguishes itself from the more general right to information and its singular focus on relationships between humans and human-created entities.

In addition, the identification of "actors" flows from Actor-Network Theory's focus on tracing the networks "on the ground" rather than incorporating assumptions or abstract theorising. Like the deliberate inclusion of non-human entities, Actor-Network Theory requires researchers to reconsider and recontextualise how they view groupings of actors within the network. What may appear to be a singular category of actors may instead be multiple actors that interact with and influence the constructed network in diverse ways. Without distinguishing between these actors, there is a risk that the individuality of different actors is lost through broad generalisation.

An example of the multiplicity of actors can be seen in relation to concerns and information requests arising from pollution levels in a part of a city. One aspect of what is involved here is natural: the way in the broader environment is being impacted on by emissions. There are clearly human factors involved too. It is human actors who cause the emissions that polluted the environment, who care about the impact of the environment and who are involved in making and answering requests for environmental information. These human actors will hold different interests in these emissions as well,[77] and will seek to access the environmental information using different methods and technologies. Through applying Actor-Network Theory, it is possible to identify all the relevant actors within the right's network. This, in turn, can help in understanding the complex interactions that occur within the right and its environmental and participative aims, identifying where mismatches arise between expectations and reality, and how these might undermine the effective exercise of the right.

1.2. NETWORKS

Another question posed by Actor-Network Theory is what constitutes a "network"? At the broadest level, the "network" discussed in Actor-

---

[77] For example, some actors will care because the pollution reflects badly on their city, while others will care because of the direct negative impact on their health or the value of their property; some may even welcome some emissions as an acceptable by-product of economic activity.

Network Theory is made up of the associations between different actors and of the ways in which these actors interact and exert influence over each other.[78] In this way, the identification of the relevant actors becomes a much more significant activity, as it is through these actors and the associations between them that the "network" is created. Identifying actors and the tracing of associations constitute the core of any constructed network.

Yet beyond this simplistic definition, there is a range of underlying aspects which make any network more complex. One such aspect is that, for Latour, Actor-Network Theory's shift to a focus on networks also allows a move away from the myth of society that is based purely on a strict top-down hierarchy.[79] A traditional approach in social research is to view society as hierarchical in nature, where certain actors have power which they can unilaterally exert over actors lower down in the hierarchy. Such an approach is particularly prevalent in doctrinal legal thinking, where great emphasis is placed on the "legal authority" of actors.[80]

Actor-Network Theory resists this pressure to impose a straightforward hierarchy upon any constructed network and its constituent actors. The associations and relationships between actors are not considered in terms of who is more authoritative, and there is no *a priori* order conferred on these relations.[81] Contrary to traditional perspectives in disciplines such as law, Actor-Network Theory posits that the "'social' is not some glue that could fix everything … it is *what* is glued together by many *other* types of connectors".[82] Similarly, the theory also posits that the influence that actors can exert over each other can change over time, with no actor holding an inherently superior position over the others.[83] This enables Actor-Network Theory to change perspectives, highlighting the fluidity of actor-networks and moving from seeking a grand, overarching rule to considering the local relationships as they operate in practice.

There are resonances here for the study of the right of access to environmental information in Scotland. The right of access to information is constructed across multiple localities, ranging from the Office of the Scottish Information Commissioner to a tourist looking at a sign about

---

[78] LATOUR, above n. 60, pp. 369–371.
[79] Ibid., pp. 371–373.
[80] See generally A. GRIFFIN, "Dethroning the Hierarchy of Authority" (2018) 1(1) *Oregon Law Review* 57; and F. SCHAUER and V. WISE, "Nonlegal Information and the Delegalization of Law" (2000) 29(1) *Journal of Legal Studies* 495.
[81] LATOUR, above n. 60, p. 373.
[82] LATOUR, above n. 58, p. 5.
[83] Ibid., pp. 5–6.

water quality on a beach. Instead of the right being used solely or mainly with the goal of participating in an abstract notion of environmental citizenship (as set out in the environmental and participative goals of the Aarhus Convention), people may be driven by motivations ranging from improving their local environment to seeking personal gain to annoyance at their local council. Rather than assuming that particular uses of the right follow the vision behind its establishment in international and Scottish law, one should look at how the (often messy) networks of actors have established rights to environmental information and the different ways in which different sorts of information are being sought and used. Actor-Network Theory's move away from hierarchy and universals towards a focus on the complexity revealed in real life is invaluable for this study.

Actor-Network Theory's challenge to hierarchical views of society is also helpful in analysing the right of access to environmental information. Rather than assuming that the legal norms in the Aarhus Convention or the role of the authorities as the guardians of environmental information place them above other actors, this allows us to think about more complex and shifting power relations. For example, it might be assumed that since they hold the information and have to be asked to disclose it, public authorities would consider that they exercise power over the members of the public making a request for information. Yet, several conversations with authorities revealed a sense that it is the requesters that hold power over them, bolstered by the legal obligations which dictate how authorities must respond, leaving them little room for discretion. The relationships in practice are thus much more nuanced than might be imagined from the simple vision that lies behind the creation of the right. More broadly, the environmental aspect of these regulations works to disrupt any anthropocentric hierarchy. All human actors are likely be significantly impacted by the environmental changes they have contributed to causing.

1.3. THE ENVIRONMENT AS AN ACTOR AND ENVIRONMENTAL POLITICS

Thinking of the environment as an actor that is significant in the right of access to environmental information, and that can be engaged with through different types of environmental citizenship, is given additional impetus by the role of environmental change in disrupting life on Earth. Recognising the environment as an actor can disrupt anthropocentric approaches to this topic. There may be nothing new in seeing the environment as playing

Chapter 2. Theoretical and Legal Frameworks

a role as a political actor, but as global heating starts to have greater impacts on everyday life, such as through the increased frequency of extreme weather events, the role of and responses to the environment as an actor are key political questions today.

Drawing on Actor-Network Theory can help to think about the role of the environment as an actor in environmental law and policy. Latour argues for those doing political ecology to engage with "the dichotomies of man and nature, subject and object, modes of production, and the environment" to "burrow down beneath the dichotomies like the proverbial old mole ... Instead of cutting the Gordian knot, I am going to shake it around in a lot of different ways".[84] Applied to the right of access to environmental information, Latour's perspective suggests that the networks around the right of access to environmental information might offer an example of the type of political ecology and environmental politics that Latour calls for bringing into being.[85] In the current context of ongoing and damaging environmental change, looking at the role of the environment as an actor in environmental law and citizenship – rather than just critiquing human-nature dichotomies, or focusing solely on the human – seems a promising approach. Indeed, this approach of recognising the environment as an actor within law can be identified in the growing trend of granting legal personhood to non-human actors, such as the Whanganui River in New Zealand.[86]

The goal of legal instruments, such as the Aarhus Convention, to build a type of environmental citizenship is potentially invaluable here, and one aim of the more detailed analyses here of how the right of access to environmental information is being used today – as well as indicating problems and limitations – is to look at hopeful signs of how the environment is being taken seriously in society and politics. Moreover, the emphasis on environmental outcomes is a crucial distinguishing feature between the right of access to environmental information and the laws securing freedom of information in the broader context, implicitly emphasising the role of the environment as an actor in itself. In this way, Actor-Network Theory may enable a reorientation from the anthropocentric view of the

---

[84] B. LATOUR, *Politics of Nature: How to Bring the Sciences into Democracy*, Harvard University Press, Cambridge, MA 2004, p. 3.
[85] B. LATOUR, *Down to Earth: Politics in the New Climatic Regime*, Polity Press, Bristol 2018, pp. 1–2.
[86] See A. HUTCHINSON, "The Whanganui River as a Legal Person" (2014) 39(3) *Alternative Law Journal* 179.

environment towards an understanding which incorporates a broader understanding of the environment as both something which acts and is acted on in environmental politics.

2. THE LEGAL FRAMEWORK: THE CONTEXT AND DEVELOPMENT OF THE RIGHT OF ACCESS TO ENVIRONMENTAL INFORMATION

In considering the right of access to environmental information and its implementation, it is also important to discuss the origins of the right and its development over the course of 50 years. The development of the right was primarily conducted at the international level, with the Stockholm Declaration acting as the initial starting point.[87] Beyond the Stockholm Declaration, Principle 10 of the Rio Declaration on Environment and Development in 1992[88] explicitly recognised both the right to access environmental information and its significance in the context of environmental degradation. Specifically, through linking access to information with opportunities to participate in decision-making processes, the Rio Declaration provided the foundation upon which subsequent legal instruments could further develop the right.

These developments came with the creation of the Aarhus Convention, which further built upon the objectives of the Rio Declaration by enshrining specific procedural rights in relation to the rights to access environmental information and to participate in environmental decision-making procedures. These procedural rights are significant in giving concrete shape to the environmental rights and aims embodied by the Rio Declaration. Indeed, the Aarhus Convention reflects the same underpinning logic of the Rio Declaration in guaranteeing these rights. This is significant – because the Aarhus Convention is the normative instrument in this area of law,[89] the environmental and participative aims embodied by the Rio Declaration are further embedded into how the right and its actors are conceptualised.

However, notwithstanding the overarching normativity of the Aarhus Convention, states are not legally obliged to comply with the Aarhus Convention unless they have ratified it. Even where ratification has taken

---

[87] Stockholm Declaration, above n. 18.
[88] Rio Declaration, above n. 19, Principle 10.
[89] See generally WHITTAKER, above n. 24.

Chapter 2. Theoretical and Legal Frameworks

place, in states with a dualist view of international law the Convention does not by itself have any force within domestic law. The UK is such a dualist state, and Scotland, as a jurisdiction within the UK, shares this approach to international law. Accordingly, while the Convention shapes the framework that is applied, the operative rights which can be asserted by individuals in the UK are to be found in the implementing measures at the national level. In Scotland, these measures are the Environmental Information (Scotland) Regulations 2004 (EI(S)R).[90]

These various international and domestic legal instruments form the legal framework under which the right of access to environmental information operates – a framework which is distinct and separate from the one which governs the general right to information under broader freedom of information laws. Yet within these instruments, there are also implicit assumptions relating to the right: specifically, what constitutes (or is explicitly excluded from being considered) an actor and how these actors interact with both each other and the right itself. It is here that Actor-Network Theory, by interrogating these assumptions, can help to understand more clearly the complexities of the interactions in real life and to construct a new network that better reflects the operation of the right in practice.

2.1. THE RIO DECLARATION

The negotiations leading up to the Rio Declaration were contextualised by the early global concerns for the environment[91] and by the work that had been undertaken prior to the Rio Conference. The Stockholm Declaration is the product of one such exercise at the international level and is important in contextualising the work of the Rio Declaration, as it established the aspirational principle of safeguarding natural resources "for present and future generations".[92] The Rio Declaration was also contextualised by the

---

[90] SSI 2004/520.
[91] J. BRUNNÉE, "The Stockholm Declaration and the Structure and Processes of International Environmental Law" in A. CHIRCOP, T. MCDORMAN and S. ROLSTON (eds), *The Future of Ocean Regime Building: Essays in Tribute to Douglas M Johnston*, Martinus Nijhoff, Leiden 2009, p. 41.
[92] Stockholm Declaration, above n. 18, Principle 2.

Intersentia 33

Brundtland Report, which further recognised and provided a definition of sustainable development which is still used to this day:

> Development that meets the needs of the present without compromising the ability of future generations to meet their own needs.[93]

It is important to note the instruments preceding the Rio Declaration, because the Declaration itself represented a notable shift in the way that information, and information rights, were conceptualised. Prior to the Rio Declaration, international law considered the accessibility of environmental information to be an issue restricted to "experts": there was a common assumption that those seeking access to environmental information needed to hold specialist expertise in order to understand the sought-after information.[94] Further reflecting this view, instruments such as the Stockholm Declaration did not explicitly mention public participation or the value of it in achieving the declared environmental goals.[95]

In contrast to that earlier view, the Rio Declaration explicitly stated that environmental information, and environmental decision-making procedures, should be the concern of and available to all concerned citizens.[96] This is enshrined in Principle 10 of the Rio Declaration, which is worth setting out in full again:

> Environmental issues are best handled with the participation of all concerned citizens, at the relevant level. At the national level, each individual shall have appropriate access to information concerning the environment that is held by public authorities, including information on hazardous materials and activities in their communities, and the opportunity to participate in decision-making processes. States shall facilitate and encourage public awareness and participation by making information widely available. Effective access to judicial and administrative proceedings, including redress and remedy, shall be provided.

---

[93] World Commission on Environment and Development, *Our Common Future* (Brundtland Report), Oxford University Press, Oxford 1987, p. 43.

[94] M. HAKLAY, "The Three Eras of Environmental Information: The Roles of Experts and the Public" in V. LORETO, M. HAKLAY, A. HOTHO, V.C.P. SERVEDIO, G. STUMME, J. THEUNIS and F. TRIA (eds), *Participatory Sensing, Opinions and Collective Awareness*, Springer, Heidelberg 2016, p. 163. This is not to suggest that this was the only view during this time; see generally S. ARNSTEIN, "A Ladder of Citizen Participation" (1969) 35(4) *Journal of the American Institute of Planners* 216.

[95] J. EBBESSON, "Principle 10: Public Participation" in J. VIÑUALES (ed), *The Rio Declaration on Environment and Development*, Oxford University Press, Oxford 2015, p. 288.

[96] HAKLAY, above n. 94.

Principle 10 contains many significant elements which have now been incorporated into the contemporary views on the right of access to environmental information and its role in environmental governance. The Principle proclaims access to environmental information as a necessary precursor to public participation in environmental decision-making procedures. Underlying this extension of participatory rights is the idea that such participation is necessary to improve the quality of environmental decisions,[97] which is key to the overarching aim of protecting the environment. A further aspect of the Rio Declaration is that unlike its antecedents, its phrasing draws attention to the twin elements within the right, both to request access to environmental information and to have environmental information proactively disclosed.[98]

Beyond recognising the link between human activities and the right to a healthy environment, the Rio Declaration also contains a range of underpinning assumptions that have shaped the right to the present day. One key assumption is that the right is primarily one which relates to the central position of humanity: that humans (or human-made bodies) are the important actors within the context of the right of access to environmental information.[99] This can be evidenced in Principle 10, which focuses on "citizens", "individuals" and "States", excluding non-human actors such as the environment itself.

Indeed, despite the Declaration's focus on protecting the environment, the environment is not considered as an entity which is valued independently from humanity. Dupuy notes that this anthropocentrism runs throughout the Declaration, with Principle 4 unambiguously reflecting the idea that: "Nature and its protection do not exist for themselves."[100] In this way, the environment is something which can only be viewed and recognised through its relationship with, and subjugation by, humanity. This view is notable in light of both the Rio Declaration and the right to information, since despite the right's aim to protect and enhance the environment, it results in the environment not being recognised as an actor within the right's actor-network.

---

[97] EBBESSON, above n. 95, pp. 290 and 307.
[98] UNEP, "Guidelines for the Development of National Legislation on Access to Information, Public Participation and Access to Justice in Environmental Matters" Adopted by the Governing Council of the United Nations Environment Programme in decision SS.XI/5, part A of 26 February 2010, pp. 5–6.
[99] P DUPUY, "The Philosophy of the Rio Declaration" in VIÑUALES, above n. 95, p. 68.
[100] Ibid., p. 69.

Another notable assumption embodied by the Rio Declaration is its construction of human actors. The terminology used in Principle 10 highlights that the Rio Declaration adopts a broad construction of the actors who engage with each other under the right. Those who want to access environmental information are defined as "citizens" or "individuals", terms which amalgamate those who want to engage with the right into a singular category of users, and do not distinguish between different motives which drive these users or their levels of expertise.[101] A notable example of this is the lack of consideration given to civil society and non-governmental organisations (NGOs), groups which are likely to engage with the right and are distinct from the "individuals" envisioned by the Rio Declaration.[102] Public authorities are also broadly defined, with different types of public authorities and the different employees working for them amalgamated into the singular label of "public authority".

To an extent, this categorisation of the human actors who engage with the right is less problematic due to the nature of the Rio Declaration. As a declaratory international instrument, the Rio Declaration was primarily focused on balancing the environmental and economic aspects of sustainable development, as well as reflecting the environmental and economic priorities of "developed" and "developing" countries.[103] Since the Rio Declaration avoids explicitly discussing specific human rights, including the right to environmental information,[104] it follows that the specifics regarding who would be using or guaranteeing these rights are not considered. Yet, despite this lack of detail, the framing of the right's human or human-made actors, and the exclusion of non-human actors, is echoed through other contemporary and subsequent normative instruments that guarantee the right.

2.2. THE AARHUS CONVENTION

By its very nature, the Rio Declaration did not prescribe exactly what is required from states to ensure public participation and access to information, nor did it create any specific obligations binding states

---

[101] The unwillingness to consider expertise as relevant may be a consequence of the shift in perspective on information rights and "expertise"; see HAKLAY, above n. 94.
[102] EBBESSON, above n. 95, p. 291.
[103] J. VIÑUALES, "The Rio Declaration on Environment and Development: Preliminary Study" in VIÑUALES, above n. 95, pp. 6–7 and 11.
[104] VIÑUALES, above n. 95, p. 58.

Chapter 2. Theoretical and Legal Frameworks

to live up to this expectation. It was therefore left to other processes to concretise the rights and obligations, and these have been pursued at the regional level. The most significant has been the Convention on Access to Information, Public Participation in Decision-Making and Access to Justice in Environmental Matters, otherwise known as the Aarhus Convention.

Agreed under the auspices of the UN Economic Commission for Europe and signed on 25 June 1998, the Aarhus Convention represents the first substantial attempt to convert the brief statement in the Rio Principles into a detailed legal framework for securing public participation and access to information and justice on environmental matters. At the legal level, any state or regional economic integration organisations can sign and ratify the Convention.[105] However, in practice, it is only states in Europe (and the EU itself) or the former Soviet Union which have currently ratified the Convention.[106] Yet, notwithstanding this limited direct application, the Aarhus Convention is the normative instrument that presents a workable set of legal rules that implements the broad principles and aspirations of the Rio Declaration.[107] In this way, it represents not just the most influential legal instrument for the right in Scotland, but also for a large portion of the world.

The objective of the Aarhus Convention is to "contribute to the protection of the right of every person of present and future generations to live in an environment adequate to his or her health and well-being."[108] On the surface, it does this through obliging states to guarantee certain procedural rights which individuals, including NGOs, can engage with in order to contribute to environmental protection efforts. However, a deeper examination highlights that these individuals are not merely free to seek to protect the environment, as the Convention also imposes a moral duty on all individuals to protect and enhance the environment for present and future generations.[109] It further sets normative expectations for how both holders of information and those seeking it will behave.

---

[105] Aarhus Convention, art. 19.
[106] Guinea-Bissau is well-advanced in its plans to accede to the Convention: see <https://unece.org/sites/default/files/2021-06/Contribution_Accession%20by%20Guinea-Bissau.pdf> accessed 19 April 2022.
[107] WHITTAKER, above n. 24, p.35.
[108] Aarhus Convention, art. 1.
[109] Ibid., Preamble para. 7. This can also be evidenced in the explicit inclusion of NGOs in relation to their ability to participate in environmental decision-making process and seek access to environmental justice, which is linked to the NGO "promoting environmental protection"; ibid., art. 2(5). See also BARRITT, above n. 21, p. 33.

This moral duty is fundamental to how the Aarhus Convention conceptualises the right of access to environmental information. Under the Convention, the right of access to environmental information is viewed as a precursor to public participation in environmental decision-making procedures, with the altruistic goal of enhancing the environment for present and future generations.[110] Public participation is thus viewed as essential in achieving the aim of a healthy environment through improving environmental protection efforts. This participative focus is supported by the other rights enshrined in the Convention: environmental information is viewed as key to securing meaningful engagement with participative processes, and access to environmental justice as key in securing the opportunity to participate.[111]

This focus on the Aarhus Convention's participative right and aims is also reflected in its design, which arranges the rights it guarantees – access to information, public participation and access to justice – into three interlocking "pillars" of rights. These three pillars are intricately linked, and the vision of concerned citizens obtaining information in order to participate in environmental decision-making lies at the core of the regime that is established. While not inherently co-dependent on each other, these pillars are mutually supportive, enabling the other pillars to operate and effectively contribute to the Convention's environmental and participative aims. In this way, the link between openness, participation and environmental protection infuses the way in which the various pillars, and the rights they represent, are conceptualised.

Access to environmental information forms the first pillar of the Aarhus Convention. Unlike the Rio Declaration, the Aarhus Convention explicitly distinguishes between the right to have environmental information proactively disclosed[112] and the right to request access to environmental information.[113] These rights are not identical and synonymous, requiring very different things from the authorities holding the information. Proactively disclosing environmental information requires the authority to take the initiative in identifying and disseminating large amounts of information and has a greater potential to reach a wider audience.

---

[110] WHITTAKER, above n. 24, p. 479.
[111] The right to information is considered to be the strongest of the three pillars: M. LEE and C. ABBOT, "The Usual Suspects? Public Participation under the Aarhus Convention" (2003) 66(1) *Modern Law Review* 80, 93.
[112] Aarhus Convention, art. 5.
[113] Ibid., art. 4.

Chapter 2. Theoretical and Legal Frameworks

By contrast, responding to requests is a purely reactive activity, governed by detailed procedural rules, but may still be onerous depending on the volume and nature of requests received, and allows interested individuals to receive information that specifically relates to their needs.[114]

The public participation pillar acts as the Convention's second pillar of rights. Encapsulating a range of opportunities for engaging in environmental decision-making procedures, this second pillar is at the heart of the Convention's desire to promote public participation as a key means of meeting its environmental aims. The Convention specifies instances when participation must be enabled and certain key steps involved, such as the publication of draft proposals and clear identification of when and how the public are to have the opportunity to make representations.[115] To ensure that the participation is meaningful, states are required to "ensure that in the decision due account is taken of the outcome of the public participation".[116] The final pillar of the Aarhus Convention is the access to justice pillar, which obliges parties to provide a legally binding procedure to enable the review of a public authority's decisions and actions in relation to the rights established under the other two pillars.[117] The access to justice pillar is notable in that it is served not only by the procedural obligations enshrined in Article 9 of the Convention, but also by the activities of the Aarhus Convention Compliance Committee, an independent body established by the Meeting of the Parties and which hears complaints relating to alleged breaches of the Convention.[118] This pillar plays a vital role in ensuring that individuals and NGOs can access environmental information, as it provides them with the means to enforce their Convention rights against the state.[119]

The three pillars are intricately linked to each other and to the vision held by the Convention of concerned citizens obtaining information to participate in environmental decision-making procedures for the

---

[114] WHITTAKER et al., above n. 40, pp. 471–472.
[115] The right to participate in environmental decision-making procedures under the Aarhus Convention extends to "specific activities" (major development projects listed in Annex I), general plans, programmes and policies, and executive regulations; Aarhus Convention, arts. 6–8.
[116] Ibid., art. 6(8).
[117] Ibid., art. 9(1) and (2).
[118] See generally UN ECE, Aarhus Convention Report of the First Meeting of the Parties: Addendum Decision I/7, ECE/MP.PP/2/Add.8 (2 April 2004).
[119] Ibid. See also J. EBBESSON, H. GAUGITSCH, J. JENDROŚKA, F. MARSHALL and S. STEC, *The Aarhus Convention: An Implementation Guide*, 2nd ed., United Nations, Geneva 2014, p. 35 and p. 223.

greater good. This is not to suggest that the Convention requires citizens to use any disclosed environmental information solely as a means of participating in environmental decision-making procedures.[120] Yet these pillars must be viewed in light of the Convention's emphasis on the benefits of public participation, derived from the Rio Declaration, namely that such participation is key to protecting and enhancing the environment.[121] As a result, there is an implicit expectation that users will seek to participate in environmental decision-making procedures.

This expectation influences how the right of access to environmental information is conceptualised: because environmental information is viewed as a precursor to public participation, its role is primarily viewed through this participative lens. However, this is just one aspect of this conceptualisation which also contains the assumptions about the actors which engage with the right of access to environmental information under the Aarhus Convention.

One such assumption is that all the relevant actors that engage with the right are either human or human-constructed entities, such as public authorities. This can be evidenced in the language of the Aarhus Convention, which refers only to "the public" or "public authorities" as entities with rights and obligations under the Aarhus Convention. This follows from the anthropocentric approach of the Rio Declaration, and evidences the Convention's primary concern in the environment through the lens of humanity, rather than considering the environment as an entity independent of humanity.[122] Within the context of Actor-Network Theory, this assumption results in the Aarhus Convention not recognising the environment or other non-human elements such as technologies as actors. This lack of recognition influences how others engage with the right to environmental information. By excluding non-human actors, there is a risk that the conceptions of the networks involved do not match what is happening in practice and that non-human entities, in particular the environment, are not paid attention by virtue of their own existence (as opposed to merely their impact on humans).[123]

---

[120] Indeed, the Convention explicitly highlights the environmental benefits of greater transparency and education the public on environmental issues; Aarhus Convention, Preamble, paras 10–13.
[121] WHITTAKER et al., above n. 40, 479.
[122] PETERSMANN, above n. 42, p. 247.
[123] See C. STONE, *Should Trees Have Standing? Law, Morality and the Environment*, 3rd ed., Oxford University Press, Oxford 2010, p. 172.

Chapter 2. Theoretical and Legal Frameworks

Another assumption in the Aarhus Convention, also reflected in the Rio Declaration, is that an adequate picture of the relevant relationships can be constructed by using broad, all-encompassing categories for the human actors who engage with the rights enshrined within it. For example, users of the right of access to environmental information are defined as "the public". The unique characteristics of different individual users are not accounted for in this term, leading to a broad homogenisation of users seeking access to environmental information.[124] Similarly, the construct of "public authorities" as actors erases the differences between different authorities, whose respective remits may be different and which may have different relationships with environmental information, and between different actors within an authority.[125]

A corollary point arising from this perspective of the Aarhus Convention is that with its emphasis on promoting public participation, the rights are provided to enable individual to engage directly with the relevant processes. For example, in disclosing environmental information, there is an expectation that public authorities are disclosing the information to the user who intends to act on it on the basis of their own motivations. Such an approach is significant not just because it emphasises the participative aims of the right; it is also significant because users who act as intermediaries, such as journalists and consultants, are not the intended beneficiaries of the rights contained within the Convention. While this does not exclude them from using these rights, they may find that their unique needs as intermediaries are not catered for within the obligations of the Aarhus Convention or its domestic implementation.

These assumptions are not merely of theoretical concern; they have an impact on how the right of access to environmental information is conceptualised and implemented. Users are imputed with wholly altruistic, environmental motives by the Convention, potentially creating tensions where public authorities feel that this motive is not held by users. Public authorities are viewed as identical to one another, leading to difficulties for users when they do not guarantee the right in the same way. While it is tempting to see these issues as being limited to the international sphere, in practice domestic environmental information regimes also reflect the Convention's framing of the right and its actors so that the concerns occur at all levels.

---

[124] One notable exception to this is NGOs, which are explicitly referred to separately to other users in the Convention; Aarhus Convention, Preamble para. 13, arts 2, 9. However, even here NGOs are broadly construed; see Chapter 3, section 2.4.
[125] For more detail on this point, see Chapter 3.

2.3. LAW IN THE EUROPEAN UNION AND SCOTLAND

The ratification of the Aarhus Convention is important to how both Scotland and the EU guarantee the right of access to environmental information. As parties to the Convention,[126] both jurisdictions are legally obliged to implement its provisions within their own legal systems. However, the Aarhus Convention itself was preceded by the EU's own efforts to guarantee the right of access to environmental information through Directive 90/313/EEC,[127] which was implemented in the UK by the Environmental Information Regulations 1992.[128] Following the ratification of the Aarhus Convention by the EU, Directive 90/313/EEC was replaced with Directive 2003/4/EC,[129] which both fleshed out the previous Directive's obligations and broadly reflected the conceptual understanding of the right to environmental information as the Aarhus Convention.[130] The UK, having ratified the Convention and still being a member of the EU at that time, was obliged to reform its environmental information regime to reflect the provisions of both the Aarhus Convention and Directive 2003/4/EC. In Scotland, this was primarily achieved through the Environmental Information (Scotland) Regulations 2004 (EI(S)R).[131] The EI(S)R continue to be in force at the time of writing, unaffected by the UK's withdrawal from the EU.[132]

---

[126] The Scottish authorities are responsible for implementing within the scope of their devolved competence the international obligations accepted by the UK, but international relations themselves are a matter reserved for the UK Government.

[127] Council Directive 90/313/EEC of 7 June 1990 on the Freedom of Access to Information on the Environment [1990] OJ L158/56.

[128] SI 1992/3240.

[129] Directive 2003/4/EC of the European Parliament and the Council of 28 January 2003 on Public Access to Environmental Information and Repealing Directive 90/313/EEC [2003] OJ L41/26.

[130] A. BERTHIER and L. KRÄMER, "The Aarhus Convention: Implementation and Compliance with EU Law", ClientEarth/European Union Aarhus Centre, Brussels 2014.

[131] SSI 2004/520. The EI(S)R do not apply to environmental information relating to matters that are reserved for the UK Government, which are thus governed by the Environmental Information Regulations 2004, SI 2004/3391, which were similarly made to implement the revised EU Directive.

[132] One element of the Trade and Co-operation Agreement governing post-withdrawal relations between the EU and the UK is a commitment to "ensur[ing] that the general public is given access to relevant environmental information held by or for public authorities, as well as ensuring the active dissemination of that information to the general public by electronic means"; Trade and Cooperation Agreement between the United Kingdom of Great Britain and Northern Ireland and the European Union and the European Atomic Energy Community (Brussels and London, 30 December 2020) (UKTS No. 8 (2021)), art. 398.

Chapter 2. Theoretical and Legal Frameworks

With both Directive 2003/4/EC and the EI(S)R being implemented because of the ratification of the Aarhus Convention, both instruments embody the Convention's environmental and participatory aims. Yet this is not to suggest that either instrument merely adheres to the obligations as set out by the Convention. Indeed, both instruments adopt a broader definition of what constitutes environmental information,[133] and take a stricter stance on the non-disclosure of information relating to emissions.[134] These deviations from the Aarhus Convention act to further emphasise the interconnectedness of "the environment" and the right's environmental aims.[135]

This substantive environmental aim is in marked distinction to the more procedural focus of the wider freedom on information provisions in Scotland that exist alongside the EI(S)R: the Freedom of Information (Scotland) Act 2002.[136] Both regimes contain obligations relating to the proactive disclosure of information and to the processing of requests for information, obligations imposed on the same range of public authorities in Scotland. Where an authority receives a request for the disclosure of information, it must determine whether the information in question is environmental or not; where a request relates to environmental information, it is the EI(S)R which take priority over the Freedom of Information (Scotland) Act 2002.[137]

The fact that Scotland has two information regimes is notable in that it reflects the dual, parallel development of the specific right to environmental information and the general right to information. The use of this parallel system can also be interpreted to reflect positively or negatively on the right to environmental information. On the one hand, in creating a specific regime, the Scottish Government and Parliament reflects an understanding that the environmental objectives of the right merit particular safeguarding within their own unique regime. Yet, on the other hand, this separation can be interpreted as the right being an "outlier" from the more ubiquitous

---

[133] BERTHIER and KRAMER, above n. 130, p. 15.
[134] Ibid., p. 44.
[135] Although this is not to suggest that the domestic implementation of the Aarhus Convention does not deviate from the Convention in other ways which are less environmentally driven; see WHITTAKER, above n. 24, p. 81.
[136] This Act applies to authorities within devolved competence under the Scotland Act 1998; for those that operate under powers reserved to the UK Government, the broadly parallel Freedom of Information Act 2000 applies.
[137] Freedom of Information (Scotland) Act 2002, s. 39(2)(a).

Intersentia 43

general right to information, in turn minimising the profile of the right to environmental information and simply creating a source of confusion for those seeing information. More prosaically, though, the existence of a separate regime for environmental information was largely driven by the need to be able to demonstrate clearly that the EU Directive had been fully implemented in domestic law.

As is expected from a domestic instrument that implements the Aarhus Convention, the EI(S)R embody the Convention's aims for the right of access to environmental information. Further still, the EI(S)R also reflect many of the implicit assumptions that underpin the Convention's understanding of the right and its expected usage in practice. These are discussed in more detail in the following section, but is worth highlighting here because it reflects a continuous strand that reaches from the Rio Declaration to the present day and has driven the development of the right and its current shape. Through charting this strand, it is possible to understand not just the origins of the right, but also the source and shape of the assumptions that underpin the right and its implementation.

3. THE LEGAL FRAMEWORK: CONTENT

Beyond charting in broad terms the development of the right of access to environmental information, and the underpinning assumptions which shaped this development, it is also important to set out the actual legal content and procedural obligations contained with the Aarhus Convention and the EI(S)R. The obligations (and associated rights) enshrined in both sets of instruments are vital for understanding the contours of the legal regime that guarantees the right of access to environmental information. It is this regime that governs how the public and public authorities deal with each other, that provides the legal rules for seeking access to environmental information in Scotland and that shape the interactions between the various actors. Consequently, the provisions of both the Aarhus Convention and the EI(S)R must be examined to provide a full understanding of the legal picture.[138]

---

[138] See generally K. DUNION, *Freedom of Information in Scotland in Practice*, Dundee University Press, Dundee 2011, Chapter 2.

Chapter 2. Theoretical and Legal Frameworks

3.1. DEFINITIONS AND SCOPE OF THE RIGHT OF ACCESS TO ENVIRONMENTAL INFORMATION

In guaranteeing the right of access to environmental information, both the Convention and the EI(S)R seek to define "environmental information" in a way that encapsulates all features of the environment and any decision-making that affects them. Delineating what information individuals and NGOs are entitled to under the right of access to environmental information, "environmental information" is defined as:

> ... any information in written, visual, aural, electronic or any other material form on:
>
> (a) The state of elements of the environment, such as air and atmosphere, water, soil, land, landscape and natural sites, biological diversity and its components, including genetically modified organisms, and the interaction among these elements;
> (b) Factors, such as substances, energy, noise and radiation, and activities or measures, including administrative measures, environmental agreements, policies, legislation, plans and programmes, affecting or likely to affect the elements of the environment within the scope of subparagraph (a) above, and cost-benefit and other economic analyses and assumptions used in environmental decision-making;
> (c) The state of human health and safety, conditions of human life, cultural sites and built structures, inasmuch as they are or may be affected by the state of the elements of the environment or, through these elements, by the factors, activities or measures referred to in subparagraph (b) above.[139]

This definition is broad and non-exhaustive, encapsulating both rural and urban conceptualisations of the environment,[140] and ensuring that a wide range of interactions between the state and the public are covered by both regimes' obligations.[141] The breadth of this definition reflects the right's aim

---

[139] Aarhus Convention, art. 2(3). This definition is carried over into EI(S)R, reg. 2(1).
[140] M. Woods, "Rural Geography III: Rural Futures and the Future of Rural Geography" (2011) 36(1) *Progress in Human Geography* 125; and D. Bell, "Variations on the Rural Idyll" in P. Cloke et al. (eds), *Handbook of Rural Studies*, Sage, Newbury Park 2006, pp. 150–151.
[141] See Ebbesson et al., above n. 119, p. 50; and *Aarhus Convention Compliance Committee Communication 2009/37* (Belarus) ECE/MP.PP//2011/11/Add.2, 12 May 2011.

Intersentia 45

of protecting the environment through promoting informed participation in environmental matters, as the definition bars restrictive interpretations of whether information is "environmental" from being implemented.[142]

The right of access applies only to information held by a public authority, fitting in with the Convention's conception of the prime role of information as enabling meaningful participation in governmental processes. "Public authority" is given a broad definition in the Convention[143] and the EI(S)R,[144] and as such encapsulates private bodies which have public responsibilities, exercise public functions or provide public services that relate to the environment. Private bodies are particularly noteworthy when discussing the implementation of the right of access to environmental information; the boundary between public authorities and other bodies can be uncertain and contested,[145] and with the growing trend in privatisation, the information regimes need to ensure that authorities cannot "contract-out" of their obligations under the right by transferring responsibilities to private bodies.[146]

While the inclusion of private bodies is the most eye-catching element of the definition, the range of public bodies covered by the definition also merits discussion. By design, the Aarhus Convention and the EI(S)R cover a range of public authorities, including the following:

- Authorities which explicitly deal with environmental matters, such as the Scottish Environment Protection Agency in Scotland.
- Central government authorities, such as the Scottish Government.
- Local government authorities, such as Angus Council.
- Authorities which ostensibly do not deal with environmental matters at all, such as Revenue Scotland.
- Publicly owned companies, such as Scottish Water.

Notably, regardless of the wide-ranging characteristics of the bodies that are considered as a "public authority" under either instrument, they are all subject to the same duties and obligations as every other "public authority", despite the differences in their operation.

---

[142] If information is not "environmental", access will be determined by the wider laws of freedom of information, notably the Freedom of Information (Scotland) Act 2002; see DUNION, above n. 138.
[143] Aarhus Convention, art. 2(2).
[144] EI(S)R, reg. 2(1), which uses the term "Scottish public authorities", but carries over the same definition.
[145] Case C-279/12, *Fish Legal v. Information Commissioner*, ECLI:EU:C:2013:853.
[146] EBBESSON et al., above n. 119, p. 47.

Chapter 2. Theoretical and Legal Frameworks

One of the reasons why the term "public authority" is defined this broadly is that every authority, to an extent, will deal with the environment and environmental information. Accordingly, the scale of the environment as an entity requires environmental information regimes to adopt a broad definition of "public authority" that includes not just authorities seen as "environmental", but also those that would not naturally be regarded as such. Drawing on Actor-Network Theory, one might view this as the environment exerting influence over the design of the legal instruments that guarantee the right of access to environmental information. As such, it is one of the rare examples where the needs of the environment are taken into account in shaping the legal framework.[147]

The broad and undifferentiated approach to defining "public authority" is matched by the approach to those who can exercise the procedural rights created under the Convention and the EI(S)R. The Aarhus Convention refers to individuals using the right of access to environment information as "the public",[148] implicitly homogenising the different individuals who seek environmental information into a singular category. This can further be identified in the Convention's explicit inclusion of everyone regardless of their nationality, domicile or status as a natural or legal person.[149] While this was adopted by the Aarhus Convention to prevent discrimination against individuals who did not live in their country of origin,[150] it also simultaneously supports the general homogenisation of users, an approach taken further by including legal persons including "associations, organisations or groups" in the definition of "the public".[151]

The EI(S)R employ the term "applicants" for any person using the right to request information,[152] which still does not take account of the differences between such users in the regime. This is important to the environmental aims of the right of access to environmental information, because through erasing and not considering the differences between users, both instruments can overlay their underpinning assumptions about users onto all of those engaging with the right. In this way, viewing the definitional provisions of both the Aarhus Convention and the EI(S)R through the lens of Actor-Network Theory is not merely an academic exercise, but also

---

[147] A further example is in relation to exceptions (see section 3.4 below).
[148] Aarhus Convention, art. 2(5); see also other provisions of the Convention.
[149] Ibid., art. 3(9).
[150] EBBESSON et al., above n. 119, p. 72.
[151] Aarhus Convention, art. 2(4).
[152] EI(S)R, reg. 2(1).

demonstrates that, at the doctrinal level, there is an oversimplification in terms of of how actors engage with each other and with the right itself, and, as a consequence of this, the different needs, motivations and capacities of different users can be overlooked with detrimental results.

3.2. THE PROACTIVE DUTY TO PROVIDE INFORMATION

A distinctive feature of the Convention, especially in comparison to more general laws on freedom of information, is the obligation on public authorities to be proactive in collecting and disseminating environmental information.[153] Whilst other more specific obligations to ensure that specific documents or pieces of information are made public will exist separately, the focus of freedom of information laws is usually purely on creating the means to request information that is not normally available.[154] The environmental information regime creates a greater obligation not just to respond to requests from specific individuals, but also to ensure that all members of society have ready access to environmental information.

Under this conceptualisation of the right of access to environmental information, the foundational role of environmental democracy shines through.[155] Specifically, the duty to disclose environmental information proactively focuses on how authorities interact with all of the public they are meant to serve and how they can create the conditions for active environmental citizenship in which the public can influence the authorities and call them to account. Information is primarily viewed as a tool to be used in the wider relationship between the public and the authorities that take decisions with a view to protecting and enhancing the environment.

This "active right" to information – so called because it requires authorities to take active steps to disseminate information as opposed to waiting passively until individual requests are received – should mean that access to information is not restricted to those members of the public already sufficiently alert and motivated and with the capacity to realise what sort of information may be available and how to seek it out. Authorities bear a responsibility for promoting environmental education and encouraging widespread public awareness of the opportunities to participate in decision-making.[156] In this way, the wider public can come

---

[153] Aarhus Convention, art. 5; EI(S)R, reg. 4.
[154] WHITTAKER et al., above n. 40, p. 471.
[155] See BARRITT, above n. 21.
[156] Aarhus Convention, Preamble, para. 14.

Chapter 2. Theoretical and Legal Frameworks

across relevant information without making any special efforts, and awareness of the availability and content of information should be more widespread.[157] All of this supports the Convention's image of an informed and engaged public serving as guardians of the environment, a more substantive goal than the focus on transparency and accountability which is at the core of wider freedom of information regimes.

3.3. REQUESTS FOR INFORMATION

In contrast to the proactive disclosure of environmental information, the "passive right" – so called because authorities are not required to do anything unless a request is made – allows individuals to request access to environmental information.[158] Every member of "the public" is entitled to submit requests for environmental information, reflecting the Convention's conception of the environment as being everyone's responsibility, with the concomitant moral obligation to ensure that it is cared for. It is this obligation that is served by all three of the Aarhus "pillars", with access to information enabling effective public participation, and both being protected by access to justice.[159] The environmental information pillar aims to create an informed society, which in turn empowers the public to participate actively and effectively in decision-making procedures.[160]

In disclosing environmental information on request, the Convention and the EI(S)R oblige public authorities to adopt an "applicant-blind" approach. Under this approach, nobody – individuals, NGOs or others – requesting environmental information needs to identify themselves or justify their request.[161] This approach seeks to ensure that no users are discriminated against for whatever reason, especially when the information they are gathering may be used to criticise or challenge the authority holding it. The approach also matches the conception of the environment as the shared responsibility of everyone with the concomitant implicit moral duty that is shared; it does not matter who submits a request

---

[157] WHITTAKER et al., above n. 40, p. 473.
[158] Aarhus Convention, art. 4.
[159] WHITTAKER et al., above n. 40, p. 470.
[160] LEE and ABBOT, above n. 111, p. 88.
[161] This is established by the absence of any requirements when making a request to provide identifying or explanatory information, and the Convention expressly states that requests can be made "without an interest having to be stated"; Aarhus Convention, art. 4(1)(a). See also EBBESSON et al., above n. 119, p. 80.

Intersentia 49

(or requests) for environmental information, as everyone who does should be doing so with the aim of protecting and enhancing the environment for present and future generations. While the Aarhus Convention does not stand in the way of information being sought for other uses, the structure of the Convention places at its core the notion of public participation driven by environmental concern.[162] Those seeking or using information for other purposes may thus be seen as misusing the right, colouring their interactions with the public authorities concerned.

In allowing the public to make requests for environmental information, neither instrument imposes many conditions on the submission of requests. The detailed procedures set out in the EI(S)R are similar but not identical to those under the wider freedom of information laws.[163] This similarity contributes to the fact that in many contexts, there is a lack of clear distinction between the environmental information and freedom of information laws, creating confusion on the part of some of those seeking to obtain information. Where the information involved is "environmental", it is the environmental information rules which must be applied.[164]

While requests must not be too general,[165] there is no obligation to adhere to a particular form of request[166] or provide personal information, such as the reason for wanting the information. Meeting the requester's needs and preferences is further supported by the obligation on public authorities to disclose the environmental information in the form requested,[167] an element that also supports those affected by disabilities or other constraints.[168] The authority is under an obligation to assist in refining the request, as well as to advise and assist the requester[169] and to transfer the request if it is another authority that holds the information sought.[170]

Under the Convention, requests for information are conceived of as enabling active participation in environmental decision-making processes

---

[162] The consequences of the applicant-blind approach in practice are discussed in Chapters 3 and 4.
[163] Notably the Freedom of Information (Scotland) Act 2002.
[164] Freedom of Information (Scotland) Act 2002, s. 39(2).
[165] Aarhus Convention, art. 4(3)(b); EI(S)R, reg. 10(4)(c).
[166] There is no requirement for requests to be made in writing; EI(S)R, reg. 5. See EBBESSON et al., above n. 119, pp. 79–80.
[167] Unless it is reasonable to provide it in another form or it is already publicly available. See Aarhus Convention, art. 4(1)(b); EI(S)R, reg. 6.
[168] EBBESSON et al., above n. 119, p. 80.
[169] Aarhus Convention, art. 3(2); EI(S)R, reg. 9.
[170] Aarhus Convention, art. 4(5); EI(S)R, reg. 14.

Chapter 2. Theoretical and Legal Frameworks

rather than being just for general enlightenment. Accordingly, under both the Convention and the EI(S)R, timeliness is important. The proactive publication of information should ensure that much environmental information is available as soon anyone wants it, but where requests are necessary, timeliness should be secured by the duty on public authorities to respond to requests as soon as possible and, at the latest, within one month,[171] which is translated as 20 working days in the EI(S)R.[172] Where the complexity or volume of the information requested justifies it, an extension of the time limit to two months (40 working days) is allowed.

While favouring the interests of the public, the Convention does recognise the burden that responding to requests for information places on authorities, although they do have in their own hands one way of reducing this by ensuring that much of the information that is in demand is proactively published. The burden is partly balanced by the power granted to public authorities to charge "reasonable fees" for disclosing environmental information on request.[173] Scottish public authorities enjoy the power to levy a "reasonable" charge for supplying environmental information, provided they act in accordance with a published schedule of fees.[174] The limitation to "reasonable" charges is important in ensuring that environmental information is not rendered inaccessible behind a paywall, thereby limiting who can participate in environmental decision-making procedures.

3.4. EXCEPTIONS

Both the Aarhus Convention and the EI(S)R limit the right of access to environmental information by allowing public authorities to withhold environmental information from disclosure if it falls under one of the listed exceptions.[175] These exceptions can be broadly classed into two categories.

---

[171] Aarhus Convention, art. 4(2).
[172] EI(S)R, reg. 7.
[173] Aarhus Convention, art. 4(8).
[174] EI(S)R, reg. 8. However, it should be noted that in practice most authorities do not charge for environmental information; see S. WHITTAKER, C.T. REID and J. MENDEL, "Charging for Environmental Information: Does Practice Match Theory?" (2018) 30 *Environmental Law and Management* 91.
[175] Notably, however, the EI(S)R requires authorities to issue their refusals to disclose environmental information in writing and to provide the reasoning for this refusal; EI(S)R, reg. 13.

Freedom of Environmental Information

The first category of exceptions is general in nature: public authorities can refuse requests if they do not hold the requested information;[176] if the material requested is in the course of completion or concerns internal communications[177] or if the request is "manifestly unreasonable" or too general.[178]

The second category of exceptions is concerned with protecting a variety of interests which may be adversely affected by the disclosure of the information requested. Some examples of such interests include the confidentiality of commercial or industrial information,[179] private information about people other than the requester,[180] and information relating to international relations, national security or public security.[181] One important reason justifying non-disclosure, which reflects the environmental aims of the right, is where disclosure would harm the environment that the information is about.[182] This exception is notable not only because it reflects the right's environmental aims, but because it demonstrates the impact that the environment has had on the design and shape of environmental information regimes. Drawing on Actor-Network Theory, this can be seen as the environment exerting pressure upon the legal framework, and those who engage with it, as an actor in its own right.

The Convention states that this second category of exclusions is to be interpreted restrictively, a position which is adopted by the EI(S)R.[183] This is reinforced by a presumption in favour of disclosure and the second category of harm-based exceptions being subject to a public interest test, requiring authorities to assess the harm arising from disclosure against the public interest served by disclosing the information.[184] Beyond the environmental exceptions enshrined in the harm-based exceptions, both the Convention and especially the EI(S)R adopt stricter rules when considering withholding information on emissions.[185] Such important

---

[176] Aarhus Convention, art. 4(3)(a); EI(S)R, reg. 10(4)(a).
[177] Provided that the exception is enshrined in national law or customary practice and taking into account the public interest in disclosing the information; Aarhus Convention, art. 4(3)(c); EI(S)R, reg. 10(4)(d) and 10(4)(e).
[178] Aarhus Convention, art. 4(3)(b); EI(S)R, reg. 10(4)(b) and 10(4)(c).
[179] Aarhus Convention, art. 4(4)(d); EI(S)R, reg.10(5)(e).
[180] Aarhus Convention, art. 4(4)(f); EIS(S)R, regs 10(5)(f), 11.
[181] Aarhus Convention, art. 4(4)(b); EI(S)R, reg. 10(5)(a).
[182] Aarhus Convention, art. 4(4)(h); EI(S)R, reg. 10(5)(g). An example might be revealing the precise location of a protected plant species at risk from collectors.
[183] Aarhus Convention, art. 4(4); EI(S)R, reg. 10(2).
[184] Aarhus Convention, art. 4(4); EI(S)R, reg. 10(1)-(2).
[185] Aarhus Convention, art. 4(4); EI(S)R, reg. 10(6).

Chapter 2. Theoretical and Legal Frameworks

qualifications are not always present in wider freedom of information legislation,[186] and are a reflection of the diffuse nature of emissions and their impact on the environment. This is another way in which both the Aarhus Convention and the EI(S)R reflect the importance of the environment in relation to the rights they guarantee, in turn further emphasising the role and interests of the environment as an actor.[187]

The existence of these exceptions to the right to environmental information is significant, as they recognise that the core environmental aims of the right will not always be met by increased public awareness and public participation, or do not always trump other legitimate interests. Indeed, the exceptions balance the competing core elements of increasing public access to environmental information and of ensuring that the right does not unduly interfere with the state's ability to govern and exercise executive powers in the public interest. In this way, the environmental objective that underlies the Convention is given clear, but not absolute, priority, maximising the opportunity for the public to fulfil their role as guardians of the environment. However, implicit in this discussion is the underpinning assumption that those who engage with the right are content with the application of these exceptions by public authorities, a view that is not reflected in the perceptions of those using the right, creating another mismatch between expectations and experience.[188]

3.5. REVIEW PROCEDURES

Reflecting the Aarhus Convention's emphasis on the accessibility of its procedural rights, the Convention obliges ratifying states to provide to those who feel that their request for environmental information has been ignored or wrongfully denied access not just to the law courts, but also to a non-judicial review procedure.[189] The importance of procedural accessibility is further reflected in the requirement to make review procedures "free of charge or inexpensive" or "not prohibitively expensive", depending on whether the procedure is non-judicial or judicial.[190] Review procedures

---

[186] E.g., Freedom of Information Act 2000, ss 26–31.
[187] This is discussed in more detail in Chapter 6.
[188] For more on this, see generally Chapter 4.
[189] Aarhus Convention, art. 9(1).
[190] Ibid., art. 9(1) and (4).

must also be conducted "expeditiously" or must be "timely", depending on the nature of the review procedure itself.[191] Such a requirement reflects the reality that many environmental decision-making procedures open to public participation operate on strict time limits so that meeting this requirement empowers individuals and NGOs seeking out environmental information to participate in these decision-making processes.

The Convention's requirements for independent review procedures to ensure that information rights are protected have been translated in Scotland into a three-stage process. Where it is thought that any of the rules have not been complied with – e.g. by withholding information or responding too slowly – the requester can make representations to the authority concerned which must carry out a review of whether it has complied, responding within 20 days.[192] If still unsatisfied, the requester can appeal to the Scottish Information Commissioner, who will determine the case and can order the authority to disclose information. A further appeal to the courts is then possible on points of law.[193] It is notable that these procedures mirror those under the wider freedom of information laws, as this mirroring blurs the distinction between the two regimes within Scotland.

The access to justice pillar is further reinforced by one of the Convention's unique mechanisms: the Aarhus Convention Compliance Committee (ACCC).[194] The ACCC is a body which monitors compliance with the Convention, both by monitoring the general level of implementation by parties and considering specific applications by individuals or groups that their rights under the Convention have been breached. It reports to the Meetings of the Parties, but has no power to provide remedies or sanctions where breaches are found. Similarly, its decisions have no direct legal force within the parties, but may be considered by national courts.[195] The existence of the ACCC nevertheless provides a route by which parties can be held to account, publicly and politically, for non-compliance and a route by which those who feel aggrieved can vindicate their position.

---

[191] Ibid., art. 9(1) and (4).
[192] EI(S)R, reg. 16.
[193] EI(S)R, reg. 17, applying the Freedom of Information (Scotland) Act 2002, Part 4.
[194] Aarhus Convention, art. 15; see also EBBESSON et al., above n. 119, pp. 222–225.
[195] E.g. *Carroll v. Scottish Borders Council* [2015] CSIH 73 [9].

4. CONCLUSION

Understanding the right of access to environmental information requires knowledge of the legal measures which serve to create and protect it in a specific jurisdiction, in this case Scotland, but also of the context of the international agreements on which those are based and the principles and aspirations which they reflect. However, the "law in the books" is often very different from the "law in practice". Uncovering what is happening in practice is vital, and the analysis of that can be aided by drawing on Actor-Network Theory to look behind the assumptions that have shaped the formal frameworks. As the following chapters will show, what happens in the real world is in many ways more complex than simply the working out of the vision embedded in the Aarhus Convention of a direct relationship between homogeneous categories of those seeking information and the public authorities that hold it. The varying motivations and capacities of those seeking information, the role of some users as intermediaries and the discretion allowed to authorities in interpreting and applying the legal rules all create a much more complex and diverse picture than that envisioned in the Convention and the laws that implement it. Such complexity creates mismatching expectations and priorities that can lead to frustrations and misunderstandings between those concerned, getting in the way of the realisation of the right's environmental objectives.

Rethinking the networks at play also draws attention to the role of the non-human actors in determining how the environmental information regime operates. In addition to reflecting on how the legal structures themselves exert influence on relationships, one important feature is the role of the environment itself. The very existence of a right of access to environmental information, distinct from wider rights to information provided under freedom of information regimes, is predicated on the significance of the environment, so that one might expect it to be a major actor throughout the relevant networks.

Yet, as will be shown, this is not the case. Notwithstanding some of the exceptions to the right, the relatively low profile of the environment contributes to the lack of a clear distinction between the separate regimes for access to environmental information and for freedom of information more widely. The overlapping of these two regimes calls into question the need for distinct information regimes and raises doubts over how far the explicitly environmental aims that inspired the creation of the right of access to environmental information are being achieved in operation.[196] In this way, a further mismatch between the expectations which underpin the right and their operation in practice is created. These mismatches are significant not just because they risk undermining the right's environmental and participative aims; they are also significant because they reflect a broader problem arising from a failure to consider the environment as an independent actor that should be more fully incorporated into regimes that guarantee the right of access to environmental information, as well as in the discussion concerning it.

---

[196] This issue is directly addressed in Chapter 7.

CHAPTER 3
PROFESSIONAL USERS

Although the environment may be intended to be the ultimate beneficiary, within the Aarhus Convention and the Environmental Information (Scotland) Regulations 2004 (EI(S)R) that give it effect in Scotland, users of the right are the actors who can claim direct benefits. It is therefore crucial that analysis of the right considers its users. It is these users who engage with the Convention's moral duty to "protect and improve the environment for the benefit of present and future generations"[197] and who exercise the right to seek access to environmental information through the proactive disclosure efforts of public authorities and the procedures set out in the EI(S)R. As a result, it is important to build both an appreciation of how the law perceives and constructs a vision of the users of the right to environmental information and an empirical understanding of who the users are and what they are doing.

1. INTRODUCTION

The starting point for understanding how the Aarhus Convention and the EI(S)R view users of the right is through the broad nature of the moral duty imposed on users to protect and improve the environment by participating in environmental decision-making processes.[198] This duty is significant because it shapes expectations regarding how and why users engage with the right. Specifically, there is an assumption that users will be directly using the environmental information they access to "observe this duty"[199] and fulfil their assumed altruistic, environmentally driven motivations for engaging with the right – a perspective reinforced by the legal instruments

---

[197] Aarhus Convention, Preamble, para. 7.
[198] BARRITT, above n. 21, pp. 27–28.
[199] Aarhus Convention, Preamble, para. 8.

that preceded the Aarhus Convention. Further, users are expected to hold the necessary expertise effectively to understand and make use of the information they access for these purposes.

Yet while the Aarhus Convention holds these assumptions regarding those using the right, they are not fully reflected in the Convention's provisions themselves. Under the Aarhus Convention, it is "the public" who can utilise its procedural rights, with "the public" being defined as:

> One or more natural or legal persons, and, in accordance with national legislation or practice, their associations, organizations or groups.[200]

This definition is broad; there is no need for a member of "the public" to have any connection to the issue in question or even to live in a state which has ratified the Convention, and the Convention explicitly recognises non-governmental organisations (NGOs) as potential users. Critically, there is no explicit exclusion of those holding non-environmental motives or those who lack the ability to understand and use the information they access, or of intermediary users such as professionals working in various careers who are not personally interested in the information being sought. The same is also true for the term "applicant" in the EI(S)R,[201] which is equally broad in its approach. There is thus no limitation to ensure that the right is exercised exclusively, or even primarily, by those who match the ideal of the environmentally engaged citizen seeking to protect or enhance the environment. Users are free to utilise their right to access environmental information in ways that differ from the expectations of the Convention and the EI(S)R – whether that be through acting as intermediaries or using the information in ways that do not contribute to, or indeed may actually detract from, the right's environmental aims. Consequently, there is a mismatch between the implicit expectations behind the right to environmental information and how the right is provided and can be (and is) utilised in practice, risking tensions between parties if users are seen as exercising the right for inappropriate purposes.

The right's underlying vision, based on the ideal of the public engaging directly with the environmental aims of the right, was perhaps too simplistic to be effective in practice. Yet through the Aarhus Convention and the EI(S)R, it has been translated into law, and users outwith the intended "public" that these instruments are designed to accommodate

---

[200] Ibid., art. 2(4).
[201] EI(S)R, reg. 2(1).

Chapter 3. Professional Users

are ill-considered – whether this is due to their intermediary role or their objectives in engaging with the right. It is here that Actor-Network Theory can play in role in identifying the use of the right in practice to unpick the assumptions and the pre-determined nature of the ideal "actors" to better reflect the actual use of the right. Indeed, far from users adhering to the expectations of the Aarhus Convention, a study of practice reveals a wide range of users, each with their own distinct means and reasons for engaging with the right. Examining practice also does more than just focus on the motives and expertise of users; it also considers the distinction between those seeking to use any environmental information directly and those who are acting on behalf of others.

As a starting point for this exploration, this chapter begins by broadly categorising users into two groups: "professional" users, who engage with the right as part of their job, and "personal" users, who do so to engage with environmental (or other) issues that impact on their lives. This broad categorisation is intended to structure the analysis in this and the following chapters. It is not intended to act as the final construction of new sets of "actors" or to identify two rigidly defined and distinct groups, as there is considerable variation within each category. Such variation and its consequences are further explored in this and the following chapters, beginning with the professional users, since, despite being less numerous, they demonstrate the starkest mismatch between the expectations that underpin the right and how the right is actually used in practice.

After identifying the professional users, this chapter builds on evidence from surveys and interviews with both users of the right and public authorities to consider how both public authorities and users perceive the motivations driving the use of the right by professional users, as well as what these users do with the environmental information accessed. Throughout the chapter, professional users are shown to have distinct motives for engaging with the right and distinctive needs in terms of how they engage with public authorities under the right. Critically, the chapter also demonstrates that these distinct needs are not recognised by either the Aarhus Convention or Scotland's environmental information regime, raising obstacles in relation to how they engage with the right. It concludes that the current approach, which conceptualises all users of the right as similar actors with similar motive and expertise, does not reflect the reality in which the right actually operates. Through challenging the homogeneous conceptualisation of users portrayed by the Aarhus Convention and the EI(S)R, this chapter highlights that such a view risks misrepresenting how these users engage with the right, and risks undermining the right's environmental and participative aims.

2. PROFESSIONAL USERS AND THE RIGHT OF ACCESS TO ENVIRONMENTAL INFORMATION

The first broad category to be considered is that of the professional users of the right of access to environmental information. While this category encapsulates a broad range of potential users, interviews with users and Scottish public authorities have highlighted some common elements which distinguish this category of users from other personal users:

- The professional user will usually be acting as an intermediary, further disseminating the accessed environmental information or acting on behalf of another.
- The environmental information sought by the professional user will (usually) not have a personal impact on their lives.
- The professional user will usually be driven by economic motives in engaging with the right, usually as part of their employment.
- The professional user will usually have expertise or expert knowledge, which allows them to engage with the right in ways not available to other users.

Some users that are categorised as "professional" may not embody all of these elements in their engagement with the right. This is not to suggest that such users belong in the "personal" user category; rather, it is indicative of the fact that any attempt to create strict, discrete categories is doomed because of the broad spectrum of users that defies efforts to create sharply define and exclusive categories.

A notable element of the Aarhus Convention and subsequent instruments is that, in guaranteeing the right of access to environmental information, the Convention emphasises the need for non-experts to use the right to directly seek out environmental information from public authorities: either through proactive disclosure under the active right or by requesting that the authority disclose the information under the passive right to environmental information. This position is adopted because of the right's participative aims; by enabling people to directly access relevant information, it allows them to then go on to participate directly in environmental decision-making procedures. This route to participation by users is important because it is thought that by introducing a plurality of viewpoints into decision-making processes, the final decision will be improved.[202] However, an implicit assumption within this position is that the participation process should not be dominated by "experts" or professionals[203] who are representing the interests of others[204] if they decide to participate in such processes.

As a result, the role of professional users in accessing and using environmental information under the right is too often discounted. Their unique needs in engaging with the right of access to environmental information are not accommodated, resulting in the potential benefits brought by a valuable class of users being underutilised. Different professional users can engage with the environmental aims of the right in ways that personal users of the right cannot: acting as information disseminators and bridging the gap between authorities and the general public.

However professional users can also impose administrative burdens on public authorities for their own commercial benefit and potentially undermine the right's environmental aims.[205] This particular mismatch between aspirations and reality can serve to exemplify the frustrations that public authorities feel when engaging with such professional intermediary users. It is this divergence between different professional users which make it necessary to consider how these distinct actors engage with the right, its overarching aims, and the procedures which guarantee the right in practice. Arising from the findings from the user and authority surveys and interviews, the professional users that will be considered in this chapter are journalists, professionals representing clients, academics, NGOs and public authorities seeking environmental information.

2.1. JOURNALISTS

The first professional users to be examined in this section are journalists. Considered to play a special role in society in scrutinising and investigating

---

[202] LEE and ABBOT, above n.111, p. 83.
[203] Moving away from earlier attitudes; see HAKLAY, above n. 94.
[204] Specifically, other human actors: the Aarhus Convention does make special provision for "non-governmental organizations promoting environmental protection", which are included in the definition of "the public concerned" so as to benefit from the rights in relation to access to justice; Aarhus Convention, art. 2(5).
[205] Such as repackaging and reselling information; see *Stirrat Park Hogg v. Dumbarton District Council* 1996 SLT 1113.

the actions of public authorities,[206] the term "journalist" has been used to describe a wide range of individuals or groups who work in news organisations and/or report news to the general public. Some classic examples of journalists would be an individual writing for printed media or a reporter investigating a story to be presented on television. However, the increased use of technology means that journalists are not restricted to the above examples. More contemporary news sources such as online media and bloggers are also covered by this definition,[207] although the inclusion of such news sources is contested.[208] The emergence of such new roles serves only to emphasise the impossibility of constructing strict and exclusive categories in this area, with the boundaries being blurred between professional and personal users and between sub-groups within each category.

The impact of these technological developments on how news stories are disseminated is representative of a broader societal change that has occurred since the Aarhus Convention was opened for signature in 1998. This is arguably most evident in how information is stored. In 1998 public authorities would store environmental information on paper in limited locations, whereas within public authorities, such information is now mostly generated, organised, stored and accessed electronically. Journalists now seek access to environmental information by browsing proactively disclosed environmental information on websites and receiving information via email rather than visiting public offices to browse a paper register. In this way, technology, as an actor in itself, has influenced how journalists and other actors engage with the right of access to environmental information.[209]

Notwithstanding these developments, the activities of journalists have contributed to society in two vital ways, regardless of whether the journalists' work was published in print, broadcast or online media (or in a combination of media). The first contribution is that journalism essentially acts as a check on public power: scrutinising and investigating the actions (or inaction) of public authorities to uncover misuses of power and hold

---

[206] See generally *Goodwin v. United Kingdom* App. No. 17488/90 (ECtHR, 27 March 1996); and *Magyar Helsinki Bizottság v. Hungary* App. No. 18030/11 (ECtHR, 8 November 2016).
[207] As the interviews for this book were only with traditional print-media journalists, this analysis will predominantly be based on such journalists.
[208] *McNally v. Saunders* [2021] EWHC 2012 (QB), [71]–[72].
[209] For further reflection on the impact of technological development, see Chapter 6, section 2.3.

Chapter 3. Professional Users

authorities to account in terms of how they exercise this power.[210] The second contribution is that of an educator and facilitator: by writing, editing and publishing news stories, journalists act to disseminate information to the general public, enabling the public to work alongside (or against) public authorities by acting on the disseminated information.[211] This activity involves not just simplifying and editing the accessed information so that only the relevant matters are presented to the general public;[212] it also involves presenting the information in a clear or entertaining way in order to ensure its accessibility.[213] Consequently, in using the right as professional users, journalists need to be more than skilled investigators; they also need to be skilled communicators and know which stories to present to their editors and the general public. This distinguishes them from other users of the right, in essence highlighting them as a distinct type of actor that engages with the right to environmental information.

While these activities are key to the role of journalists in society, how they interact with the right of access to environmental information is less explored. First, in line with the educational role of journalism, journalists act as intermediaries between public authorities and the public; they transform the information they have sought under the right, editing the relevant information and presenting it in a way that is broadly accessible to the general public (or their more specialised audience). While the Aarhus Convention and the EI(S)R do not prohibit intermediaries from using the right to gather environmental information for dissemination to other individuals,[214] both regimes do not tailor their procedures to reflect the potential use of the right by such intermediaries.

This lack of attention flows from the Convention's focus on interested individuals directly being given the environmental information in which they are interested. A justification for this approach is that it prevents the

---

[210] This is encapsulated in the "monitorial" and "radical" roles that can underpin the activities of journalists; see C. CHRISTIANS et al., *Normative Theories of the Media: Journalism in Democratic States*, University of Illinois Press, Urbana 2009, pp. 139–157 and 179–195.

[211] This is encapsulated in the "facilitative" and "collaborative" roles that can underpin the activities of journalists: see ibid., pp. 158–178 and 196–218.

[212] The same broad considerations apply to those servicing a specialised audience rather than the general public, e.g. when writing for a practitioner audience or those in an industrial sector, although the starting point may be different.

[213] See generally A. MOWSHOWITZ, "On the Market Value of Information" (1992) 43 *Journal of the American Society for Information Science* 225.

[214] The Convention does mention "the importance of making use of the media and of electronic or other, future forms of communication", but does not recognise an independent role for the media; Aarhus Convention, Preamble, para. 15.

environmental information from becoming distorted by a third party and ensures that the individual knows that they are receiving the information as it is held by the authority. However, such a justification does potentially overstate the desire of individuals to access information directly from the source and understate the potential role and value of intermediaries in disseminating such information.

A potential consequence of this focus on individuals directly accessing information from public authorities is that the role of journalists in disseminating environmental information has raised concerns felt by both individuals and public authorities in Scotland. At the innocuous level, some individuals felt that journalists were merely seeking to "fill up column spaces"[215] rather than upholding the lofty ideals of reporting on pertinent environmental news and issues. More fundamentally, other users felt that the editorial methods of journalists would alter the meaning of the information discussed in their articles:

> [F]or me it depends on the thing [environmental information of interest] but I just generally find that getting solid information, and by that I mean not information that's reported by sort of biased media ... getting solid information can be quite difficult.[216]

Scottish public authorities also noted similar concerns:

> [I]t [the right of access to environmental information] is abused by media. It is abused because they pick up on a story and they just put this little bit in without the full picture.[217]

> [J]ournalists, like I say, fair play to them, but then it's frustrating if you give them context ... But then, it can be frustrating if you give out context but then it's used in a totally different way and you think that's really not what I said.[218]

This evidences a belief that, whether due to pressure to attract and hold an audience, a lack of skill in summarising and re-presenting unedited information to the general public or malicious intent, there is a risk that the environmental information disclosed to journalists will not be accurately presented to the public. Phrased in the context of the role of

---

[215] Interview with User No. 9.
[216] Interview with User No. 2.
[217] Interview with Public Authority No. 4.
[218] Interview with Public Authority No. 10.

Chapter 3. Professional Users

journalists, there is a suspicion that their educational activities are tainted by the commercial realities of their job.

In this way, the intermediary nature of how journalists use the right can be perceived by other users and public authorities as something that detracts from and gets in the way of disseminating environmental information accurately and in a non-partisan way. Nervousness about how journalists will be presenting information and the impact of the publicity created can interfere with the operation of the right of access to information, as shown by the Scottish Government's practice at one stage of treating requests from journalists differently from other requests, seeking higher-level clearance before responding to requests for information.[219]

Yet, notwithstanding such doubts, journalists and their intermediary nature can also act to contribute to the actualisation of the right's environmental and participative aims. While those interviewed noted the potential concern with relying on journalists, they also noted that journalists did act "to inform the public" and hold public authorities accountable in line with their role as a check on public power:

> [T]o be quite honest actually I kind of think councillors are more accountable to the papers than they are to the public![220]

Journalists themselves perceive their role in this way:

> We've had a lot of scrapes, environmental corruption otherwise and things like that ... You have to be giving the people the information and that's why it's become so important for me to dig up all sorts of info and publish it.[221]

Consequently, in terms of how journalists seek to use and engage with the right of access to environmental information, there is a strong element of trying to ensure that public authorities are transparent and accountable. These accountability aims are more commonly attributed to the aims of the general right to information, but they are also equally relevant to the aims of the right to environmental information. This overlap between the two

---

[219] Scottish Information Commissioner, *Intervention Report: Scottish Government* (13 June 2018, Scottish Information Commissioner). The report is available at the Scottish Information Commissioner's website: <http://www.itspublicknowledge.info/home/AboutSIC/WhatWeDo/Intervention201702016ScottishGovernment.aspx> accessed 19 April 2022.
[220] Interview with User No. 9.
[221] Interview with User No. 7.

Intersentia 65

regimes and the desire for holding public authorities to account can lead to difficulties in distinguishing between the two regimes in practice.

A point of distinction between the two regimes is that journalists can contribute to the specifically environmental goals of the right to environmental information beyond the scrutiny of public authorities. The educational aspects of journalism enable journalists to proactively engage with individuals who may not themselves actively seek out information from public authorities. Indeed, as journalists generally have a much wider audience than public authorities when disseminating information, they can typically engage with a larger number of people. In turn, this can lead to a greater number of individuals participating in environmental decision-making procedures, enhancing the participative aims of the right in a way that would be impossible for public authorities to do alone.

However, these positive aspects of journalism do not lessen the suspicion of public authorities towards journalists in their intermediary role and the lack of support, if not implicit discouragement, in relation to how the Convention and the EI(S)R regard them. Beyond the potential for journalists to distort the meaning of disclosed environmental information, this suspicion can also be sourced from the mixed motives of journalists in engaging with the right.

As highlighted in the above quote, one reason why journalists engage with the right is to hold public authorities to account – an altruistic motive, driven by a passion for good governance and accountability which aligns with the motivational expectations of the Aarhus Convention, although not its distinct environmental objective. Indeed, for some journalists, this altruistic element constitutes the reason why they decided to work as a journalist:

> I had no intentions of becoming a reporter which is, to all intents and purposes what I've become. I just wanted to initially serve on a community [body] and help people. ... When I saw that was not what was happening, that's when I started realising that freedom of information requests could help me get information that I'm not being given.[222]

Such journalists are driven by the public interest in ensuring that the general public are informed and are able to scrutinise the actions of public authorities when they make decisions, whether these impact on the environment or otherwise. These journalists, who are driven by their

---

[222] Ibid.

Chapter 3. Professional Users

passion for their topics of interest, align with the normative expectations of the Aarhus Convention despite acting as intermediaries.

Yet, despite the positive impacts of journalists driven by these altruistic motivations, because such journalists may not be driven by a specifically environmental motive, their use of the right will not always be wholly aligned with the expectations of the Aarhus Convention and the EI(S)R. The focus of these journalists is more on the general values of governmental transparency and accountability, values which are better reflected in the wider right and laws on the general right to information rather than the specific right to environmental information. This is relevant because such journalists are merely incidentally engaging with the right to environmental information, and any contributions to the right's environmental aims are a by-product of that engagement.

Further deviating from the expectations of the Aarhus Convention and the EI(S)R is the fact that (at least for those in the traditional media) the reason that journalists are able to promote public scrutiny of public authorities is because doing so is part of their job as a journalist. This employment aspect of their engagement with the right is significant:[223] because they are paid to conduct these investigations, there is an independent (although often overlapping) economic motive which underpins their use of the right. Such considerations also impact on commercial news outlets and journalists who work for them, as they will select and edit stories which align with the interests, and to some extent the preferences, of their paying readers.[224]

This is not to ignore the journalists who are driven to publish articles due to their passion for the environment, nor to undermine journalists who are driven by both their altruistic interest and economic considerations. Indeed, even journalists driven by purely commercial motivations can have beneficial effects for the environment if their actions (albeit driven by commercial motives) serve to raise awareness of environmental issues. However, such economic considerations do entail a departure from the altruistic motivations envisaged for users of the right. There is a potential mismatch between the expectations of pure altruism embedded in

---

[223] Some journalists may be technically self-employed, but the financial aspect to their motivation remains the same.
[224] Such considerations do not account for news outlets or journalists who are not beholden to such economic concerns and write in accordance with their own interests. Yet even here it is possible that the desire to maintain a readership may influence which information is presented to readers and how it is presented.

the Aarhus Convention, the experience of public authorities who feel that journalists "abuse" the right, and the experiences of journalists themselves. This can cause tension in terms of how journalists engage with the right and the willingness of authorities to go beyond their legal obligations in order to provide further assistance to them. A distant, or at worst hostile, relationship can hinder how journalists access environmental information and hence their ability to contribute, whether directly or indirectly, to the right's environmental aims.

A final element of how journalists engage with the right of access to environmental information is their distinctive methods of engaging with the right and the environmental information accessed. Journalists, because of their expertise in asking questions and investigation, tend to have an enhanced ability to phrase requests for environmental information:

> But the good thing I would say about requests from journalists is they tend to be pretty clear.[225]

In addition, journalists are generally more able to understand the environmental information disclosed to them compared with "personal" users of the right. Developed from their professional duties and expectations as journalists, this enhanced capacity is important for understanding the information disclosed to them as well as their ability to edit and refine the information enhancing the extent to which it is made presentable to the wider public. These distinguishing characteristics when compared to other users of the right are significant, because they enable journalists to make better use of the right and to benefit from it in a way that is unavailable to other users.

Further contrasts between how journalists and other users engage with the right can be drawn in how journalists actually request access to environmental information. In addition to being able to submit requests under domestic environmental information legislation, journalists are also able to request environmental information directly from media officers. While the journalist is requesting information from the same authority as other users, going through the media officer confers various advantages:

> I'll often call up the media officer and say "I want to find out about what you did about this field [are] you going to let developers have it or not?" Now I could do

---

[225] Interview with Public Authority No. 10.

Chapter 3. Professional Users

a FOI request[226] but I'm writing an article, my editor wants it by Friday. I want this information now, if you don't give it to me and get it to me now, I'll simply write in my first article that the Council refused to supply it.[227]

This evidences the fact that journalists can threaten wide dissemination of a story without the authority having an input in order to hasten the disclosure of environmental information. The ability to hasten the disclosure of information is not one generally shared by other users of the right, either professional or personal, and is directly connected to the journalist's professional role in society and the impact that publishing the story could have on the authority. The interviewee noted that this threat does not always work, but this does not lessen the relevance of this approach or the fact that the option to use this threat is available to journalists in a way that is not the case for other users.

Journalists' unique relationship with authorities and means of engaging with the right may often be positive in terms of spreading environmental information and stimulating awareness of and interest in environmental issues, but it can also give rise to problems. In order for a story to be attractive and considered "good" journalism, it must either provide new information or be an exclusive story. This need for originality and speed in publishing stories is a core element of how journalists work, but it is not reflected in the legal framework or in how public authorities operate in terms of guaranteeing the right.

Starting with proactively disclosed environmental information, because it is available to everyone a journalist cannot necessarily use it to justify the novelty or exclusivity of their story, although a detailed study of information that is available to others but has not been examined in the same depth may allow for a sufficient head-start in front of others who may seek to mine the same sources once a story has been broken. Similarly, when submitting requests for environmental information, while there may be an expectation of exclusivity in the dialogue between journalists and public authorities, this exclusivity is quickly lost when the authorities record the disclosure in their publicly available disclosure log. This absence of exclusivity is emphasised by the adherence of public authorities to the applicant- and motive-blind nature of the right, which precludes them from

---

[226] Note that this is a simple example of reference to freedom of information (FOI) being used as a comprehensive shorthand for the technically distinct rights to access information under the separate freedom of information and environmental information laws.
[227] Interview with User No. 7.

treating journalists differently from other users by delaying the publication of requests on disclosure logs:

> But we do have ... a disclosure log where every time we release information, we then ... circumnavigate it to our central digital team who then put that on our website. ... And in terms of how we deal with them [requests], we treat them the same no matter who they come from.[228]

Consequently, the unique needs of journalists in engaging with the right are not reflected in the operation of the right by public authorities.

The ways in which journalists engage with and use the right may be undermined in other ways. In contrast with the apparent adherence to the applicant- and motive-blind approach, some Scottish public authorities do distinguish between journalists and other users in processing and responding to environmental information requests. This was done through clearing the disclosure of the requested information to a higher-ranking official, such as a Scottish Minister, before disclosing it to the journalist.[229] This process delayed the disclosure of environmental to journalists, contrary to domestic[230] and international law,[231] and acts as an example of journalists being targeted for their unique identity and relationship with the right. Notably, this practice was still being discussed in 2019:

> [T]he only differences is if it's a press inquiry, then we'll run it past the comms guys just to make sure we've got potential lines in case there's coverage and interest there.[232]

The existence of these parallel processing procedures is emblematic of the tensions between journalists and public authorities in terms of how journalists exercise their right to access environmental information. Scottish public authorities are keenly aware of the influence of journalists, and the use of these parallel procedures could be portrayed as a means adopted by public authorities to redress the perceived imbalance of power. Yet such procedures run contrary to the spirit of the Aarhus Convention.

---

[228] Interview with Public Authority No. 13.
[229] Scottish Information Commissioner, above n. 219.
[230] EI(S)R, reg. 5; if nothing else, seeking the additional clearance meant that requests were probably not being complied with "as soon as possible".
[231] Aarhus Convention, art. 4.
[232] Interview with Public Authority No. 13.

Chapter 3. Professional Users

Such a mismatch is a consequence of the Aarhus Convention consciously excluding the identity of the user in its provisions, and highlights the tension between the applicant-blind approach embedded in the law and the reality of how different users engage with the right in practice. This stems from the assumption that the applicant- and motive-blind approach does not act to the detriment of any users of the right. Yet this is not always the case in practice, both because this uniform approach can hinder those with a unique relationship with the right and because the authorities will sometimes impose internal obstacles in request processing due to the identity of the user. Ultimately these issues serve to detract from how journalists can engage with the right, and in turn from how they can contribute to the right's environmental and participative aims.

2.2. PROFESSIONALS REPRESENTING CLIENTS

The second category of professional users is professionals who engage with the right on behalf of clients hiring their services. In the context of the right of access to environmental information, these professional users will tend to be environmental consultants engaging with planning decisions or lawyers seeking information to protect or further their clients' legal interests. Environmental information can be relevant when representing clients in matters other than those with a specifically environmental focus. For example, lawyers may be seeking information on conditions at the relevant location when seeking compensation for damage which an authority is accused of causing,[233] or indeed the background conditions for other incidents.

The relationship between this category of professional users and their clients is fundamental in terms of establishing how they use and engage with the right of access to environmental information and involves a further set of actors whose roles can be better understood with the benefit of Actor-Network Theory. Driven by their client's interests and instructions, these professionals, like many journalists, are not personally impacted by the matters on which they are seeking environmental information, nor are they personally interested in the information; rather, through representing their clients, these users are acting as intermediaries, using their expertise to access environmental information to provide advice and represent their clients' best interests. In this way, Actor-Network Theory provides the

---

[233] Ibid.

impetus to distinguish between the two actors and their relationship – the commercial relationship between professional users, as actors engaging with the right, and the clients who hire these professionals – and highlights the intermediary nature of these particular professional users.

However, while this intermediary role does bear some similarities to that of journalists, there is a key element of their respective roles which distinguishes the nature of their intermediary duties. This element is the relationship with the client whom the intermediary is representing. For journalists, this relationship is with a broader public, a diffuse relationship that results in a wider degree of discretion as to how journalists act as intermediaries. Conversely, professionals representing clients have a direct one-to-one relationship with their clients, who can provide explicit instructions as to their interests and goals. As a result, these professionals use the right "in the service of [their] clients",[234] replicating how "personal" users directly engage with public authorities under the right (albeit with greater expertise and knowledge).

A further distinguishing feature is that this category of professionals is more likely to participate in formal environmental decision-making procedures. Indeed, in order to represent their clients' interests, professionals will often have to act on the environmental information disclosed to them. Examples of such actions are participating in planning procedures to ensure a development is given planning permission or:

> [M]aking objections or representations of some sort. Usually within a statutory framework.[235]

This contrasts with the relationship between journalists and the public, where journalists are unlikely to directly participate in such environmental decisions due to the nature of the profession.[236] In this way, these professional users are more likely to contribute to the participative aims of the right and the Aarhus Convention more broadly. Such differences further contribute to the broad spectrum of users who engage with the right of access to environmental information. This, in turn, highlights

---

[234] Interview with User No. 15.
[235] Ibid.
[236] However, this is not to suggest that some journalists do not have an indirect effect on environmental decision-making processes: journalists such as George Monbiot can impact on decision-making processes even where they do not directly participate in such processes.

Chapter 3. Professional Users

the need to resist efforts to place users into simple, definitive categories constructed by the Aarhus Convention's expectations, and shows the value of unpicking these preconceptions and the more complex relationships that exist in practice.

Nevertheless, as with the intermediary relationship between journalists and the public, there are risks which come with professional users accessing environmental information on behalf of another. As discussed previously, with any intermediary there is the risk of the meaning of the environmental information being distorted, but in the context of professional representatives there is an additional risk: that the representative will seek out environmental information which their client does not need. This may be as the result of an abundance of caution and a desire to make sure that no relevant material is missed, but the suspicion is that some professional representatives will do this to artificially increase their workload and charge their client more for their services, or at least are not unhappy if excessive caution produces that result. One interviewed public authority explicitly highlighted this risk:

> We do get quite a few requests that are from solicitors on behalf of clients. And I suppose sometimes we do wonder whether it really is on behalf of the client. How close the solicitor's request [is] to what the client really needs.[237]

Excessive, wide-ranging requests for environmental information run the risk of delaying the advice provided to the client, as the authority may produce a large volume of irrelevant information that the professional user will have to consider. There is a further risk that these requests will sour the relationship between the authority and the professional user, as the authority may need to spend a large amount of resources processing a request it believes is not valuable for the professional user's client. Seeking access to environmental information that is unnecessary to advise the client may not be done in bad faith, but this does not lessen the negative impact of such errors in practice.

The intermediary nature of how this category of professionals engages with the right of access to environmental information also impacts on their motives for engaging with the right. In representing the interests of their clients, these professionals' primary motivations are economic: they seek to be paid for their work in representing their clients' interests.

---

[237] Interview with Public Authority No. 11.

Such considerations are antithetical to the altruistic expectations embedded within the Aarhus Convention and the EI(S)R, fundamentally contrasting with the moral duty to "protect and enhance the environment" enshrined in both regimes.

Yet it must be noted that because these professionals are generally obliged to follow the instructions of their clients,[238] the motivations of these clients are relevant for determining the ultimate use of the right and the environmental information disclosed under it. If a client has instructed a solicitor to try to block a factory from being built to protect the nesting site of birds, the solicitor's engagement with the right will then be in line with the implicit moral duty found in the Aarhus Convention. Conversely, if the same solicitor is instructed by another client to seek permission to build a golf course on an area that is protected by law on the basis of its environmental importance, then the solicitor will be acting in a way that directly conflicts with the Convention's environmental aims and implied moral duty to protect and enhance the environment.

Consequently, whether or not this category of professionals adheres to the normative elements of the Aarhus Convention depends to a significant extent on the motivations of their clients.[239] Such a relationship is different from the intermediary relationship between journalists and the public, which is not driven by such clearly articulated motives (whether supporting or conflicting with environmental objectives). It should be noted that in practice most clients seeking professional services do not appear to have altruistic motivations, and instead seek to protect their personal legal rights or commercial interests.[240] As a result, the involvement of the professionals who represent them will likewise normally not be serving purely environmental goals. However, there will be cases where an altruistic motivation is in play, aligning some professional representatives with the altruistic expectations of the Aarhus Convention. Such diversity further emphasises the broad spectrum of users that engage with the right, even within this single sub-category of professional users.

---

[238] There are exceptions to this, such as where the professional's client requests the professional to do something that is illegal or contrary to the standards of the professional's regulatory body.

[239] As with journalists, there are those in this category whose activities and choice of work are driven more by their personal motivations than by any financial rewards.

[240] This aligns with this book's findings on the motives of personal users seeking to access environmental information and to participate in environmental decision-making processes; see Chapters 4 and 5.

A further distinction to be made between the intermediary relationships of professional representatives and journalists is the central role of payment. Regardless of whether the client's motives are environmental, altruistic or personal, if they do not have the funds to pay their representative, then the representative will generally not engage with the right on their behalf:

> I may have had cause [to recommend that a client appeal to the Scottish Information Commissioner] on one or two occasions, when I would have said to a client, "Yes, I think it's worth appealing here" but they, you know, haven't had enough money [to pay me to do it on their behalf].[241]

This economic element is crucial to the way in which this category of professionals engages with the right of access to environmental information. Unlike journalists, professional representatives will either be paid or seek an enforceable right to be paid before providing their services. Consequently, if the client is unable or unwilling to pay them, the representative will not engage with the right on behalf of the client, regardless of their motive. Such financial outlay is more likely to arise where the client is driven by a commercial or strong personal motive, so that this use of the right tends to be driven by financial gain rather than environmental protection, contrary to the aims of the right to access environmental information. The irony is not lost of public authorities when a right created to be used in the public interest to achieve environmental benefits is used to further purely private interests that may cause environmental harm.

However, there are exceptions to this rule: professional representatives who are willing either to work pro bono, i.e. for a reduced or no fee for clients unable to afford the normal charges, or to accept lower fees to work for causes they believe in. Encapsulating bodies such as the Citizens Advice Bureau and lawyers who provide pro bono representation, these professionals are not driven to advise clients by economic remuneration or personal gain. As pro bono representatives are less driven by economic motivations, there is a greater likelihood of them being driven by altruistic motivations.

Yet it must be highlighted that pro bono representatives are still bound by the wishes of their clients, and that their clients' motives still provide the primary driving motivation in their engagement with the right. Clients seeking pro bono representation may do so for environmental, public interest reasons. However, equally, they may be seeking such representation

---

[241] Interview with User No. 15.

for more personal motives, such as protecting their homes, contrary to the altruistic aspects of the right to access environmental information. It is also possible that, regardless of an altruistic element in the client's motives, their issue is not related to the health of the environment, but to other public interests, such as respecting the rule of law when environmentally beneficial activities are challenged because they fall outwith the strict legal powers of the statutory body responsible. Such conflicts are emblematic of the (potentially) contrary interests of humanity and environmental protection. This highlights not only the problems in ascribing characteristics to a broad category of personal users that these professional consultants represent,[242] but also the potential mismatch between the expected use of the right and its use in practice to further non-environmental goals.

A final element to consider in terms of how this category of professionals engages with the right of access to environmental information is the expertise that they can apply. Indeed, as this expertise is the reason why these professionals are hired to represent the interests of their clients, it constitutes a fundamental aspect of how they utilise and engage with the right. Such expertise can take various forms, but is commonly considered in terms of the ability to access and understand the disclosed environmental information.

In accessing environmental information, professionals who are representing clients might be expected to have developed a working knowledge of where to access proactively disclosed environmental information. However, this is not always the case, with some of these professionals submitting requests for environmental information which has already been proactively disclosed or asking for an excessively wide tranche of environmental information:

> So what it means is whilst many ... professional users, we'll call them that, professional users will look at that and find it in the first place some don't find it or they just send you an email because my name's on the website and then I just redirect them to the website.[243]

Such a divergence between different professional representatives indicates that professional representatives are not all equally as knowledgeable as each other, further blurring the distinctions which can be drawn between each individual actor within this category of users.

---

[242] This is further discussed in Chapter 4.
[243] Interview with Public Authority No. 6.

The differences between individual professionals are further demonstrated by the personal connections that some of them have with public authorities, allowing them to bypass the domestic environmental information legislation. When information has not been published, some professionals may be able to gain access to it not through the formal legal procedures, but by making an informal request to someone they know in the relevant authority. Critically these personal connections are held only by some professional representatives and can degrade over time. This adds an additional differentiator between different professional representatives, reinforcing the significance of the user's identity in using the right, even when dealing with professional as opposed to personal users.

Professional users representing clients are not uniformly expert, do not all have access to the same informal ways of supplementing or by-passing the formal procedures and will be guided by the endlessly varied motives of the clients they are serving. All of these factors will influence how each individual professional user engages with the right to access environmental information and their relationship with the authorities that hold it. While it is important to recognise the differences between each professional user, and thus not to homogenise them, a shared characteristic is that how they engage with the right will often be markedly different from that of an ordinary member of the public. Again, this evidences that any simple vision of engaged citizens directly seeking information, such as that embodied by the Aarhus Convention and the EI(S)R, falls well short of capturing the much more varied practice, motivation and expertise of users in the real world.

2.3. ACADEMICS AND STUDENTS

The third category of professional users who engage with the right of access to environmental information comprises academic users and students working or learning in higher and further education, as well as in secondary and primary schools. However, while both teachers and students are categorised here as academics, there is a nuanced distinction between how and why they engage with the right. This, in turn, contributes to the diversity of users who utilise the right of access to environmental information and introduces further actors whose distinct characteristics need to be considered.

Before moving on to discussing this category of users, it is beneficial to highlight how these users actually engage with the right. Students have a simpler motive for wanting to access environmental information: they are likely engaging with the right in order to inform their interests or, a more commonly identified motive, to complete work assigned to them during their education:

> When students turn up to do this, or it's the latter part of the term where they're supposed to put in their dissertation or their project, oh boy do we get swamped with endless requests.[244]

> [A student society] is one of the student societies, one of the national student societies, and we do receive a request from [the student society] from time to time.[245]

Such uses are not intermediary in nature, embodying the more direct relationship between user and information envisaged by the Aarhus Convention and the EI(S)R.

In contrast with students, academics have a more fluid relationship with their status as intermediaries. In certain instances, academics do clearly act as intermediaries between public authorities and the general public, acting to interpret, refine and communicate relevant environmental information to those interested in it. However, in other aspects of their academic role, academics will publish work that is aimed at other academics and not the general public. Such works are usually less accessible to the general public,[246] both in terms of the language used and in the public availability of academic publications.[247] Further, in their role as teachers, academics will likely only be engaging with students who have enrolled on the relevant university programme. As a result, academics oscillate between directly engaging with the public as intermediaries and retreating into more specialised spaces of communication.

However, academics can also engage with the right with the intention of directly contributing to decision-making procedures and governance. Such direct engagement could be in appearing before parliamentary committees and responding to official consultations, challenging policy

---

[244] Interview with Public Authority No. 15.
[245] Interview with Public Authority No. 9.
[246] Although academics may hope that these publications are read by a wider audience.
[247] The drive towards open access publishing is making more academic output accessible to the public rather than being available in subscription-only publications, but few, if any, non-specialists take advantage of this.

decisions adopted by local authorities or providing evidence to Government consultations:

> [I've made] submissions to calls for evidence or consultation documents around policy changes and so on.[248]

This is not to suggest that journalists, professional users representing clients or other professional users cannot engage with public participation mechanisms or public consultations; rather, it is to emphasise that their jobs or roles do not lend themselves to such direct participation in the same way that being employed as an academic enables these users to engage with these participatory processes. Consequently, academic users can more easily switch between acting as an intermediary, which is not directly encouraged by the Aarhus Convention or the EI(S)R, and as direct users, which is supported by these instruments.

The next element to consider with regard to how academics and students engage with the right is their driving motivation. While the right presumed that those using the right are doing so for altruistic reasons, in practice academics may be driven by less altruistic concerns. Like other professional users, both academics and students are partially driven by self-serving economic considerations – making their living or enhancing their career prospects – rather than always living up to the altruistic ideal that lies behind the right. As is the case with other professional users, this may or may not be combined with a desire to pursue environmental enhancement,[249] but again highlights the complex reality of diverse actors making use of the Aarhus Convention and the EI(S)R. It is here that Actor-Network Theory helps in unpicking this diversity. Through helping distinguish between different academic actors and how they engage with the right, Actor-Network Theory highlights the different ways in which actors who initially appear to be similar are actually driven by different motives and use the accessed information in different ways. This is not only valuable in identifying the how the right is used in practice; it also challenges the broad conceptualisation of users that is adopted by the right and hinders efforts to identify whether the right's environmental and participative aims have been achieved.

---

[248] Interview with User No. 14. Individual academics may, of course, be driven to participate through strong personal concerns, as in the case of the petitioner in *Walton v. Scottish Ministers* [2012] UKSC 44, who challenged a major road development.

[249] Indeed, as with other categories of users, some academic use may be for purposes that are inimical to the environment.

The final element to consider in terms of how academics engage with the right is the expertise that they can apply to seeking out proactively disclosed environmental information and submitting requests for environmental information, and even more in understanding the significance of the information obtained. In terms of proactively disclosed environmental information, many Scottish public authorities indicated that, in order to get full use of the proactively disclosed information, users needed a special degree of expertise:

> [I]t makes sense to provide open data sets, which the public can then manipulate and download and, you know, kind of, deal with themselves. I must admit ... I suspect for a lot of people who are perhaps not confident with manipulating data and understanding data and analysing data, I suspect that that's actually not terribly helpful to them, and that they'd probably prefer, kind of, some sort of summary information.[250]

Academics are better placed to hold this expertise and be able to use the opportunity to analyse the information than other users of the right. Simply making information available to the public does not mean that it is always truly accessible; for some sorts of material, only a few have the expertise to make the most effective use of what can be accessed. Indeed, revealing lots of data can obfuscate rather than clarify the position for most (or sometimes all) people, whilst any summary risks distortion or hiding crucial details.[251] The expertise of academics who can analyse data and explain its significance thus has a special place in making the right of access to environmental information truly effective. Similar considerations of expertise also underpin how academics submit requests for environmental information, as their familiarity with the subject area enhances their ability to phrase their request.[252]

While considerations of expertise do arise in the other professional users' engagement with the right, they take on a special significance in the context of academics. Academics are considered to be experts in their

---

[250] Interview with Public Authority No. 9.
[251] In relation to Environmental Impact Assessment, this dilemma is addressed by requiring the disclosure of both the full environmental report and a "non-technical summary of the information": Directive 2011/92/EU of the European Parliament and of the Council of 13 December 2011 on the assessment of the effects of certain public and private projects on the environment [2021] OJ L26/1 (as amended), art. 5(1).
[252] It should be noted that this may not be the case for students who, by virtue of being in the process of learning about a subject area, may not hold this expertise.

Chapter 3. Professional Users

respective topics and thus better informed and more able to interpret and use the environmental information that is disclosed to them, either proactively or on request. Yet there is no recognition in the Aarhus Convention or the EI(S)R of the differing capacities of users to make use of what is disclosed. Other considerations relevant to academics, such as the need on occasions for a quick response in order to publish within a deadline or prepare for a consultation, are equally not considered. This further represents the applicant- and motive-blind approach of the right of access to environmental information seeking to treat all users the same, despite the clear differences in motive and ability to engage with the right. While academics are not detrimentally affected by this to the extent that journalists have been, it does further highlight the tensions between the right's aspirational and intended usage, and how it is used in practice.

2.4. NON-GOVERNMENTAL ORGANISATIONS (NGOs)

Another set of professional users that seeks access to environmental information are NGOs. These are significant in the context of the right of access to environmental information because the role of environmental NGOs in achieving the right's aims is explicitly recognised by the Aarhus Convention itself.[253] The spotlight placed on environmental NGOs by the Aarhus Convention is based on the assumption that such NGOs hold altruistic, environmental aims and have specific expertise in environmental matters. In this way, the Convention has constructed an idealised version of an environmental NGO actor, one which complies with the right's normative environmental and participative aims.

However, this uniformity between different NGOs does not exist in practice. At the fundamental level, not every NGO using the right is primarily environmental in nature; some NGOs are concerned about disability rights, others are focused on preventing development on a local piece of land and others on promoting the interests of sectors of industry or groups of businesses. Such a range of NGOs means that not every NGO will hold environmental concerns at the centre of its operation. Indeed, for some NGOs, as for some individuals, harming the environment may be

---

[253] Aarhus Convention, Preamble, para. 13. The EI(S)R do not place special emphasis on NGOs within their own provisions, marking a distinction between them and the Aarhus Convention.

Intersentia 81

justified by benefits gained elsewhere.[254] As such, not every NGO will fall within the broad environmental interest category envisaged in the Aarhus Convention.

Even within environmental NGOs, there are conflicting aims and views which act to contradict the view of NGOs working as one collective force.[255] There is a clear divide between large environmental NGOs, such as Greenpeace and Friends of the Earth, and local environmental groups. Such a divide is caused by the different levels of resources and expertise available to them, as well as the differences in terms of the scope of their concerns and their relationships with the state and how they raise funds.[256] Consequently, the distinctions which can be drawn between international and local environmental groups further splinter the assumptions regarding the unity of environmental NGOs.

With such a broad spectrum of environmental NGOs engaging with the right of access to environmental information, there is an issue in determining whether NGOs generally engage with the right as intermediaries or as direct users of the information disclosed to them. On the one hand, some activities, such as information campaigns or mapping pollution hotspots to create a publicly available map, serve to refine and present the information sourced from public authorities to the general public.[257] Such intermediary activities, notwithstanding any positive impacts, do not align with the Aarhus Convention's and the EI(S)R's preference for users to directly engage with public authorities and use the disclosed information themselves.

However, the same NGOs which conduct information campaigns or refine environmental information can also use the information to inform protests, participate in decision-making procedures or initiate

---

[254] Although it should be noted that NGOs are unlikely to explicitly draw attention to harms caused by their actions.
[255] An obvious example is when the promotion of renewable energy threatens sites important for biodiversity.
[256] This is true even within NGOs of a similar status. See V. TIMMER, "Greenpeace Be Nimble, Friends of the Earth Be Quick: Agility, Adaptive Capacity and the Organizational Effectiveness of International Nongovernmental Organisations", presented at the 2005 Berlin Conference on the Human Dimensions of Global Environmental Change International Organisations and Global Environmental Governance, 2–3 December 2005.
[257] E.g. as advocated in Environmental Defense Fund, *Making the Invisible Visible: A Guide for Mapping Hyperlocal Air Pollution to Drive Clean Air Action* (2019) <https://www.edf.org/sites/default/files/content/making-the-invisible-visible.pdf> accessed 19 April 2022.

Chapter 3. Professional Users

legal challenges; indeed, for some such as ClientEarth, taking such action is the primary focus of their activity. These activities do align with the expectations of the Aarhus Convention, as it constitutes users directly accessing environmental information from public authorities and using it to participate in official governmental processes. Thus, NGOs can act as both intermediaries and direct users, depending on what activities they are undertaking with the disclosed environmental information. Such duality cannot be explained through adhering to the homogeneous conceptualisation of users inherent to the Aarhus Convention. Instead, it can be better understood through Actor-Network Theory's more nuanced conceptualisation of these users and their relationships, overcoming the mismatch between the expected and actual uses of the right that undermines the current understanding of the right based on the simpler vision that lies behind its creation.

A further presumption regarding NGOs derived from the Aarhus Convention is their motives for engaging with the right. Generally, under the Aarhus Convention, NGOs are expected to act in the public interest, which the Convention defines as protecting and enhancing the environment for present and future generations. This motive is evidenced in how some NGOs engage with the right in Scotland under the EI(S)R, but other groups are driven by different issues such as more local concerns:

> Maybe like local campaign groups that are maybe they think their town needs a new bypass, or they are not happy with road layouts, or the way that the traffic light sequencing lights.[258]

Such local concerns can sometimes align with the environmental aims of the right, but may also be coloured by more selfish, parochial interests. For example, if a local NGO, in order to protect the economic value of nearby homes, opposes the development of a road through an environmentally sensitive area, then they are aligned with the environmental aims of the Aarhus Convention. However, the same parochial motives can become misaligned with those of the Convention where such resistance prevents a development which has a broad positive impact on the wider environment at the expense of specific properties or a very local area, e.g. opposing new water treatment facilities that will prevent the discharge of untreated sewage at times of heavy rain. Local interest groups themselves thus take a range of positions, with very different environmental implications.

---

[258] Interview with Public Authority No. 13.

The motivations which drive local NGOs are interesting because they are emblematic of the tenuous link underpinning the assumption that users must hold altruistic, environmental motivations in order to have a positive impact on the environment. As demonstrated in the above paragraph, the same parochial motivation against development can have a positive or negative impact on the environment depending on what sort of project is proposed. This disconnect is further emphasised in relation to NGOs representing different interests, such as those of a sector or industry where, depending on the specific sector involved, self-interest may or may not align with environmental objectives. In this way, the relationship between NGOs, public authorities and the environmental and participative aims of the right are much more complex than initially assumed.

Further, even where NGOs are purely concerned about the quality of the wider environment rather than their local area, economic concerns can impact on how they engage with the right. On a practical level, NGOs with limited staff (if any) and funds will find it more difficult to submit, track and act on requests for environmental information than larger, well-funded NGOs. An additional economic consideration for NGOs arises where they receive some funds from the state. Many NGOs that are in receipt of state funds, through direct support or as a payment for services, fear that the act of submitting a request under the environmental information regime or appealing a decision of non-disclosure will be viewed as confrontational, harming the relationship between themselves and the state, and risking cuts to their funding.[259] Such considerations do not affect all NGOs, but this lends further significance to the structure of the NGO and its finances and the diversity of experience, which is not reflected in the provisions of the Aarhus Convention or the EI(S)R.

The final characteristic which is implied in the Aarhus Convention and in its domestic implementation is that all NGOs hold expertise in environmental matters, enabling them to meet the participative and environmental aims of the Convention. This assumption rests on the basis that all NGOs have a similar level of expertise – an assumption which seems unlikely to reflect the experience of different NGOs, whose levels of expertise and resources will vary considerably. Such a position is not to suggest that local NGOs cannot hold expertise or effectively engage with

---

[259] W. DINAN, K. SPENCE and H. HUTCHENSON, "Imperfect Information: Experiences and Perceptions of the Use of Freedom of Information in the Scottish Voluntary Sector – Qualitative Research Report" (Scottish Information Commissioner, 2012).

public authorities; rather, it reflects the greater availability of resources (and likely expertise) held by some (likely larger and more prolific) NGOs compared to others (such as ad hoc local groups formed in response to unwelcome development proposals).

This in itself may influence the effectiveness of the exercise of the right, as by assuming that all NGOs have the same levels of knowledge and experience, the Aarhus Convention fails to reflect the differentiation which exists between NGOs in practice. By applying this broad assumption, it creates the possibility for NGOs which meet these expectations to dominate non-governmental activities within the environmental sector.[260] While not inherently detrimental to environmental protection efforts, the elevation of these NGOs could create a false impression of how well these particular NGOs contribute to the right's environmental aims. It can also risk other NGOs being underappreciated within the legal processes, diminishing their opportunity to effectively contribute views to environmental decision-making procedures and help to protect the environment. This is not to suggest that all NGOs will contribute to these environmental aims. Through attributing altruistic motivations to all NGOs, there is a risk of assisting NGOs that have no intention of contributing to the protection of the environment. While engaging with these complexities arising from the diversity within NGOs is difficult, it must be done in order to break down barriers to participation and ensure that the impact of individual NGOs on the right's environmental and participative aims in practice is clear.

2.5. USERS FROM WITHIN THE PUBLIC SECTOR

The final category of professional users to be considered is those connected to other public authorities. In interviews with Scottish public authorities, two specific sets of users within this professional category were expressly highlighted: other public sector employees and parliamentary researchers. These professional users are unusual because there is an expectation that the right will be not used by individuals as part of their work for the public sector.[261] Yet, as there are no limitations on who can use the right, there is

---

[260] LEE and ABBOT, above n. 111.
[261] The definitions of "the public" and "the public concerned" are broad enough to include public authorities or those working for them, but clearly envisage the public as being distinct from the governmental set-up; Aarhus Convention, art. 2(4), (5).

nothing preventing public authorities from using the right for their own purposes.[262] Despite the assumption that public authority employees do not need to use the right of access to environmental information, some such employees use the right in their professional capacity. Viewing this interaction through Actor-Network Theory provides the means by which the underlying assumption of the right can be challenged. Through conceptualising public authority employees not as "users" but as a specific actor operating within the right, Actor-Network Theory can help identify the reality of how the right is used. Further still, the theory can facilitate challenges to the idea that public authorities can act only as holders of environmental information, a conceptualisation which underpins the relationship between the general public and public authorities under the right.

In examining the role of users who work within the public sector, some of whom engage with the right in an intermediary capacity, it is important to distinguish between the two sets of users highlighted in interviews with public authorities. The first are parliamentary researchers. These professional users seek to access environmental information as part of their job to assist Members of Parliament and Members of the Scottish Parliament through conducting research to find information to use during parliamentary questions and other political activities. Although separate from the government, these users are also very different from members of the general public. Such users clearly act in an intermediary role, with the issues that doing so brings, as discussed above.

The second set of users are public authority employees from other authorities. It was noted in interviews that there is a general convention against any widespread practice of one authority requesting information from another by using the formal mechanisms (under either access to environmental information or wider freedom of information laws) rather than other channels, but this does happen on occasions. The employees involved are professional users seeking to access environmental information in order to achieve the task set by their employer and again are very different from the public at large. As such, this further contributes to the existence of a broad spectrum of users – a spectrum which resists being categorised and eschews the simple categorisation of users embedded in the Aarhus Convention and the EI(S)R.

---

[262] This section does not consider public sector employees who use the right for their own personal purposes, such as resolving personal grievances. Such users are categorised as "personal users" and are discussed in Chapter 4.

Chapter 3. Professional Users

Recourse to the right to request environmental information is particularly notable in relation to those working for other authorities, since it suggests a failure on the part of the state to hold the information in the right place or to provide it proactively. The Aarhus Convention contains an obligation for public authorities to hold the environmental information that is relevant to their functions.[263] By seeking from others access to environmental information supposedly relevant to their functioning, authorities are tacitly admitting that they have failed to hold or provide to their employees all the relevant environmental information. Within the interviews, there is evidence that other public authorities sought to access environmental information relevant to their functions because they themselves did not hold it:

> I mean, I don't think we have ever had any core Government bodies asking us for information, it is usually local authorities and normally parliament.[264]

Such gaps in the records of public authorities, or in what is readily available to parliamentarians, may point towards unrealistic expectations originating from the Aarhus Convention, or it may indicate a failure of communication between public authorities to share all the relevant environmental information that they need. Whatever the background, the legal position enshrined in the Aarhus Convention creates an obligation to hold the necessary information. Regardless of funding limitations, staffing problems or other administrative issues that can arise, the obligations imposed by the Convention, and the assumptions underpinning them, remain legally binding. This is not to suggest that public authorities are failing to govern effectively; instead, this may reflect the reality of the public sector being made up of various bodies, rather than a unified whole as envisioned by the Aarhus Convention, justifying the use of Actor-Network Theory to deconstruct the full variety of actors involved.

Perhaps somewhat surprisingly, questions also arise in terms of the expertise of these users in engaging with the right. A point of interest highlighted by the interviews is that, despite their expertise on the workings of public administration, users within this category can sometimes fail to

---

[263] Aarhus Convention, art. 5(1): "Each Party shall ensure that: (a) Public authorities possess and update environmental information which is relevant to their functions ..."
[264] Interview with Public Authority No. 13.

effectively phrase their requests for environmental information. This was particularly true with regard to parliamentary researchers:

> The parliamentary researchers I think is a classic example because we will get parliamentary researchers, and we have actually got something going on at the moment where in the last week, they have sent us 40 requests ... All asking for huge wide-ranging information.[265]

What this demonstrates is that that despite the expertise one might expect to be held by parliamentary researchers, this expertise does not necessarily extend to knowing the best methods to access environmental information. It also hints at a frustration that such a lack of expertise results in an expenditure of time and effort that might be deployed to deal with requests from "genuine" members of the public. This problem over expertise also stands in contrast to experience of the other professional users of the right, who do (although not invariably) apply expertise in ensuring that requests are specific and easily understood. Whatever the explanation for such apparent lack of expertise in refining requests – whether a lack of experience and guidance for those in what are often short-term posts or a sense that the role justifies gathering broad information – it does further add to the conclusion that the current vision of users of the right does not adequately reflect the broad spectrum of users who actually use the right in practice.

The fact that users from within the public sector are exercising the right to access environmental information is rather unexpected in view of what drove the right's creation. Both the right and the legal instruments that embody it specifically seek out the views of those outwith public authorities – it is through the participation of actors outside the public sector, who hold insights that a public authority does not, that improvements will be made in how the environment is protected.[266] Users working for public authorities are unlikely to provide this insight as they are actors originating from within the public sector, and thus are unlikely to contribute to the right's environmental aims in the way that is intended. This further highlights the mismatch between the intended uses of the right and the actual uses of the right in practice.

---

[265] Ibid.
[266] See Chapter 5, section 2.

3. CONCLUSION

While the Aarhus Convention and the EI(S)R set out a detailed and specific set of procedural obligations for public authorities, they are significantly less nuanced in their expectations for who will seek to exercise the right of access to environmental information. Indeed, looking towards the originating instrument of the Rio Declaration, both legal instruments imply certain characteristics that "intended" users should have: they should be members of the public wishing to use the information to participate in environmental decision-making processes; they should be driven by altruistic environmental considerations and they should be seeking to access environmental information for themselves and able to make use of the information obtained.

This is not to suggest that the drafters of the Aarhus Convention or the EI(S)R would have been surprised by users who do not meet these normative expectations using the right. The definitions used and the absence of any provisions limiting the right from being used in ways that do not match the ideal[267] suggest a willingness to accept that anyone should be able to use the right for whatever purpose. Nevertheless, the environmental information regimes have constructed a particular understanding of the characteristics users of the right should hold to best engage with its environmental and participative aims, and these expectations can seep into how the right is guaranteed in practice. Therefore, the arising mismatches can lead to tensions between the user and the authorities that guarantee the right.

Professional users of the right are particularly affected by this view of users because they do not fit within the normative expectations set by the Convention or the EI(S)R. The intermediary role of such users, in addition to their economic motives and lack of personal connection to the information, runs contrary to the "ideal" user envisioned by the Convention. This is not explicit within the Convention or the EI(S)R themselves; indeed, the Convention recognises "the importance of the respective roles that individual citizens, non-governmental organizations and the private sector can play in environmental protection".[268] Yet the "one-size-fits-all" framework introduced through these instruments' applicant- and

---

[267] For example, the adoption of the applicant- and motive-blind approach that precludes any need to explain why information is being sought, as discussed in Chapter 4.
[268] Aarhus Convention, Preamble, para. 13.

motive-blind procedures does not adequately address the unique needs of these different users (e.g. the speed and exclusivity desired by journalists) or their driving motives for engaging with the right. Ultimately, the right and its legal instruments have constructed an idealised actor: a singular category of users that directly access environmental information and are best placed to achieve the right's aims, and that cannot be found within those acting as professional users.

Of course, there is a risk of uncritically adopting the alternative view that specific classes of professional users merit a bespoke regime in order to best accommodate their needs and enhance their ability to engage with the right's environmental and participative aims. Even designing several tailored schemes for groups of users may serve only to complicate things in a way that adds burdens which outweigh the benefits achieved. Such a position also follows the same line as the Aarhus Convention and the EI(S)R in terms of failing to respect the full diversity of practice by creating pre-determined categories, this time working on the assumption that professional users, acting as intermediaries, will be driven by environmental motives and be better positioned than other users to engage with and further the right's environmental and participative aims. This will not always be true. Personal users are becoming increasingly interested in and knowledgeable about environmental matters, and how to engage with them matters, whereas some professional users do not always have (or have the capacity to) show the well-honed skills that the best of their colleagues deploy in seeking information. Nevertheless, the fact that such a proposal can be viably mooted suggests that there is an issue with how the current regimes conceptualise users of the right as the one broadly similar category of actors with similar characteristics.

The fact that neither the Aarhus Convention nor the EI(S)R explicitly recognises the potential for intermediaries to engage with the right's goals does place professional users in an uncomfortable position. As actors they sit uneasily within the expectations of the right that shape the relevant environmental information regimes, embodying the mismatch between the intended and actual uses of the right. Actor-Network Theory helps to distinguish between different users in a way that highlights not only their unique motives, expertise and ability to engage with the right, but also their divergence from the vision of the ideal user that underpins the right. Such a mismatch has real consequences, the most evident of which being the willingness of professional users to bypass the formal information disclosure mechanisms through relying on professional contacts to accelerate the process.

Chapter 3. Professional Users

These gaps between how the right operates in practice and the expectations regarding users of the right could be viewed as simply the vagaries of real life and the consequence of a decision to opt for a single, simple legal framework that can cope, more or less well, with a wide range of circumstances. This may be a sound decision, but that conclusion should be reached after a proper consideration of the consequences in practice. Professional users are able to contribute to the right's environmental and participative aims in ways that the "intended" users of the right cannot, and the current approach both raises obstacles in terms of how they engage with the right and can have a negative influence how other actors view these users. However, because the right is targeted at a wide audience, including both "professional" and "personal" users, the vision for the right and the right's implementing legal instruments overlook both the unique benefits and individual needs that such professional users have in accessing environmental information. In treating every user identically, the Aarhus Convention and the EI(S)R seek to broaden the availability of environmental information at the expense of the unique needs of "professional" users and the costs and benefits of those deserve greater attention.

Shifting perspective from professional users of the right, the current applicant- and motive-blind approach is likely adopted as a means to help "personal" users of the right. In contrast to professional users, personal users are less likely to have the levels of expertise by which to access and understand environmental information or have alternate means which bypass the formal environmental information regulations. In this way, the applicant- and motive-blind approach arguably prevents professional users from becoming privileged actors within the context of the right. Yet in seeking to assist personal users, both the Convention and the EI(S)R paper over the differences between professional users of the right, broadly homogenising them as actors and hindering how they engage with the right of access to environmental information. Yet, as the closer analysis enabled by Actor-Network Theory shows, the broad homogenisation of users and public authorities does not match practice, where there are not two distinct sets of actors, but an endless variety of individual actors with different motives, levels of expertise and relationships with other actors within the context of the right itself. The diversity of professional users that engage with the right to environmental information has a substantial impact on how the right is both used and guaranteed in practice. But such diversity, and divergence from the expectations of the right, is not limited to professional users: there is also an unrecognised diversity in how personal users engage with the right in practice.

CHAPTER 4
PERSONAL USERS

The previous chapter focused on professional users of the right to access environmental information and highlighted the stark mismatch between the expectations which underpin the right's intended use and how the right is actually used in practice. Professional users serve as a clear example of this mismatch because the underpinning assumptions which animate the right and its legal regimes do not cater for this minority category of users. However, considering this mismatch in that context also provides the opportunity to identify whether the same is true for "personal users". Personal users – the majority of those using the right – are more likely to be engaging directly with the environmental information held by public authorities and with the right's environmental and participative aims. Yet, as with those in the professional user category, the individual actors within this second group are also diverse in terms of what motivates them, how they use information obtained and their levels of expertise in engaging with public authorities and the right itself. Thus, mismatches such as those identified in the context of professional users also arise in relation to personal users.

1. INTRODUCTION

The differences between personal users are key to how they experience and engage with the right of access to environmental information. These differences can be split into two themes. The first of these relates to the motive of personal users, referring to what drives these users to engage with the right and seek access to environmental information. The second theme relates to the levels of expertise that different users hold, encapsulating different aspects such as the ability in seeking proactively disclosed information, drafting and submitting requests for environmental information, and understanding any information accessed under the right. Such variety distinguishes different personal users from each other, creating a complex tapestry of personal users who are each engaging with the right in their own way and for their own reasons.

This variety lies at the heart of this chapter. Although each individual personal user will engage with the right differently, the assumptions embodied by instruments such as the Aarhus Convention and the Environmental Information (Scotland) Regulations 2004 EI(S)R do not account for these differences. In terms of what motivates personal users, the normative expectations that underpin the right of access to environmental information assume that individuals are driven by the desire to fulfil the right's implicit moral environmental and participative aims.[269] Beyond this, the right also assumes that all users have a degree of trust in how the public authority discharges its obligations under the right. Both assumptions shape the provisions of the Aarhus Convention and the EI(S)R, which in turn can generate conflict between the user and the public authority where these expectations are not met.

There are further expectations regarding the expertise levels of individual users. Broadly, the right assumes that all users will hold sufficient expertise to engage with public authorities and understand any environmental information that they access from the authority. Indeed, a starting point is that citizens will know of their right to access environmental information, distinct from any other entitlements under freedom of information laws. The Convention and its domestic implementation through the EI(S)R do qualify this to an extent by obliging authorities to provide advice and assistance where necessary.[270] However, this in turn also raises practical questions relating to identifying the need for assistance and whether the user will be happy to accept the assistance offered.

These expectations construct an idealised user of the right: one who can effectively engage with the right's environmental and participative aims. When viewed through the experience of personal users, these expectations are shown to be not wholly aligned with how many users actually engage with the right. The mismatches that can arise in practice can have unintended consequences on how the right is guaranteed, with environmental information regimes not accounting for these deviations or seeking to resolve them. Ultimately, this can have a detrimental impact on both users, who are engaging with the right in a way that is not wholly supported, and public authorities, who may feel that their limited resources are being wasted by users who are "abusing" their rights.

---

[269] Aarhus Convention, Preamble, para. 7. See also Principle 10 of the Rio Declaration, above n. 19; and BARRITT, above n. 21, pp. 39–72.

[270] Aarhus Convention, art. 3(2); EI(S)R, reg. 9.

Chapter 4. Personal Users

Actor-Network Theory can help to identify the mismatch between the expectations of the right and the reality of its use, unpicking the implicit conceptualisation of "users" adopted in relation to the right by identifying how it fails to reflect how users actually engage with the right in practice. This also allows the analysis to highlight the points of tension between users and public authorities and the reasons why such tensions arise. Ultimately it is these tensions which have a negative impact on how the right of access to environmental information is guaranteed; exploring the source of these tensions is the first step to better guaranteeing the right in order to secure its environmental and participative aims.

This chapter is structured to reflect the different stages of the journey personal users go through when engaging with the right of access to environmental information. The chapter begins by highlighting the different motives which drive personal users to engage with the right of access to environmental information. It then moves on to discuss how personal users seek out proactively disclosed environmental information and directly request access to environmental information from public authorities. From this, the chapter explores the obligation imposed on public authorities to provide advice and assistance to users. It then concludes by considering how users receive and understand environmental information that they have accessed by virtue of the right.

2. MOTIVE

Individual users of the right will all have reasons for wanting to access environmental information. However, not all users will have the same motive (or motives) for using the right. Indeed, the motives which drive different personal users to engage with the right will differ depending on their surrounding circumstances, their trust in the public authority and their views on the matter to which the information relates. Further complexity is introduced by the fact that personal users are often not driven by a singular, unitary motive. Instead, they are often driven by multiple motives which coalesce into a specific reason for wishing to engage with the right of access to environmental information at a particular moment. This range of different motives reflects a key aspect of the right in practice: there is no one unifying or overarching motive that drives users to seek access to environmental information.

The variety of user motives is not reflected in the Aarhus Convention or the EI(S)R, both of which adopt an applicant-blind approach that pays no heed to the motive and identity of the user seeking access to the information. One reason for this approach is that the right is founded on the implicit moral duty to protect and enhance the environment.[271] As both instruments assume that all users are seeking to discharge this moral duty, there is no need for public authorities to inquire into the motives of those users who are seeking to access environmental information. Further, more practical justifications for this approach are that it avoids an additional stage that might provide a hurdle to seeking access and, in particular, restricts the ability of public authorities to treat requests unfavourably due to the identity of the requester or the reason for seeking information.[272]

Regardless of these justifications for the motive-blind approach, the motive driving users to engage with the right permeates the entirety of the process. Interactions between users of the right and public authorities are subtly (or not so subtly) influenced by the reasons underpinning why the user seeks to access the desired environmental information. For example, an authority's attempt to assist a user in refining a broadly phrased request is likely to be perceived differently by a user motivated by a belief that the authority is trying to hide embarrassing data and by a user simply struggling to phrase their request effectively.

This is not reflected in how the Convention or the EI(S)R construe "users", with the relevant terms defined in a way that reflects a conceptualisation of users as a singular category of actors that trust and act alongside authorities for the benefit of the environment. Mismatches between a user's motivations and the expectations of others can lead to misunderstandings and dissatisfaction between personal users and the authority, which undermine how the right of access to environmental information is guaranteed and risks hindering the environmental and participatory aims of the right itself. As will be shown in this chapter, the identification of these divergent motives is key to understanding how the right to access environmental information is utilised, why it diverges from the right's underpinning expectations and what the impact of these divergences is on how the right is guaranteed.

---

[271] Aarhus Convention, Preamble, para. 7. See also generally BARRITT, above n. 21.
[272] G. MICHENER and K. RODRIGUEZ, "'Who Wants to Know?' Assessing Discrimination in Transparency and Freedom of Information Regimes" Fourth Global Conference on Transparency Research, Lugano, Switzerland, 4–6 June 2015.

2.1. PERSONAL USERS, MOTIVES AND THE IDEALS OF THE AARHUS CONVENTION

Key to understanding the intended operation of the right of access to environmental information is the implicit assumption that personal users engage with the right in order to discharge their moral duty to protect and enhance the environment.[273] Sourced and continued from its origins in the Rio Declaration,[274] this assumption embodies the presupposed relationship between individuals, public authorities and the environment itself – that public authorities are viewed as trusted holders of environmental information, requiring scrutiny but generally acting in the best interests of the public. Yet perhaps more significant is that this assumption also embodies the idea that users are a singular set of actors, driven by broadly similar environmental motivations and hold similar, positive views on public authorities.

This conceptualisation of users is generally not evidenced in practice, which reveals an increasing sense of distrust in the state[275] and a greater willingness to oppose decisions made by public authorities.[276] One reason for this is that, far from only holding altruistic environmental motives, personal users are generally driven by a broader range of motives. While some personal users are driven by environmental concerns, aligning with the expectations of the right, these motives are often not the primary motive which drives users to engage with the right. There is thus a general mismatch between the expectations of the right, and its embodiment within the Aarhus Convention and the EI(S)R, and the motives which drive the majority of personal users to engage with the right of access to environmental information, potentially calling into question what is being achieved by the establishment of the right.

A frequent spur for users to seek to use the right was events where the public authority has played a role in causing (or failing to prevent) a negative impact on the user, the area in which the user lives or the area that the user has a connection with:

> I was concerned that not enough is being done to tackle the issue of vehicle idling, especially outside schools.[277]

---

[273] Aarhus Convention, Preamble, para. 7.
[274] Rio Declaration, above n. 19, Principle 10.
[275] This is discussed in more detail in section 2.2 below.
[276] See generally V. NIELSEN, H. NIELSEN and M. BISGAARD, "Citizen Reactions to Bureaucratic Encounters: Different Ways of Coping with Public Authorities" (2021) 31(2) *Journal of Public Administration Research and Theory* 381.
[277] Interview with User No. 10.

Such motives emphasise the desire of the user to influence the public authority in some way, usually to take a specific course of action or to change a course of action in order to remedy a problem identified by (and possibly affecting) the user in some way. The direct connection between the personal user, the environmental information sought and a problem affecting the user is significant because it was the most common recurring motive in personal users' reasoning for engaging with the right to access environmental information. A further point of interest is that while there may be broader environmental concerns embedded within this motive, the primary focus on how the authority is acting means that many such motivations would fit equally well under the rationale for the wider freedom of information laws as under the specific environmental information regime.

In addition to this personal motive, there were two other motives which were commonly brought up. The first of these were broader concerns regarding the governance of the public authority, in particular the desire to ensure transparency and accountability in the exercise of their powers:

> So as a Council tax payer I was pretty annoyed about that and wanted to find out what had gone wrong.[278]

This motivation even more clearly aligns with the objectives of the wider movement towards freedom of information rather than the more specific environmental aims of the right to environmental information. However, that latter element was represented by the second recurring motive, which was a concern for the environment:

> I've seen over the past ten years a massive decline of insect species and also wildlife.[279]

> I do it because it's an environmental matter, because if the food bin gets tipped over it's not going to be recycled. If the bin without a lid is full of paper and cardboard it's now wet, it's not going to get recycled. So it's an issue the council should be addressing systemically.[280]

Some users are driven by an altruistic concern for the environment, aligning with a vision of users acting as engaged citizens seeking to protect

---

[278] Interview with User No. 6.
[279] Interview with User No. 4.
[280] Interview with User No. 8.

Chapter 4. Personal Users

and enhance the environment. Indeed, with the range and multiplicity of motives driving personal users, it would have been surprising if a genuinely altruistic concern for the environment was not significant for some users.

This variety is further revealed when the motivations of personal users are examined in more detail. While there is a temptation to categorise these driving motives into broad groups such as "personal motives" or "environmental motives", in reality many users will hold multiple different motivations. An example of this can be where the environmental concerns that drive some personal users are located within their own local area and are about a matter which directly concerns them, such as recycling:

> [I]f we're recycling all this stuff, is our council tax bill going down a wee bit, if they're making money off the environmental side of it?[281]

Such an overlap of motives means that any number of users may be driven to engage with the right at least in part out of a concern for the environment. The existence of this environmental motivation in many users' desire to engage with the right is significant because it suggests that the right and its legal instruments are successful in encouraging and enabling individuals to engage with the moral duty to protect and enhance the environment.

Nevertheless, it could also be argued that due to this overlap, it is likely that any user who is engaging with these environmental concerns is also doing so for personal reasons. These personal reasons may indeed run counter to the aim of environmental improvement. A user may seek information on action taken in relation to their local area in order to oppose it, since despite its positive impact on the environment, it has a detrimental impact in another aspect of their life, e.g. objecting to major waste water infrastructure designed to tackle harmful discharges to rivers or the sea, but requiring construction on open land near a person's home.[282]

The Aarhus Convention and the EI(S)R do not limit the exercise of the right to those who can demonstrate an environmental motive that aligns with their overall environmental and participative objectives. In this way, regardless of the driving motives of personal users engaging with the

---

[281] Interview with User No. 11.
[282] Discussions on this tension between local and wider environmental concerns can be identified in the academic discussions on NIMBYism; see P. DEVINE-WRIGHT, "Rethinking NIMBYism: The Role of Place Attachment and Place Identity in Explaining Place-Protective Action" (2009) 19(6) *Journal of Community and Applied Social Psychology* 426.

right, there are no legal obstacles that hinder how they engage with the right. However, this deviation from the altruistic, environmental ideals embedded within the right does suggest that the animating environmental motive is absent from how the right is actually used. Such a mismatch arises from the treatment of personal users as a singular category of users, viewing them as broadly similar actors with no distinguishing features between them. This failure to accurately characterise the range of users has the potential to affect the relationship between users and public authorities. Moreover, the lack of a clear environmental motive in many cases undermines the distinction between the right to environmental information and the general right to information, and therefore the need for the two separate regimes that support them.

2.2. PERSONAL USERS, MOTIVES AND TRUST

In considering the motives of users who engage with the right of access to environmental information, the degree of trust (or lack thereof) between the personal user and the public authority merits further attention. Whereas for professional users, dealings with the public authority are on a formal and business-like basis, for personal users, the relationship is much more direct and personal. As previously highlighted, many personal users seek to engage with the right on the basis of an action or "wrong" that has been inflicted upon them and/or the broader public by the authority in question. This initiating event for the user's interest in the right is important because the interviewed users often expressed some degree of distrust of the authority and its willingness to engage with them in relation to the perceived issue.

One of the invisible assumptions which underpin the operation and implementation of the right is trust. Both the Aarhus Convention and the EI(S)R position public authorities as bodies which act and operate in the public interest.[283] Therefore, users are expected to trust public authorities to be acting properly in terms of how they guarantee and implement the right to environmental information. It is important to note that this assumption of trust does not blind the Convention or the EI(S)R to the possibility of

---

[283] Aarhus Convention, Preamble, para. 17. This is not explicitly mentioned in the EI(S)R, but as an instrument derived from the Aarhus Convention, it follows that they adopt the same perspective.

authorities misusing their powers, either by mistake or intentionally; both regimes contain obligations to provide review procedures by which users can challenge how public authorities guarantee the right to information,[284] and enabling scrutiny to ensure that authorities are working appropriately is an element of the public participation that is promoted. Nevertheless, the trust that is assumed to underpin the interactions between personal users and authorities still manifests within the provisions of both regimes, with one of the key aspects being the unspoken assumption that users of the right will interpret any interactions with an authority in good faith.

The distrust that some users feel is therefore significant and affects how users engage with public authorities under the right, because it influences how they perceive any interactions between themselves and the authority. Either the information published by an authority or its response to a request for information may be perceived as insufficient and reflective of a deeper issue:

> So generally it'll be no, I'm dissatisfied because either you haven't given me all the information and I think you've got it. Or you've told me that you haven't given me information and I don't believe you. So you're lying to me.[285]

> A locked spreadsheet. And they said oh oh that's the way we do it ... luckily I knew how to, I had the expertise to basically unlock the so-called locked down data that was in there. And very very interesting data. But then, I asked myself did they do that on purpose?[286]

The same reaction also extends to interactions following a request for environmental information:

> They give you answers that are so stupid and so [are] there to, you know, obfuscation and just, "should go away"-type answers.[287]

Acting as evidence to contradict that assumption of trust that underpins the right to environmental information, the views of some users challenge both this unspoken assumption and the broad conceptualisation of users

---

[284] Aarhus Convention, art. 9 and Preamble, para. 18; EI(S)R, reg. 17.
[285] Interview with Public Authority No. 11, discussing the reasons driving requests they receive for internal reviews of their initial response to a user requesting information.
[286] Interview with User No. 10.
[287] Interview with User No. 5.

as a singular set of actors with similar characteristics. It is important to highlight that sometimes these negative views are justified: public authorities are capable of acting in ways which are uncooperative, which in turn negatively impacts on the interactions between them and members of the public. Yet in the context of the right of access to environmental information, whether or not these negative views held by users are justified or not is irrelevant. Beliefs and opinions held by personal users can negatively influence how they perceive interactions with public authorities regardless of the validity of these views. This in turn makes interactions between both actors significantly more difficult to navigate – a difficulty emphasised by the lack of support and guidance provided on this issue by the Aarhus Convention and the EI(S)R.

This mismatch between the expectations of the right and the reality of how different users interact with public authorities is of real concern to how the right of access to environmental information is guaranteed. If a user does not have confidence in the response provided by an authority to a request for information, the legal framework does provide means to take the matter further by using the review and appeal procedures or by making further requests for related information, but such responses may be seen as confrontational. The authority that may be confident that it has dealt with the request properly can be surprised by the subsequent challenge or request that requires further resources to process. The very fact of being suspected of not having been fully open may itself trigger a more defensive response to future requests, exacerbating this poor relationship and undermining the overall aims of the right.

What exacerbates this issue is the lack of recognition within the right itself regarding the potential lack of trust between users and public authorities. Through conceptualising users as a singular category of actors, both the Convention and the EI(S)R paper over any of the individual issues and problems which may impact on communications between users and public authorities. Some recourse for dissatisfied or distrusting users is provided, but ultimately, by conceptualising users in this way, the right does not fully recognise the mismatch between its ideals and the reality of its implementation, harming the environmental and participative aims which underpin it. These issues further reflect the mismatch between the ideals of the right and the reality of how it is guaranteed and used in practice, and continue to be relevant throughout the entirety of the user's engagement with the right and its environmental aims.

3. SEEKING ACCESS TO ENVIRONMENTAL INFORMATION

Moving beyond a mere desire to access environmental information, the next step for personal users of the right is for them to seek out the information from the public authority. This can be done in one of two ways. The first is that the personal user can identify whether the authority has proactively disclosed the environmental information through its communication channels – often through the authority's website, but potentially also through offline channels such as a brochure, leaflet or even a notice board.[288] The second method that a user can employ is to submit a request for environmental information directly to the authority under the relevant environmental information legislation, a method shared with the wider laws on freedom of information.

Both methods are enshrined within the Aarhus Convention[289] and the EI(S)R,[290] which oblige public authorities both to proactively disclose environmental information and to respond to requests for environmental information. It is important to distinguish between these two aspects of the right of access to environmental information: this is because they are each implemented through different procedures, service different needs of users and act as different entry points for individuals seeking access to environmental information.

While both sets of obligations and procedures are seeking to respond to the different needs of users, one common aspect that both have to contend with is the varying levels of expertise held by different users. Users are generally expected to be able to navigate an authority's communication channels to find the relevant environmental information, and to be able to submit requests which sufficiently describe the environmental information that they are looking for. However, not all users hold this expertise or have the time to do this, and indeed different public authorities may adopt different approaches to discharging their duties to both proactively disclose and respond to requests for environmental information, so that experience in one context may not be applicable elsewhere. The obligation to provide advice and assistance to those making requests (see section 4 below) does show some recognition that some users may need help, but

---

[288] E.g. the notices giving details of water quality at bathing beaches: Bathing Waters (Scotland) Regulations 2008, SSI 2008/170, reg. 8.
[289] Aarhus Convention, arts 4–5.
[290] EI(S)R, regs 4–5.

the initial assumption creates a potential mismatch between the expertise actually held by users and the expertise that users are expected to hold, creating possible points of tension and frustration between users and public authorities when interacting under the right.

3.1. PROACTIVE DISCLOSURE

The obligation on public authorities to proactively disclose environmental information is established in Article 5 of the Aarhus Convention and regulation 4 of the EI(S)R. There are a range of procedural obligations associated with this right,[291] but the core element of this right is that the authorities must disclose this information without waiting to receive a request from a member of the public. While this may initially seem obvious and innocuous, this proactive requirement marks a big change from the former position where only that information covered by specific statutory provisions requiring publication had to be disclosed.[292] Interactions under this aspect of the right will be markedly different from those when a specific request is being made.

A notable point about the sheer amount of information being proactively published under the right is that the fact that it is being made available in fulfilment of a legal obligation is obscured. Authorities do not label specific information as being published in pursuance of their legal obligations under the Aarhus Convention and the EI(S)R, and tend not to distinguish between what they are legally required to publish and other material being made available. Moreover, proactive publication tends to be undertaken without the involvement of the teams responsible for handling access to environmental information or freedom of information more widely. This leads to the true impact of the obligation to publish becoming hard to assess and hidden from the public, the vast majority of whom will not realise that when they look at certain material, they are doing so as beneficiaries of a legal right to environmental information.[293]

In terms of individuals using the right to access proactively disclosed environmental information, the fact that the information is proactively disclosed means that the impetus of taking the first steps is imposed on

---

[291] Aarhus Convention, art. 5(2)–(3) and 5(3)–(9); EI(S)R, reg. 4.
[292] See Chapter 1, section 1.
[293] This proved a stumbling block in terms of trying to recruit people for the surveys and interviews for this project.

Chapter 4. Personal Users

the public authority. This makes it significantly easier for users both to discover and access information that has been made available, whether they were already interested and engaged with the topic or if their interest was sparked by seeing the information that is available. This is important for understanding how personal users interact with the right, because it is often the first method that personal users will utilise when seeking to access the desired environmental information.

There is a logic to the idea that proactively disclosed environmental information is the first "port of call" for users who wish to access environmental information under the right. The whole point is to provide the public with easy access to relevant information.[294] Consequently, even though the public is using the right unknowingly, it follows that proactive disclosure is where many personal users will begin when seeking environmental information. This can be illustrated through the internet traffic statistics provided by one of the interviewed public authorities. The authority noted that from April 2018 to March 2019, its website recorded 887,590 visits. These statistics can be contrasted with those from City of Edinburgh Council, a comparatively larger authority, which recorded an unusually high demand, but still only 1,169 requests for environmental information over the same period of time.[295] Noting that these statistics do not account for information proactively disclosed offline (such as leaflets and notices), it can be seen that many, many more people are engaging with the authorities' proactively disclosed material than through direct requests for information. One explanation for this gap between users seeking proactively disclosed environmental information and users submitting requests for environmental information is that the majority of users were able to find the environmental information that they were seeking. While alternative explanations do exist,[296] the explanation based on successfully finding the information does align with both the theoretical use of the right of proactive disclosure and the interviewed users' experience with such information.

---

[294] WHITTAKER et al., above n. 40, p. 472.
[295] Scottish Information Commissioner January–December 2018 Statistics Report. This number of requests was the highest number of requests received by a single authority (of any sort) over this period of time, highlighting the significantly larger reach of proactively disclosed environmental information. This pattern is further reflected in subsequent years in the statistics gathered by the Scottish Information Commissioner; above n. 52.
[296] For example, it may be that users were unable to find the environmental information they desired, but did not wish to submit a request for environmental information, did not know how to do so or just never got round to it.

Intersentia 105

Nevertheless, it is important to highlight that not every personal user has the same experience in accessing proactively disclosed environmental information. One core aspect of this obligation to proactively disclose environmental information is that the information must be "effectively accessible".[297] While what constitutes "effectively accessible" is an ongoing debate,[298] a common thread in discussions is that public authorities are granted a broad discretion in terms of how they proactively disclose environmental information.

To an extent, this discretion can be beneficial, as the public authority can tailor its proactive disclosure strategy to best reflect its purpose, the type and format of the environmental information held, and what would be most beneficial to users of the right. However, public authorities may utilise this discretion in ways that may inadvertently require users to hold certain types of expertise, expertise that if not held would restrict their ability to access the proactively disclosed information.

One aspect of assumed expertise which may not in fact be held is that users may be unaware of how much environmental information authorities have proactively disclosed. While there is a minimum amount of environmental information that authorities must proactively disclose,[299] this list is not exhaustive. Generally, public authorities are keen to proactively disclose as much environmental information as possible, both for economic and environmental reasons:

> [I]t's in our interests to let people self-serve as much as possible, because … we're always being challenged, in terms of resourcing.
>
> [I]n terms of engaging people and, kind of, getting their interest in nature and what's happening, and understanding the role of nature in a number of different areas of things that happen in Scotland, whether that's planning, tourism, recreation, things like that, it's important to, kind of, get that information out there.[300]

---

[297] Aarhus Convention, art. 5(2); see also art. 5(3) on electronic disclosure. The word "effective" is not included in the EI(S)R, but an obligation with regard to making information available electronically is; see EI(S)R, reg. 4(1).

[298] Task Force on Access to Information under the Aarhus Convention, "Draft Decision VI/1 on Promoting Effective Access to Information" ECE/MP.PP/2017/8. We do not consider here the further needs of those with various disabilities, or the related obligations on authorities under equalities legislation.

[299] Aarhus Convention art. 5(1), (3); EI(S)R, reg. 4(2).

[300] Interview with Public Authority No. 7.

Chapter 4. Personal Users

Yet, counterintuitively, this may cause issues for the user if they are unable to find the environmental information that they are seeking. The ability of users to access proactively disclosed environmental information broadly assumes that the user holds the expertise to navigate the authority's channels of communication.[301] If a user is unable to do this, then they will have significant difficulty engaging with this aspect of the right:

> [G]enerally speaking, my – it's not easy to find the information within Council systems. Eh, and I – I get ... you know, I've only got so much time and so much mental capacity to fight through systems.[302]

Whereas in the early days of the Aarhus Convention, the "systems" referred to would have been paper-based files and registers, now material is held electronically. This requires different expertise on the part of the user and distances them physically from a source of assistance, highlighting the impact of technology as an actor in shaping the network involved in delivering the right to environmental information.[303]

These issues relating to expertise can be further emphasised where a user is seeking proactively disclosed environmental information from different public authorities. As public authorities have been granted a wide level of discretion, different authorities may decide to adopt different systems and methods to proactively disclose environmental information. While such differences may be based on validly divergent views and concerns, they pose a challenge to users who have to learn the peculiarities of how each authority complies with its duty to disclose information:

> [A]nd I find it quite difficult with local authority websites that it's very difficult to navigate because they're all built in different ways.[304]

At the core of this discussion regarding the accessibility of proactively disclosed environmental information are two key points. First, whether environmental information is "effectively accessible" or not is often determined by the expertise held by the user in seeking to access environmental information, and their ability to navigate the different communication channels of public

---

[301] Examples of this include the need for a user to navigate an authority's website or to understand the organisational structure adopted by the authority in storing its proactively disclosed environmental information.
[302] Interview with User No. 5.
[303] See Chapter 6, section 2.3.
[304] Interview with User No. 12.

authorities. Yet this is not reflected in either the Aarhus Convention or the EIS(R), which take no account of how far the personal characteristics of users' impact on how they engage with the right.

Second, a common recurring aspect within the proactive disclosure of environmental information is the role of technology. The enhanced role of technology can be considered beneficial due to the increased use of technology in society and the easier accessibility of online dissemination compared to proactive disclosure via paper register.[305] Yet the use of technology is a double-edged sword, as it also requires a greater familiarity with technology and online browsing that not every user will have. In recognising the conflict in terms of how technology is to be adopted in relation to the right of access to environmental information, it is clear that technology will continue to have an influence on how the right is guaranteed in the future.

3.2. DISCLOSURE ON REQUEST

The other way that users can seek access to environmental information is to submit a request to a public authority asking it to disclose the desired information. These requests act as an initiator for public authorities, which must process and respond to the request for environmental information while complying with a range of procedural obligations.[306] While users are not subject to many obligations when submitting a request for environmental information, their request must be sufficiently clear in terms of describing the requested environmental information.[307] As a result of this requirement, how a user phrases their request, and whether or not they have the skill and expertise to phrase their request in sufficiently clear terms, becomes a potential point of contention between personal users and public authorities.

The procedures involved are largely similar to those when seeking information under the freedom of information laws, contributing to the lack of distinction in many minds between the two regimes. This is further exacerbated by the fact that many active users seek out both environmental and non-environmental information, and therefore make use of both routes when seeking out information. It is also notable that other

---

[305] See Chapter 6, section 2.3.
[306] Aarhus Convention, art. 4; EI(S)R, regs 5–14.
[307] Aarhus Convention, art. 4(3)(b); EI(S)R, reg. 10(4)(c).

actors beyond users and public authorities view these separate rights as interchangeable. The WhatDoTheyKnow website, as an actor that facilitates the submission of requests to public authorities, also does not distinguish between the right to environmental information and the general right to information. Consequently, this method of engaging with environmental information acts to further compound the interchangeability of the right to environmental information and the general right under freedom of information legislation.

Although the assumption behind the way in which the right has been established is that users will largely have the expertise to identify the information they wish, in discussing how users engage with the right, public authorities noted that there was a great degree of variation in the ability of personal users to effectively seek access to environmental information:

> There are some people who know their subject in detail and who knows precisely what bit of information they are after. There will be other people who perhaps aren't quite sure what they are after or who don't state what it is in a clear way.[308]
>
> I think sometimes when people come to us they don't necessarily understand the legislation and they don't word their questions very well and we have to sort of go back and help them to frame things and maybe, have a vague idea of what they want.[309]

Generally, public authorities noted that personal users often struggled with phrasing their requests in a clear way and in understanding how much information the authority holds on a specific topic.[310] These perceived issues with requests submitted by personal users do not have a minor effect; if a request does not meet the required standards, then the authority is entitled to refuse to process the request.

In order to reduce this problem, the Convention and the EI(S)R do oblige public authorities to provide advice and assistance to the user in order to help them reformulate the request.[311] However, the provision of this advice and the reformulation of the request does require the use of resources from the authority and more time and effort from the user,

---

[308] Interview with Public Authority No. 16.
[309] Interview with Public Authority No. 5.
[310] Either through requesting access to information the public authority did not hold or by requesting information without realising the amount of information the authority held on the relevant topic.
[311] Aarhus Convention, art. 3(2); EI(S)R, reg. 9.

delaying their access to the desired information. This can be problematic if the personal user has limited time to access and read the environmental information, such as where there is a deadline for providing input into an environmental decision-making procedure. The lack of expertise can thus damage the effectiveness of the right and its participative aims, even when the information is ultimately supplied.

The provision of this advice and assistance is also predicated on the assumption that users are happy to receive this advice. This may not be the case in practice; even where the user trusts the authority, personal users may resist the authority's interpretation of their requests and have confidence in their own ability to phrase requests for environmental information appropriately:

> It was quite easy just to frame a question and send it in by email.[312]

Some personal users are more circumspect in their ability to phrase requests for environmental information:

> I suspect … some of my own questions could have been phrased better to … or if I'd understood better what … the basis on – on which public authorities can refuse to answer questions I might not have wasted time on some of the questions I'd asked.[313]

This variation between different personal users' opinions on their ability to phrase requests for environmental information is notable because it further resists the broad conceptualisation of users as a single category of actors with broadly similar capacities to engage with the right. Personal users are not uniform in their ability to engage with the right to request information and are not all equally willing to listen to the advice and assistance provided by public authorities. This contrasts with the lack of discretion given to public authorities in terms of how they approach such requests; they are required to offer advice and assistance regardless of whether the user believes they need that assistance or not.

On the one hand, this approach does make sense: in helping personal users to narrow down and specify their requests, public authorities are not only aiding the user but are also protecting their internal administrative processes from having to process overly wide or vague requests for

---

[312] Interview with User No. 6.
[313] Interview with User No. 1.

environmental information. However, if a personal user receives advice after submitting a request that they feel is sufficiently clear, then they may refuse to engage with the advice provided by the authority or start correspondence about this issue, distracting from the original point of the request. This is particularly true where the personal user does not trust the authority, as they may perceive this advice as the authority attempting to divert the requester's attention or to hide information.

It is important to note that a simplified conceptualisation, treating a whole category as if they share the same attributes, is not limited to the ways in which public authorities respond to users. In detailing their experiences with submitting requests for environmental information, users often focused on their knowledge (or lack thereof) and how public authorities perceived this knowledge. Omitted from these discussions was any consideration of differences in how authorities store information, an important element in terms of whether a request was viewed as appropriate or not. By omitting this aspect and focusing on their own skills, users were homogenising public authorities as a singular category of actors, a conceptualisation which is not borne out in practice.

Ultimately, this leads to tensions between different users and public authorities due to mismatches in expectations from each actor – an issue which is emphasised by the limited amount of information users have to provide about themselves in submitting a request upon which authorities can provide advice and assistance. This tension is particularly problematic in this early stage of the request process as future interactions can be negatively influenced, particularly where the user views the authority as seeking to divert their attention from the requested information. In this way the provision of advice may act to disengage users from seeking to access environmental information under the right in practice rather than encouraging them as is intended.

4. ADVICE

The duty to provide advice and assistance is one of the key points of interaction between users and public authorities in guaranteeing the right to environmental information. The intention behind this duty is to oblige authorities to support users in seeking access to environmental information, in turn making the right more accessible to everyone.[314] While promoting

---

[314] EBBESSON et al., above n. 119, pp. 62–63.

the accessibility of the right is an admirable goal, this seemingly value-neutral duty does contain a range of unspoken assumptions about the relationship between users and public authorities.

First, the duty sits alongside the wider procedures which place public authorities as the arbiter of what constitutes a "valid" engagement with the right; authorities are the actors with the necessary knowledge and expertise to determine the correctness of the user's attempt to utilise the right. This can be problematic where users do not wish to be given advice,[315] either because they feel they do not need it or because they do not trust the advice given or the authority itself. Where users hold this belief, authorities providing advice and assistance may be arguably failing to appreciate the distinction between the "idealised" user and the user that they are actually engage with. This in turn can lead to prolonged correspondence, recourse to reviews and appeals, and users having their lack of trust reinforced to the point where they give up on the right to information as a reliable and useful way of furthering their concerns.

Second, the emphasis placed on the role of public authorities as sources of advice and assistance fails to recognise that these authorities are not the sole source of advice available to users. The ability of users to assist one another is broadly set aside due to the implicit conceptualisation of users as a singular set of actors who, generally, need advice and assistance from public authorities.[316] Yet in practice users often look to one another for advice, and in some instances may be better placed to act as sources of advice than public authorities. There is a parallel here with the role of intermediaries, where the underlying vision based on the direct relationship between users and authorities again ignores the part that other actors can play in shaping the relevant interactions in ways that support or obstruct the environmental and participative goals behind the right. Such a parallel is important to highlight because it further evidences the potential risk to the right's aims that can arise from misunderstanding how users engage with the right and other actors.

---

[315] The same applies to the similar duty to provide assistance under the Freedom of Information (Scotland) Act 2002, s. 15, where it has also been noted that on occasions authorities "have been less than helpful" in fulfilling this obligation; DUNION, above n. 138, pp. 54–55.

[316] For more on the impact of technology in enabling users to communicate with and advise each other, see Chapter 6, section 2.3.

4.1. ADVICE PROVIDED BY PUBLIC AUTHORITIES

In relation to the provision of advice and assistance to users seeking environmental information, the Aarhus Convention explicitly imposes clear obligations on public authorities to provide such advice:

> Each Party shall endeavour to ensure that officials and authorities assist and provide guidance to the public in seeking access to information, in facilitating participation in decision-making and in seeking access to justice in environmental matters.[317]

This obligation is more strongly phrased in domestic implementations of the Convention. For example, the EI(S)R phrase this obligation in the following way:

> A Scottish public authority shall provide advice and assistance, so far as it would be reasonable to expect the authority to do so, to applicants and prospective applicants.[318]

Examining the text of these legal instruments is valuable because, on the surface, the obligation appears to be fairly simple: where an authority perceives that a user needs assistance, they are obliged to provide advice that reflects the unique issues faced by the user. An example of this is where an authority advises a user to reformulate a request so that it complies with the procedural requirements established by the Convention and the EI(S)R.[319] However, this simplicity conceals a mismatch between how the right, and the actors interacting with it, are conceptualised in theory and in practice.

The source of this mismatch is the "applicant-blind" approach that is adopted by the right of access to environmental information. A critical element of this approach is that public authorities cannot consider the identity of the user or their motivations for engaging with the right when providing advice and assistance.[320] Yet while this approach does help to

---

[317] Aarhus Convention, art. 3(2).
[318] EI(S)R, reg. 9(1).
[319] Especially the specific obligation to assist in relation to requests formulated in too general a manner; ibid., reg. 9(2).
[320] See generally Aarhus Convention, art. 4; E. FISHER, "Exploring the Legal Architecture of Transparency' in P. ALA'I and R. VAUGHN (eds), *Research Handbook on Transparency*, Edward Elgar, Cheltenham 2014, pp. 64–65 and 69.

protect users and their requests from being discriminated against due to the user's identity, it conflicts with the duty to provide effective advice and assistance, since fulfilling this duty requires the authority to consider the characteristics of the user in order to provide advice tailored to the specific capabilities and goals of that user.[321] This creates a tension in trying to balance the two approaches, a tension that is keenly felt by public authorities when they are providing advice to users:

> So, sometimes it will feel like ... that's when it can be a really difficult dynamic, 'cause they then feel like you're not really being helpful, because the bottom line is, you know, you can sometimes read a request and think mm, that's really not the right question, but you need to ask me the right question, you know.[322]

This is not to suggest that these public authorities are considering the identity and expertise of the user when determining whether to disclose the requested information. The interviewed authorities often specifically emphasised the desirability of adhering to the applicant-blind approach when processing requests for environmental information, as well as the fact that not doing so would be a breach of the law.

However, this embedding of the applicant-blind approach further emphasises the difficulty of judging actual users against the right's fixed ideal of what a user should be doing. The authority has to set aside the identity of the user when processing their requests, but simultaneously has to take into account their identity when offering advice and assistance, a contradiction that is created by the Aarhus Convention and the EI(S)R without being recognised. By not explicitly distinguishing between these separate processes, this approach blurs the line between what is considered appropriate and inappropriate when authorities disclose environmental information and respond to users seeking advice and assistance. This can, in turn, discourage authorities from trying to ascertain what a user really wants to find out and why, limiting the assistance offered to users who may have appreciated additional help.

A further point regarding the provision of advice and assistance is that the Aarhus Convention implicitly assumes that users of the right will be happy to accept the advice of the public authority in question.

---

[321] In the context of the wider freedom of information regime, this was noted in *K v. Information Commissioner* EA/2014/0024; and P. GIBBONS, "Mythbusting FOI" (2019) 16(1) *Freedom of Information* 4.

[322] Interview with Public Authority No. 10.

In being tasked with providing advice and assistance, the Aarhus Convention is placing public authorities in a paternalistic role, where the authority guides the user towards appropriately engaging with the right.[323] Yet there are various difficulties with this view. One such difficulty, which has already been discussed, is where users are provided with unwanted advice and assistance. Another overarching difficulty in providing advice generally is that users may not trust the authority or the advice given:

> [T]he responses I've had are as broad as the ... you know sometimes they are, sometimes they don't even know ... it takes you a while to get them to ... even understand what your question is and what you're looking for.[324]

The framework for the right to environmental information embodied by the Aarhus Convention and the EI(S)R envisages an authority's provision of advice and assistance as a positive feature supporting the right, not as something that may drive some users away. Yet once it is appreciated that a lack of trust in the authority is one potential driving motivation for users seeking access to environmental information in the first place, that negative result is not so surprising. The circumstances of the individual user, including their degree of trust, are thus important for how users interpret offers of advice and assistance from the authority. As the right and its legal instruments fail to consider this perspective, the risk that tensions will arise between users and public authorities due to this mismatch in expectations is ever-present. The practical impact of these tensions can be the submission of complaints and appeals relating to the conduct of the authority, or even users becoming disenchanted with the right. This is problematic, as these consequences can undermine the implementation of the right and its environmental and participative aims.

4.2. ADVICE PROVIDED BY OTHER USERS

While environmental information regimes place public authorities as the primary sources of advice and assistance, this does not mean that they are the sole method by which users can seek out and receive such help.

---

[323] Aarhus Convention, Preamble, para. 8.
[324] Interview with User No. 5.

Whether driven by convenience (including where internet searches direct them)[325] or by a lack of trust in the authority, the source from which personal users may get advice with regard to the right to environmental information is other users.

The primary method by which users receive advice from other users is from the internet. Websites such as WhatDoTheyKnow allow users to share their requests and the responses from public authorities, and respond to questions posed by other users.[326] Freedom of information blogs also provide a source of user-derived advice,[327] although these are often run by professional users and thus differ from the advice provided from personal users. These sources of advice are valuable to personal users who are less confident in their own ability to discover information and want support in either accessing published material or seeking to submit a request for environmental information:

> Right. To be fair ... I might not have made ... these requests if I had not come across this site [WhatDoTheyKnow], because they make it so easy ... and they ... they extended my knowledge about ... you know, who is obliged to reply ... and under what circumstances and so on and so forth. So, full credit to the people who run it.[328]

Such sources of advice and assistance run in parallel to that provided by public authorities, and users are not restricted to relying on one source of advice. Indeed, in proactively seeking environmental information or submitting a request to an authority, users may seek advice and assistance from multiple users they can contact remotely, and then benefit from advice from the authority itself.

A key element here has been the development of technology, with there being a generally positive view towards using technology as a means of widening access to users and making it simpler to engage with the right and the authorities which guarantee it.[329] WhatDoTheyKnow

---

[325] The lack of awareness of a specific right to environmental information increases the likelihood of those taking the first steps being directed to more general, user-inspired, sources of advice.
[326] WhatDoTheyKnow, <https://www.whatdotheyknow.com/> accessed 20 April 2022.
[327] E.g. P. GIBBONS "FOI Man", <https://www.foiman.com/> accessed 20 April 2022.
[328] Interview with User No. 1.
[329] E.g. Aarhus Convention, art. 5(9); UN ECE, "Report of the Second Meeting of the Parties Addendum Decision II/3 on Electronic Information Tools and the Clearing-House Mechanism", ECE/MP.PP/2005/2/Add.4 8 June 2005.

Chapter 4. Personal Users

in particular enables users to form an online community to exchange knowledge[330] on the basis of real, unedited interactions between users and public authorities. In this way, the role of technology as an actor which (as will be discussed in Chapter 6) influences how users and other actors engage with the right is highlighted.

Yet this use of technology by users does not come without complications. The use of websites such as WhatDoTheyKnow has altered the relationship between users and public authorities.[331] Any communication between a user and a public authority now has the potential to be shared and commented on by any number of other users, often without the employee who is processing the user's request being aware of this. This fundamentally alters the dynamic between the two communicating parties, as both users and authorities may alter how they communicate with each other on the basis that their communications will be viewed and judged by a wider audience,[332] such as those visiting WhatDoTheyKnow. In turn, this can affect how both parties communicate with each other, impacting on how public authorities guarantee the right of access to environmental information.

A further complication is that the advice provided by other users may not always be correct and useful.[333] This has been evidenced where users follow a set of guidelines when drafting requests for environmental information:

> In my directorate there's a set of 11 questions, standard set that comes from Martin's Money Website. If you want to claim compensation for [damages], ask these 10 questions. So we get a lot of them in that format, but they're not actually asking for anything. They're asking for three years' worth of records, you don't actually need three years' worth of records …[334]

There is a risk that a general template for requests does not properly identify the specific environmental information that the user wishes to

---

[330] R. JAYANTI and J. SINGH, "Pragmatic Learning Theory: An Inquiry-Action Framework for Distributed Consumer Learning in Online Communities" (2010) 36(6) *Journal of Consumer Research* 1058.
[331] See Chapter 6, section 2.3.
[332] In psychology this is known as the Hawthorne Effect. This is discussed in the context of the general right to information in K. WALBY and M LARSEN, "Access to Information and Freedom of Information Requests: Neglected Means of Data Production in the Social Sciences" (2011) 18(1) *Qualitative Inquiry* 31, 36–37.
[333] Although the same may be true of advice from authorities See, in the context of freedom of information requests, DUNION, above n. 138, p. 54.
[334] Interview with Public Authority No. 13.

access, instead seeking access to a broad range of information that contains material both relevant and irrelevant for the user. Such broad requests can also interfere with the operations of the authority, which either has to process these broad requests or seek to narrow the request down through discussions with the user. While users with limited experience may feel more confident in submitting a request if they follow a template, there is a risk that such a user cannot distinguish between "good" and "bad" templates for submitting requests and end up being worse off than approaching the authority and benefiting from its obligation to offer advice and assistance.

The ability of users to seek advice from other users, whether professional or personal, is important as it highlights the mismatch between how users engage with the right in practice and the broad conceptualisation of users as a singular category of actors with similar levels of expertise. The Aarhus Convention and the EI(S)R focus on the ability of public authorities to provide advice and assistance, but they may not always be best placed to provide advice to all users. There is a further complication in that users, when seeking advice from other users, expose the emails between them and the authority online, placing more pressure on how both actors communicate with each other alongside bringing potential benefits in terms of openness. While this does not undermine the benefits of users receiving advice and support from each other, the ways in which this approach can alter and shape communications between users and authorities under the right is not reflected in the legal frameworks.

5. RECEIVING AND UNDERSTANDING ENVIRONMENTAL INFORMATION

For users of the right of access to environmental information, the core of the right is the getting hold of the desired environmental information, whether it is already published or has to be sought by means of a request. This is true regardless of the motive driving the user to seek the environmental information, how they seek the information and the user's level of expertise. Yet while this is ostensibly as simple as whether or not the authority has disclosed the information in some form, there are a range of legal and practical considerations which can influence how this is done and how effective such disclosure can be, not least in relation to furthering the participative objectives which are so prominent here.

One such consideration specific to the passive right to environmental information is that public authorities are not obliged to disclose every piece of environmental information that they hold. Both the Aarhus Convention and the EI(S)R entitle public authorities to refuse a request to disclose environmental information for a number of reasons,[335] including where the request is formulated in too general a manner,[336] where the information is still in the process of being completed[337] or where it jeopardises the interests of persons working with or being regulated by the authority.[338] These exceptions can prevent a user from accessing the environmental information that they desire, causing tension between them and the authority. This is particularly true in the context of the further "manifestly unreasonable" exception,[339] which enables authorities to set aside the applicant-blind approach and consider the history and personal characteristics of the user when processing their request.

A further consideration is whether personal users are able to understand the environmental information that is disclosed to them, either proactively or by request. While environmental information regimes are primarily focused on the disclosure of environmental information, minimal attention is paid to how a user actually reads and understands the environmental information disclosed to them. This could be considered an oversight, as in order for users to effectively contribute to the environmental and participative aims of the right, they need to be able to understand the environmental information given to them. Yet this apparent oversight may be seen as simply a concomitant of the simple vision lying behind the creation of the right of access. This continues the trend of the underpinning expectations of the right shaping and influencing the design of the legal regimes which guarantee it, as well as hindering the effective implementation of the right where these expectations do not match with how the right is used in practice.

5.1. NON-DISCLOSURE OF ENVIRONMENTAL INFORMATION

Within the context of the right of access to environmental information, there are three possible outcomes for the right. The first of these outcomes

---

[335] See Chapter 2, section 3.4.
[336] Aarhus Convention, art. 4(3)(b); EI(S)R, reg. 10(4).
[337] Aarhus Convention, art. 4(3)(b) and (c); EI(S)R, reg. 10(4).
[338] Aarhus Convention, art. 4(4)(g); EI(S)R, reg. 10(5)(f).
[339] Aarhus Convention, art. 4(3)(b); EI(S)R, reg. 10(4)(b).

is that the authority has fully disclosed the environmental information sought by the user, either proactively or on request. This outcome is one which users of the right seek through utilising their right to environmental information, which suggests that when it happens, users will be happy with the results of their engagement with the right.[340]

The second outcome is that public authorities refuse to disclose any of the environmental information sought by the user, an outcome which is clearly undesirable from the perspective of the user. This outcome is closely related to the third potential outcome, where the authority discloses only some of the environmental information sought by the user. In the context of authorities not proactively disclosing the sought-after information, users can simply request that the authority disclose the desired environmental information.[341] However, where authorities refuse to disclose environmental information on request, the only recourse available to the user is to challenge the decision of the authority to withhold the requested information.

It is important to re-emphasise that public authorities are permitted to refuse to disclose environmental information only when that information is covered by one of the exceptions listed in the legal provisions.[342] The Aarhus Convention establishes the default position that environmental information is to be disclosed[343] and in line with this position, the use of the exceptions is tightly controlled. Any decision to withhold environmental information is not merely a whim of the authority; rather, it should be a carefully considered decision taken on the basis of the pre-existing legal tests.

However, personal users who have had environmental information withheld from them often do not perceive the position in this way. Rather, personal users are often aggrieved by the refusal to disclose environmental information, seeing the decision to withhold as unjustified and as evidence that the authority is hiding information solely on the basis that it reflects

---

[340] Although it should be noted that for some users, the disclosure of the requested information will be unsatisfactory if it does not further lead to an outcome that they desire or if, for example, it is presented in a way they find unhelpful: see generally Chapter 5.

[341] Alternatively, if there is a specific legal obligation to disclose the particular environmental information (e.g. the Local Government (Scotland) Act 1973, ss 50A–50K), then the user can oblige the authority to proactively disclose the desired information.

[342] Aarhus Convention, art. 4(3); EI(S)R, regs 10–11.

[343] Aarhus Convention, art. 4.

Chapter 4. Personal Users

poorly on itself. As illustrated by the following quote, users can feel this way even where the authority specifies the basis on which it refuses to disclose the requested environmental information:

> So I wrote to them, freedom of information, "how long has the camera been there, what difference has been made" that kind of scenario. The answer I got back to about 4 questions was it's not in the interest of the environment to answer your question. Because it does nothing; it's section bluff of the Panic Act.[344]

Part of this reaction to the withholding of environmental information might be dissatisfaction at being unable to access the desired environmental information. However, the language chosen by personal users to describe such decisions by public authorities suggests a lack of trust in the authority and the reasoning for withholding the desired information.

This lack of trust manifests itself even where the authority discloses some of the environmental information requested by the user. Users are primed to expect the full disclosure of environmental information, both in terms of the legal provisions of the EI(S)R[345] and with transparency acting (and expected by many of the public to act) as a core component of "good governance".[346] As a result, any refusal to disclose environmental information is a breach of expectations, regardless of the basis for the withholding of the requested information, and may lead to a lack of confidence in the process for obtaining information.

A particular exception where a lack of trust can have a significant impact on the relationship between a personal user and a public authority is the "manifestly unreasonable" exception.[347] This allows public authorities to refuse to process a request for environmental information where they believe that the request is manifestly unreasonable. The term

---

[344] Interview with User No. 5. The exception mentioned is found in Aarhus Convention, art. 4(4)(h); and EI(S)R, reg. 10(5)(g).

[345] The starting point is that "a Scottish public authority that holds environmental information shall make it available when requested to do so by any applicant"; EI(S)R, reg. 5(1).

[346] See generally M. Fenster, "Transparency in Search of Theory" (2015) 18(2) *European Journal of Social Theory* 150; and S. Grimmelikhuijsen et al., "Do Freedom of Information Laws Increase the Transparency of Government? A Pre-registered Replication of a Field Experiment" (2018) 1(2) *Journal of Behavioural Public Administration* 1.

[347] Aarhus Convention, art. 4(3)(b); EI(S)R, reg. 10(4)(b).

"manifestly unreasonable" is not defined by the Aarhus Convention, the EI(S)R or any previous environmental information regimes that utilised it.

In considering the scope of the manifestly unreasonable exception, both the Upper Tribunal[348] and the Court of Appeal[349] have detailed four factors which public authorities can consider when applying the exception:

(1) the burden (on the public authority and its staff);
(2) the motive (of the requester);
(3) the value or serious purpose (of the request); and
(4) any harassment or distress (of and to staff).

These factors are important in the context of users and a (potential) lack of trust because, unlike the other exceptions within Aarhus Convention and the EI(S)R, authorities must consider factors specific to the users themselves rather than the information that they requested. In essence, the manifestly unreasonable exception "allows" authorities to discard the applicant- and motive-blind approach – a potentially troubling idea for users who do not trust public authorities to act in accordance with the relevant environmental information regime or in the public interest generally.

Ironically, while the right and its implementing instruments do not account for the issues in discarding the applicant- and motive-blind approach, public authorities are very aware of the issues that can arise in applying this exception. What this can lead to is authorities being hesitant in terms of applying the exception:

> [A]nd, of course, it depends, then, how much more work it is, because there is a point at which it can become manifestly unreasonable.[350]

> Or it could end up that would be when we would use manifestly unreasonable. Because, just because of the scope [of the request] is huge.[351]

The contradictory approaches contained within this exception create tensions within the authority itself and between the authority and the user

---

[348] *Craven v. Information Commissioner* [2012] UKUT 442, [19], [78]–[79]. See also *Beggs v. Scottish Information Commissioner* [2018] CSIH 80.
[349] *Dransfeld v. Information Commissioner; Craven v. Information Commissioner* [2015] EWCA Civ 454, [64]–[73], [79].
[350] Interview with Public Authority No. 9.
[351] Interview with Public Authority No. 11.

Chapter 4. Personal Users

who may have their requested environmental information withheld. An authority which applies the exception has to consider whether doing so will unduly narrow the ability to access environmental information, but conversely an authority which does not apply the exception may have to bear the disproportionate resource costs of dealing with a (very) few overly demanding users. While environmental information regimes grant them the power to make this judgment, it does not provide an internally consistent approach to help authorities make this decision in practice.

While the manifestly unreasonable exception is emblematic of a variety of mismatches within the intended and actual uses of the right, all of the exceptions are implicit in placing public authorities as trustworthy bodies in the context of the right to environmental information. Public authorities are positioned as bodies which act in the public interest, not only when publishing and disclosing information, but when deciding to withhold it as well. Indeed, they are expressly required to balance the public interest in disclosure with that protected by the exceptions.[352] Public authorities may have good reasons for withholding environmental information.[353] Yet not every user trusts public authorities to act in the public interest, and where this trust is not held, it can change the relationship and the tone of the interactions between both parties. Users can begin to distrust the responses given by authorities, leading to them initiating review procedures more readily than they might otherwise have done.

Such divergent views from different personal users highlight the practical impact that trust, and the assumption that users will trust public authorities, can have in terms of how the right is implemented in practice. It is important to note that these findings are not suggesting that there is a general dissatisfaction with how public authorities conduct themselves or provide public services. However, some users do appear to distrust authorities and how they guarantee the right of access to environmental information,[354] contrary to the broad generalisation implicit within the Aarhus Convention and the EI(S)R. This is significant because if users have a negative experience when they are refused environmental information,

---

[352] Aarhus Convention, art. 10(4); EI(S)R, reg. 10(1).
[353] For example, not disclosing information relating to badger surveys on the basis that doing so would put the protected species at risk: Scottish Information Commissioner, Decision 044/2007, *Mr G Crole and Transport Scotland*, 8 March 2007.
[354] It is also notable that much of the Freedom of Information literature mentions the need to re-establish trust in the government; see B. WORTHY, "More Open But Not More Trusted? The Effect of the Freedom of Information Act 2000 on the United Kingdom Central Government" (2010) 23(4) *Governance* 561, 575.

an experience heightened by a lack of trust, then that negativity can permeate throughout other interactions with the authority; in particular, where the user utilises the environmental information to participate in environmental decision-making procedures.[355] From the perspective of public authorities, participation in such decisions is designed not only to improve the final decision, but also to enhance confidence in and acceptance of the decisions being made.[356] Yet none of these benefits will be secured if users are suspicious about the veracity of the authority arising from their (potentially legitimate) refusal to disclose environmental information.

5.2. UNDERSTANDING DISCLOSED ENVIRONMENTAL INFORMATION

The right of access to environmental information is primarily concerned with the mechanics of disclosing environmental information, whether they relate to how environmental information is proactively disclosed or how requests for environmental information are processed by public authorities. However, beyond the disclosure of environmental information, neither the Aarhus Convention nor the EI(S)R contains any obligations to explain the environmental information that is accessed under the right. This is because both instruments assume that those using the right will hold the requisite expertise to understand the information they access.

It is important not to understate the origins of this assumption. In the first "era" of the right of access to environmental information, there was a general assumption that such information was only of interest to experts.[357] This belief is notable because experts, due to their familiarity with the relevant subject, are assumed to have sufficient expertise to understand the information disclosed to them. While the Rio Declaration, the precursor to the Aarhus Convention, marked a shift in the intended audience for environmental information, this assumption was never challenged. Instead, all users were assumed to hold sufficient expertise to understand the information disclosed to them – in essence, broadly conceptualising users as a single, similar category of actors with similar

---

[355] On this topic, see Chapter 5.
[356] See F COENAN "Introduction" in F COENAN (ed), *Public Participation and Better Environmental Decisions: The Promise and Limits of Participatory Processes for the Quality of Environmentally Related Decision-Making*, Springer, Heidelberg 2009, p. 2.
[357] HAKLAY, above n. 94, p. 163.

levels of expertise. As a result of this, it is simply assumed that providing access to environmental information without further support will deliver the right's environmental and participative aims.

The impact of this assumption can be seen in the design of the Convention and the EI(S)R, which do not contain any obligations to produce summaries of or explanatory guidance for any information disclosed under the right. This is in contrast with other similar obligations to produce environmental information, such as for environmental impact assessments, which do impose an obligation to provide a non-technical summary[358] that is accessible to laypersons.[359] Consequently, in order for users to effectively use their right to access environmental information, there is an implicit requirement that users hold the requisite expertise and knowledge to understand the environmental information proactively or reactively disclosed to them.

There are educational obligations enshrined within instruments such as the Aarhus Convention. The Convention does contain a general obligation imposed on public authorities and states to promote environmental education and environmental awareness amongst the public.[360] However, this education focuses primarily on the procedural rights enshrined in the Aarhus Convention and on "imparting environmental awareness, ecological knowledge, attitudes, values, commitments for actions, and ethical responsibilities for the rational use of resources and for sound and sustainable development".[361] Highlighting the specific procedural rights available to individuals and the general need to recalibrate humanity's relationship with the environment is clearly important. However, in the specific context of understanding disclosed environmental information, this overarching education is unlikely to provide the expertise and knowledge to better enable users to understand the environmental information that they access through the right. Consequently, these educational obligations

---

[358] Aarhus Convention, art. 6(6)(d); in Scotland, see, for example, the Town and Country Planning (Environmental Impact Assessment) (Scotland) Regulations 2017, SSI 2017/102, reg. 5(2)(e).
[359] EBBESSON et al., above n. 119, p. 152.
[360] Aarhus Convention, Preamble, arts 8 and 9 and art. 3(3). There are no similar educational obligations in the EI(S)R.
[361] M. POPPE, G. WEIGELHOFER and G. WINKLER, "Public Participation and Environmental Education' in S. SCHMUTZ and J. SENDZIMIR (eds), *Riverine Ecosystem Management: Science for Governing Towards a Sustainable Future*, Springer, Heidelberg 2018, p. 443, discussing the Rio Declaration, but of equal relevance to the Aarhus Convention.

are unlikely to fill the expertise gap that some users may experience in seeking to understand the environmental information that has been disclosed by public authorities.[362]

The mismatch between the expected and actual expertise of personal users is not merely theoretical in nature; it has a real impact on how personal users engage with public authorities and exercise their right to access environmental information. The gap caused by the lack of support from the authority post-disclosure of the environmental information means that some users of the right will be unable to understand the information that has been disclosed to them. Upon failing to understand the environmental information disclosed to them, users may feel dissatisfaction with the right and with how the authority responded to their request. Such dissatisfaction may dissuade users from further engaging with environmental matters, undermining the right's environmental aims.[363]

Another possible outcome is that users may seek further assistance from the public authority to understand the disclosed information. As there is no formal obligation or procedure to provide this assistance, these users looking for further assistance may end up making further requests as an indirect way of seeking assistance:

> Or what you might be doing is going back, which is what I was, I'm doing something at the moment, you've already had this information in another request, but it's not been made blindingly obvious in our original response that actually the information you were looking for was already with you but we didn't identify it.[364]

> Because we've had requests for this, you can tell they still don't understand all the information they've been given, but it's within their scope, even if it's been clarified. And they're still asking for more information.[365]

In essence, this means that personal users may utilise their procedural right to request access to environmental information as a means of obtaining

---

[362] There is a broader discussion to be had about the distinction between knowledge of a subject area and knowledge of the local area to which the information relates. Both sets of knowledge are valuable in contributing to the Aarhus Convention's aims, but are outwith the scope of this text.
[363] On the need to consider the capacities of the recipients of legally disclosed information in a specific context, see C. REID, M. LLOYD, B. ILLSLEY and B. LYNCH, "Effective Public Access to Planning Information" [1998] *Journal of Planning and Environmental Law* 1028.
[364] Interview with Public Authority No. 15.
[365] Interview with Public Authority No. 11.

additional support to better understand information previously disclosed. Such support is not provided for under the Aarhus Convention or the EI(S)R due to the underpinning assumptions regarding the expertise and similarities between different users, and may result in an additional burden for authorities who are not obliged or sufficiently equipped or resourced to provide the sort of support that might be needed. The co-opting of these procedures for an unintended purpose highlights a mismatch between the pre-constructed role of users as actors holding the requisite expertise and the actual expertise held by individual users of the right. Where users fail to understand the information disclosed to them they are given limited additional support, which in turn hinders their ability to participate in environmental decision-making procedures[366] and to help protect and enhance the environment – both fundamental aims of the right of access to environmental information.

6. CONCLUSION

As has been made clear throughout this chapter, the image of the "ideal user" which lies behind the legal framework for the right of access to environmental information does not match with how users engage with the right in practice. The extent to which professional users diverge from this ideal was evident in the previous chapter, but even when considering the personal users who may be expected to come closer to the ideal of the environmentally active citizen, the mismatch is obvious. The variation between different personal users' expertise and motives creates an almost infinite range of users, who engage not just with public authorities but also with each other. The legal regime thus has to cope with a reality very different from the ideal for which it was designed.

The use of environmental information regimes is not and should not be limited to those "ideal users", but the decision to implement a single, uniform framework for all users, based on a general conceptualisation of the "ideal" user, colours the whole picture. This is not to suggest that all consequences from this approach are negative. By assuming that every user trusts public authorities enough to accept advice and assistance from them, the Aarhus Convention and the EI(S)R make this advice easier to access when required. Ultimately, both regimes adopt this broad

---

[366] Chapter 5 offers a broader discussion of how users do use accessed environmental information to participate in environmental decision-making procedures.

conceptualisation not to punish those who deviate from its ideals, but to construct a workable environmental information regime which guarantees the right for the greatest number of users.

However, this approach, based on an implicit uniform conceptualisation of users, does create problems for those who deviate from the assumptions which underpin this conceptualisation. This is equally true for personal users as it is for professional users. Personal users, despite being the intended audience for the right, encounter various obstacles in engaging with the right due to how they deviate from the right's underpinning assumptions. Such issues place public authorities in a difficult position: having to assist the user and understand points of tensions without guidance from the Aarhus Convention or the EI(S)R on to how navigate these unspoken, yet impactful, assumptions regarding the characteristics of the user.

It is valuable to highlight the tensions between these different procedures because they evidence a complicated relationship between the constructed ideal of a user who adheres to the right's underpinning assumptions and the personal users who actually use the right in practice. This tension is particularly notable because the applicant-blind approach can be a significant barrier to how personal users engage with the right. The reason for this is that the applicant-blind approach, and the assumptions it embodies, do not reflect the varying levels of expertise that personal users hold and the divergent motives which drive them to access environmental information. It could be argued that an approach which more explicitly recognises these differences may better guarantee the right in practice.

This is not to suggest that the Aarhus Convention or the EI(S)R are seeking to undermine how personal users engage with the right; the procedural obligations were, and still are, revolutionary in guaranteeing the right of access to environmental information, and the applicant-blind approach prevents authorities from discriminating against users on the basis of their identity or motive. However, the negative impact that such an approach can have on users seeking to utilise their right to access environmental information is problematic. The vision of the engaged and capable citizen worried about prejudice that might arise from revealing their interest takes priority over the interests of those who have different needs, either for more support at all stages or because of the professional nature of their interest. The aim of both the Convention and the EI(S)R is to promote the use of the right by "regular" people in order to galvanise a general environmental movement among the population,[367] an aim which

---

[367] Aarhus Convention, Preamble, para. 14.

Chapter 4. Personal Users

is hindered by the obstacles put in place by the applicant-blind approach and the categorisation of users as a singular set of actors.

Considering the diversity of use in practice, the choice of a "one-size fits all" approach based on the construction of users as a singular actor is at times detrimental to how the right is guaranteed in practice. Indeed, both the Aarhus Convention and the EI(S)R recognise this in terms of how they deviate from this ideal within their provisions, albeit inconsistently. Significant change would, however, require a major change of approach to one which consistently considers the characteristics of those using the right and enables public authorities to identify (or seek to identify) these characteristics to better assist users and guarantee the right to environmental information. Such a shift in perspective would require a modified range of procedural rights and obligations and raises a range of questions regarding its implementation in practice.[368]

In order to recognise how the right actually operates in practice, there is a need to critique how the right conceptualises "personal users" as an actor within the actor-network created by the right of access to environmental information. Actor-Network Theory, through its treatment of individual users of the right as distinct actors, helps challenge the right's broad conceptualisation of "personal users" as a singular, uniform category. The new perspective granted through Actor-Network Theory is valuable, as it provides an explanation as to why different users engage with the right in different ways, and for different reasons, in contrast to the right's conceptualisation of users. Yet this critique raises a further question: if users do not adhere to a single set of idealised norms in terms of how they engage with environmental information procedures, then is it likely that they will use the disclosed information in a way that aligns with the right's environmental expectations?

The environmental dimension, or rather the lack of it, is a further key point to emerge from this chapter and the preceding one. The legislative provisions and the practical issues that arise focus on the relationships between the human actors and human constructs such as websites. Most of these do or could apply equally to the wider laws on freedom of information. Yet, as noted earlier, the existence of a separate regime for access to environmental information is predicated on there being a different, more substantive goal that goes beyond the transparency and accountability objectives behind freedom of information in general. If the

---

[368] See further the discussion in Chapter 7, section 4.

Intersentia 129

aim of protecting and improving the environment is not central to how the networks created by the Aarhus Convention and the EI(S)R are operating, the justification for a separate regime is called into question.

Examining this issue calls for a deeper consideration not just of how and why information is accessed but also how it is used. The next chapter explores how well actual practice matches the aspiration of providing access to information as a precursor of increased public participation in environmental decision-making. After that has been examined, further consideration can be given to the wider question. In light of the challenges to the expectations that underpin the right of access to environmental information, is the right working as intended to protect and enhance the environment?

CHAPTER 5
INFORMATION AND PARTICIPATION

The right of access to environmental information has been the focus of this book so far, but this right does not operate in isolation. Linked to the right of access to environmental information is the right to participate in environmental decision-making procedures. Broadly defined as ensuring the ability for individuals to participate in environmental decisions made by a public authority, the development of this right and its role in protecting and enhancing the environment has occurred in parallel with the right of access to environmental information. Indeed, at the extreme, the right to access information can be presented as a subsidiary matter, existing merely to ensure that public participation can be effective. How far the use of the right to access environmental information is in practice linked to the exercise, and effectiveness, of the right to participate – and the broader efficacy of public participation – are therefore crucial to exploring what these rights are achieving.

1. INTRODUCTION

The parallel development of the rights to access environmental information and to participate in environmental decision-making is evidenced in the Rio Declaration, which boldly asserted that: "Environmental issues are best handled with the participation of all concerned citizens."[369] The Rio Declaration was notable not just for this assertion, but for also explicitly linking the provision of environmental information with the ability to effectively participate in environmental decision-making procedures.[370] This position was generally adopted in subsequent legal instruments, particularly the Aarhus Convention, and represented a broader trend

---

[369] Rio Declaration, above n. 19, Principle 10.
[370] Ibid.

towards viewing human rights and "environmental participatory rights" as a connected set of rights.[371]

Yet the stark clarity of the assertion made by the Rio Declaration masks the fact that there is considerable uncertainty over what such participation is supposed to achieve and how it should be made possible. As Lee and Abbot noted: "Participation has a very strong pull on environmental policy making, but its meaning and aims are rarely made clear."[372] The rationale for promoting participation has been subject to considerable debate, reflecting a divergence in how public participation, and its aims, are conceptualised, with different levels of empowerment for the public involved.[373] Although many of these differing views are not incompatible, different conceptions of what is being sought will affect the ways in which the arrangements to provide and support participation are designed, and how well they operate. Mismatches between the ideals themselves, and between the ideals and the mechanisms chosen to give them effect, will produce a framework that is inconsistent and ineffective.[374]

The interlinking of the rights to access environmental information and to participate in environmental decision-making procedures is critical. Yet the research set out in the previous chapters has shown that many users are not primarily (or at least not only) driven to seek environmental information by altruistic environmental motives, and it is therefore unlikely that many will engage with environmental decision-making processes solely to protect and enhance the environment (in the absence of additional motivations). Further, users may not even be utilising the right of access to environmental information to participate in decision-making procedures at all or may have preferred views as to the outcomes of such participation which reduce rather than enhance environmental protection.

This mismatch between expectation and reality at the intersection of the rights to access environmental information and participate in environmental decision-making procedures can lead to increased dissatisfaction with the arrangements. Users may be required to follow procedures that do not meet their needs, whether as inexperienced users requiring sustained support at all stages or as professional users with their own needs, while authorities may resent the effort devoted to making

---

[371] See J. SIMILÄ, "The Evolution of Participatory Rights in the Era of Fiscal Austerity and Reduced Administrative Burden" in JENDROŚKA and BAR, above n.64.
[372] LEE and ABBOT, above n. 111, p. 86.
[373] See section 2.2 below.
[374] J. STEELE, "Participation and Deliberation in Environmental Law: Exploring a Problem-Solving Approach" (2001) 21(3) *Oxford Journal of Legal Studies* 415.

Chapter 5. Information and Participation

information available when it does not result in the benefits for decision-making that are said to justify the burdens involved. Such dissatisfaction can lead to a decreased interest in accessing environmental information or participating in environmental decision-making procedures, and a lack of enthusiasm for making the system work as well as it could, potentially undermining the environmental protection aims of both rights.

This chapter considers how users have utilised environmental information accessed through the right of access to environmental information, highlighting how both the right to environmental information and public participation are perceived and used in practice. It focuses on the small minority of members of the public who have chosen both to engage with the right and participate in environmental decision-making procedures. This focus on a minority raises (but does not answer) the wider question of how far the lack of widespread uptake of the right's participative aims indicates a failing of the right to effectively promote public participation in environmental decision-making procedures. A further point arises from the breadth of the definition of environmental information and the existence of separate obligations to make certain information available to the public, in some cases long pre-dating the recognition of a right to access environmental information. In such circumstances, covering, for example, many of the formal processes of local authorities,[375] the picture is muddied by the fact that it is not possible to attribute the disclosure of information exclusively to the legal framework on either environmental information or wider transparency and participation.

This chapter first sets out the rationale which underpins the right to participate in environmental decision-making procedures and how it links to both the right to access environmental information and the wider aim of protecting and enhancing the environment through public participation. This section then analyses public participation through the theoretical framework provided by Arnstein's Ladder of Participation, before applying this theory to the provisions of the Aarhus Convention. The chapter then moves on to explore how both users of the right and public authorities view the uses of the environmental information accessed under the Aarhus Convention and the Environmental Information (Scotland) Regulations 2004 (EI(S)R). It does this by identifying how users utilise environmental information accessed under the right and whether this usage meets with each actor's respective expectations. It concludes by considering the extent to which these expectations align or diverge from the ideals behind the

---

[375] Local Government (Scotland) Act 1973, ss 50A–50K.

Aarhus Convention, and what this means in terms of the role of the right in terms of protecting and enhancing the environment.

2. THEORIES OF PUBLIC PARTICIPATION

Within the context of environmental law, public participation is primarily conceptualised as the means by which individuals interact with public law decision-making processes that impact on the environment. Similarly, the conceptualisation in the Aarhus Convention and the EI(S)R views the purpose of such participation as enabling individuals to "assert the right to live in an environment adequate to health and well-being, and to fulfil [their moral] duty to protect the environment".[376] This environmental element is vital to the conceptualisation adopted by the Convention and the EI(S)R, but is not the only way to consider public participation. Public participation can also be considered in isolation from any environmental considerations. From this non-environmental perspective, the focus is more on the relationship between public authorities and the public, with aspects such as the legitimacy of decisions made by the authority taking centre stage. As such, it aligns closely with the goals of the wider freedom of information laws and their objectives of transparency and accountability.

These different views of public participation are important for a variety of reasons. First, while a decision itself may have an impact on the environment, the users who access environmental information to engage with policy-making processes may not be viewing the process through this environmental lens. Divorcing the environmental aims of the right from the action of participating in decision-making procedures undermines the theoretical basis of the right to environmental information. This, in turn, further muddies the distinction between the right to environmental information and the general right to information.

Second, through setting aside specifically environmental considerations, it is possible to make use of the broader work done in analysing and constructing theoretical frameworks that further explore other aspects of public participation. In particular, and without a specifically environmental dimension, Arnstein's Ladder of Participation considers the extent of which public participation can deliver (or fail to deliver) empowerment, and the suitability of different forms of public participation. These broader

---

[376] EBBESSON et al., above n. 119, p. 120.

considerations are very relevant to public participation in environmental decision-making procedures and to how the Aarhus Convention conceptualises public participation in its own provisions.

2.1. THE RATIONALE BEHIND PUBLIC PARTICIPATION

Several strands of argument provide a rationale for encouraging public participation:

> Some value public participation in its own right as a form of enriched citizenship and accountability, others because of the legitimacy it confers on decision-making, the improved representativeness of decisions it secures or the more efficacious policy outcomes that can result.[377]

These strands of argument each deal with a distinct perspective on public participation and its value, each emphasising different "virtues" and benefits of engaging with the public. At the core of these diverse perspectives is the shared assertion that public participation is "a good thing". Yet it is important to distinguish between what "good things" constitute the core arguments underpinning the value of public participation. In their analysis of participation in the context of environmental impact assessment, Glucker et al. do this through categorising the elements of these perspectives into three distinct categories: normative, instrumental and substantive.[378]

The normative rationale focuses on the benefits for the citizens who are able to exercise their right to participate. Some of these are fairly direct, in that those affected are able to have some influence over decisions that have an impact on their environment. This is particularly important for marginalised and disenfranchised groups, who may otherwise be excluded (whether deliberately or not) from inputting into decision-making procedures. In the direct sense, this rationale for creating specific procedures is seeking to overcome barriers to public participation, such as the status of the interested individual, the availability of contacts or capacity to participate.[379] Less directly, participation is seen as enabling citizens

---

[377] R. Fox, "Engagement and Participation: What the Public Want and How Our Politicians Need to Respond" (2009) 62(4) *Parliamentary Affairs* 673, 674.
[378] A. Glucker et al., "Public Participation in Environmental Impact Assessment: Why, Who and How?" (2013) 43 *Environmental Impact Assessment Review* 104.
[379] Capacity can also be constrained by limits on participants' expertise in either constructing or presenting in the required format a case that may involve technical matters and on access to the finance needed to acquire and deploy such expertise.

to exercise active citizenship and further as a means of social learning, helping to build a more confident and capable civic society that can make fuller use of the various opportunities available to engage in public affairs.

The instrumental benefits rationale focuses primarily on the legitimacy of decisions adopted by public authorities. Public participation is seen as generating legitimacy for the decisions that are taken, since all of those affected have had the opportunity to have their voice heard and to comment on the material on which the decision-maker has been working. The extent to which legitimacy is achieved will depend on how far the public's views are, and are perceived as being, in fact considered. Nevertheless, especially when rolled in with the transparency and accountability that public participation is intended to provide, in a democratic system a process with some degree of open public participation will be regarded as better than a closed decision-making procedure.

This links with the third rationale: the substantive benefits of public participation on the quality of the final decision taken. These benefits rest on the additional inputs which can be provided by embracing contributions from the public at large. Such inputs can supplement (or even contradict) the knowledge and data gathered and held by the limited number of actors directly involved in developing policy or promoting or deciding on proposed projects. At the factual level, residents can add local knowledge to the information already held by either authorities or developers, particularly in relation to the impact of changes over time and of occasional events such as flooding or the presence of non-resident species. Testing the robustness of the information put forward by others is a further significant element, especially in the environmental assessment process, where a key step is the exposure to public scrutiny of the documents forming the environmental impact assessment report presented by the proposers of a project.[380] The public input extends beyond factual information to provide insights on values and preferences. Such matters have a major part to play in taking environmental decisions,[381] and again direct public participation

---

[380] The precise procedure and terminology vary, but central to the environmental impact process is the requirement on the proposer of a project to prepare a report identifying the likely impacts of the project, a report which is subject to public and expert scrutiny, and is a major (but not decisive) consideration to be taken into account in determining whether or not the project will be approved; see J. HOLDER, *Environmental Assessment: The Regulation of Decision Making*, Oxford University Press, Oxford 2004, chap. 6.

[381] Royal Commission on Environmental Pollution, *Twenty-First Report: Setting Environmental Standards* (Cm 4053, 1998).

creates an opportunity for such inputs to be made regardless of the obstacles, filters and biases created by the standard representative or other intermediary procedures in the governmental structures.

Each rationale that underpins public participation is notable in that they can be wholly divorced from the environmental considerations and goals that are intrinsic to the rights of accessing environmental information, to participate in environmental decision-making processes and the regimes which implement these rights. This can be significant in influencing the expectations of users and public authorities; because these rationales can be independent from any environmental concerns, expectations may not be influenced by any environmental factors. For public participation, as for access to information, the Aarhus Convention and the EI(S)R are based on the need to do something special for environmental matters. However, because public participation overlaps with motivations and concerns which are not environmental in nature, there is a risk that the use of a distinct environmental information regime will cause confusion when distinguishing it from the general right to, and the desire to promote, public participation.

Yet in highlighting this, it is important to note that the reason why any of the broader underpinning rationales are seen as important may not be wholly separated from a concern about the environment. Individuals may be worried about the quality of decision-making not as an abstract concern about governance, but because of the very real impact on substantive decisions that affect the environment. In this way, while it is important to understand these rationales independent of the Convention's environmental aims, it is also important to recognise that there is an environmental element to public participation too.

2.2. PUBLIC PARTICIPATION AND ARNSTEIN'S LADDER OF PARTICIPATION

The established rationales and the perceived benefits that public participation is seen to bring to environmental decision-making procedures are valuable for understanding why public participation has established such a hold over decision-making procedures over the last few decades in domestic and international law.[382] However, while these rationales have

---

[382] See generally SIMILÄ, above n.371.

been evidenced in public participation mechanisms, they are abstract in nature: they assume a unified understanding of what constitutes "improving" a decision made by a public authority, an agreed-upon definition of legitimacy, and a single understanding of how public participation mechanisms should be designed and utilised.

As is the position with access to information, these assumed understandings, and the potential to deviate from them, are significant, as there is a danger that any mismatches in understanding will lead to frustration and disengagement if expectations are not fulfilled. If the individual actors engaging with each other under the right do not share the same vision or assessment of the process, few, if any, of the objectives may be met:

> There is a danger that we may find ourselves in the worst possible situation. Frustration on the part of publics with legally required participation processes results in less engagement by affected communities and increases the superficiality of those processes; policy makers are also frustrated and resort to tick box bureaucratic exercises rather than seeking genuine opportunities for the public to influence development. This risks becoming a self-perpetuating vicious circle. This sense that there is a hollowness in participatory exercises at the consenting stage for major projects is reinforced by the very low expectations for public participation in the high level policy discourse.[383]

The risk of such a vicious circle places emphasis not only on the purpose but also on the methods of participation and what they can achieve. In this way, it is important not to consider public participation as a single idea, with one method of implementation. Rather, it is a multi-faceted concept that can be understood in different ways by different people, and with a range of ways to be implemented in practice.

One significant theoretical framework which considers the form and function of public participation mechanisms is Arnstein's Ladder of Participation.[384] Setting the foundation for much of the following research on public participation,[385] Arnstein put forward the view that

---

[383] LEE and ABBOT, above n. 111, p. 60.
[384] ARNSTEIN, above n. 94.
[385] For example, K. COLLINS and R. ISON, "Jumping off Arnstein's Ladder: Social Learning as a New Policy Paradigm for Climate Change Adaptation" (2009) 19 *Environmental Policy and Governance* 358 and C. SLOTTERBACK and M. LAURIA, "Building a Foundation for Public Engagement in Planning: 50 Years of Impact, Interpretation, and Inspiration from Arnstein's Ladder" (2019) 85(3) *Journal of the American Planning Association* 183.

Chapter 5. Information and Participation

public participation is primarily a means by which power is redistributed between the state and citizens.[386] From this starting position, Arnstein further posited that in order to effectively redistribute power, public participation processes need to allow citizens to affect the outcome of a decision; processes which do not allow this are "empty" and "frustrating" for citizens, and act as a way to legitimise outcomes without redistributing power.[387]

Perhaps the most long-lasting aspect of Arnstein's work is the Ladder of Participation, which visually illustrates the different types of public participation and the extent to which they allow for citizens to influence the outcome of decision-making processes. At the broadest level, the higher up the ladder a decision-making process is, the more power is redistributed to the public, in turn empowering them and fulfilling the objective of public participation as understood by Arnstein.[388]

Figure 1. A Diagram Illustrating Arnstein's Ladder of Participation[389]

8	Citizen Control	Degrees of Citizen Power
7	Delegated Power	
6	Partnership	
5	Placation	Degrees of Tokenism
4	Consultation	
3	Informing	
2	Therapy	Non-Participation
1	Manipulation	

Source: S. ARNSTEIN, "A Ladder of Citizen Participation" (1969) 35(4) *Journal of the American Institute of Planners* 216, 217.

Arnstein's work continues to be the basis for how public authorities view and design their own public participation procedures.[390] This is not to imply that there are no issues with Arnstein's theoretical framework. Indeed,

---

[386] ARNSTEIN, above n. 94, p. 216.
[387] Ibid., p. 216.
[388] Ibid., p. 217.
[389] Ibid.
[390] See, for example, *The Report of the Working Group on Citizen Engagement with Local Government* (Department of the Environment, Community & Local Government, Dublin, 2014), where the different rungs on the ladder are helpfully linked to particular participation mechanisms that reflect them; <https://www.socialjustice.ie/sites/default/files/attach/civil-society-article/3393/wgcereport.pdf> accessed 20 April 2022.

Arnstein herself notes that the visual illustration is an oversimplification of a wider range of issues which can impact upon the success of a participatory process.[391] However, subsequent work has highlighted some additional flaws within Arnstein's framework.

Implicit within the Ladder of Participation is that the idea that the metric by which public participation can be judged as successful is the extent to which citizens can influence the final decision taken by the public authority.[392] Yet this implicit underpinning belief is flawed. One issue is that this approach assumes that citizens being given more influence over the final decision directly correlates to an improvement in the substantive merits of the decision being taken.[393] Such an approach not only focuses on the "substantive benefits" rationale of public participation, discarding the normative and instrumental rationales, but rests on an assumption that is often questionable, especially in relation to complex, multi-faceted issues which involve highly technical and long-term considerations.

Another issue is that Arnstein assumes all members of the public want to become more involved in taking the final decision. This amalgamates the public into a singular category of similar actors, glossing over differences between how individuals view and interact with participatory decision-making processes.[394] A final critique that can be made of Arnstein's model is that it assumes that all users are unified in their desired outcome for a decision-making process, which further unduly amalgamates the public into a singular category of actors. In reality, the public may hold sharply contrasting views on the relevant issues, contrasting views which are more or less soundly based and which cannot be reconciled. Public participation may be able to guarantee that such divergent views are represented in the decision-making process, but is unlikely to produce an outcome that all are happy with.

These critiques illustrate that "public participation" can mean many things, and that implementing public participation in practice is complex. Of course, this also has an impact within the specific area of environmental law and participation in environmental decision-making processes. Arnstein's theory not only shines a light on what to consider in terms

---

[391] For example, racism: ARNSTEIN, above n. 94, 217.
[392] C. HAYWARD, L. SIMPSON and L. WOOD, "Still Left out in the Cold: Problematising Participatory Research and Development" (2004) 44(1) *Sociologia Ruralis* 95, 99.
[393] J. TRITTER and A. MCCALLUM, "The Snakes and Ladders of User Involvement: Moving beyond Arnstein" (2006) 76 *Health Policy* 156, 162.
[394] HAYWARD et al., above n. 392, pp. 100–101.

of empowerment and public participation, but can also illuminate the expectations that are embedded within the Aarhus Convention.

3. PUBLIC PARTICIPATION, ENVIRONMENTAL INFORMATION AND THE AARHUS CONVENTION

Public participation and the underpinning rationales play a significant role in the construction of the Aarhus Convention and the procedural obligations enshrined within it. The basis for the Aarhus Convention is that promoting public participation in environmental decision-making procedures will lead to individuals being able to assert their right "to live in an environment adequate to [their] health and well-being" and to fulfil their moral duty to protect and enhance the environment.[395] The Aarhus Convention therefore guarantees both the right for individuals to participate in environmental decisions and the right to environmental information; without such information, individuals will have limited knowledge upon which to effectively participate in environmental decision-making procedures.[396]

These ideas are expressed in the Preamble to the Aarhus Convention.[397] However, it is notable that the Preamble does not restrict itself to a single rationale to justify its focus on public participation. It references the substantive benefits of improving the "quality and the implementation of [environmental] decisions",[398] of promoting transparency in the exercise of public power[399] and in improving the legitimacy of decisions,[400] matching the rationales identified by Glucker et al. Far from limiting itself from a single rationale, the Aarhus Convention incorporates a range of rationales in terms of how it conceptualises public participation and the benefits it can play in protecting and enhancing the environment.

However, this broad acceptance of the different rationales and benefits of public participation brings with it some issues regarding expectations and interpreting the intent behind the Aarhus Convention. With the Convention's recognition of various different rationales for justifying public

---

[395] Aarhus Convention, Preamble, paras 7–9.
[396] Ibid., para. 8.
[397] Ibid., paras 7–16.
[398] Ibid., para. 9.
[399] Ibid., para. 10.
[400] Ibid.

participation, it is possible for different people to interpret the aims of the Convention in different ways[401] or to highlight different rationales when unpicking the Convention's various strands.[402] As each of the rationales is adopted by the Aarhus Convention and recognised within the Preambular paragraphs, each individual's interpretation of the Aarhus Convention and the goals of public participation can be considered valid despite the substantial differences between them.

This can be problematic, as different interpretations of public participation and its rationales can lead to divergent expectations regarding public participation in decision-making procedures. From the perspective of transparency, the public authorities concerned may feel that they have achieved the objectives of participation by sharing information and giving opportunities to contribute to their decision-making processes. At the same time, though, members of the public may feel deeply frustrated if they have been denied the fuller collaboration that they thought was their due in order to ensure the legitimacy of the process. The presence of mismatched expectations as to the different roles of the parties within the procedures will lead to miscommunication and dissatisfaction that affects not only the authority's decision-making process, but also the right to participate itself.

The potential impact of this mismatch of expectations is not limited to the satisfaction with public participation processes; it also impacts any associated processes and rights which lead up to and promote the right to participate in environmental decision-making procedures. Critically, one such associated set of processes and relevant right is the right of access to environmental information. Users of the right to environmental information will use the right on the basis that they will be able to utilise the accessed environmental information to achieve their desired goals. If that goal is to make use of public participation procedures to influence a decision that is being adopted by a public authority, then any failure to influence that decision may be seen as reflecting poorly on the effectiveness of the right of access to environmental information.

This will be the case despite the fact that the immediate outcome desired from the procedures implementing the right of access to environmental

---

[401] A. Hough, "The Public Participation Principle: Effective Implementation of Aarhus Participation Rights by the European Union Legal Framework" (2017) 25 *Environmental Liability*, 3, 4.

[402] E.g. highlighting "input legitimacy" and "output legitimacy": ibid., p. 4; C. Abbot, "Losing the Local? Public Participation and Legal Expertise in Planning Law" (2020) 40 *Legal Studies* 269, 274.

information is the proactive or reactive disclosure of environmental information. While the right is designed to lead into public participation processes, it is not designed to contribute to participatory processes in and of itself. Yet, in terms of the expectations of users, this disconnect may be irrelevant. Where a user wants to become involved with a decision-making process, there is an intrinsic connection between the right to access environmental information and the right to participate in environmental decision-making procedures. If a user's expectations about one of these rights is unfulfilled, either through the information the user is seeking not being disclosed or the outcome of the decision-making process not aligning with their views, then this dissatisfaction will spread to the other, connected right.

The ambiguity over how the Aarhus Convention views and represents these views on public participation also carries over to the "empowerment" aspects of the Convention. Intrinsic to the Aarhus Convention is the idea that the provision of environmental information and opportunities to participate in environmental decisions would empower the public.[403] Yet there are limits to this empowerment. Under the Convention, public authorities must seek the view of the public prior to taking an environmental decision[404] and must incorporate these views into the reasoning for their decision.[405] However, while input from the public must be able to influence the substance of the final decision,[406] there is no obligation imposed to ensure that every decision taken by an authority reflects the views of those who participated.

This would place the Aarhus Convention's right to public participation within the "consultation" rung of Arnstein's Ladder of Participation: a form of public participation which, by itself, Arnstein did not recognise as a valid form of public participation due to the lack of direct influence citizens have on the final decision.[407] This is further reinforced by the fact that the Aarhus Convention prioritises the role of the public authority as the final decision-maker. Citizens, acting as users of the Convention's rights, are not conceptualised as actors who will have the final say in a

---

[403] M. MASON, "Information Disclosure and Environmental Rights: The Aarhus Convention" (2010) 10(3) *Global Environmental Politics* 10, 13–14.
[404] Aarhus Convention, art. 6.
[405] Ibid., art. 6(8).
[406] EBBESSON et al., above n. 119, p. 120.
[407] ARNSTEIN, above n. 94, p. 219.

decision-making process; rather, they are characterised as actors who can contribute to the decision-making process, and whose contributions must have the "possibility" of influencing the final decision.[408] In this way, the provisions and default perspective of the Aarhus Convention result in users being unable to reach the highest rungs of participation as established by Arnstein.

Notwithstanding this, the Aarhus Convention does not prevent the creation of decision-making procedures where citizens are granted control over the decision that is taken. The Convention only establishes the minimum level of procedural rights that states must guarantee, and public authorities are free to design and introduce public participation mechanisms that allow for the public to have more control over the final decision.[409] This means that public authorities are free to redistribute their decision-making power and cede control of the final decision-making power to citizens.

However, this freedom also enables a degree of ambiguity to develop in terms of the expectations of public participatory processes. The freedom of states to go beyond the provisions of the Aarhus Convention has an aspirational quality. States are tacitly encouraged to move beyond the mere legal requirements of the Aarhus Convention by the idea that the Convention protects the "minimum" level of rights required to achieve its environmental aims.[410] This enables states to develop their procedures over time and to match different participatory processes to different sorts of decisions, but creates a degree of uncertainty as to the extent to which public authorities should be expected to be empowering citizens. Should authorities be complying with the minimum requirements and limit citizens to contributing to decision-making processes, or should they be seeking to redistribute power to a greater extent than the minimum requirements? Different actors, whether they be users or public authorities, can answer that question differently and these different expectations can each be considered as legitimate on the basis of what is said in the Aarhus Convention. This then sets the stage for different actors to hold conflicting and mismatching expectations regarding the rights guaranteed by the Convention.

---

[408] EBBESSON et al., above n. 119, p. 120.
[409] Ibid, p. 19.
[410] Ibid.

4. USING ENVIRONMENTAL INFORMATION: THEORY AND PRACTICE

The normative, instrumental and substantive rationales for public participation are key for how the right, and its implementing legal regimes, conceptualise both the right to environmental information and the linked right to participate in environmental decisions. Both the Aarhus Convention and the EI(S)R are underpinned by the assumption that users, driven by altruistic environmental motivations, seek environmental information to participate in environmental decisions to fulfil their duty to protect and enhance the environment. Yet this assumption about the driving motivation of users is not entirely correct.

Similarly, there are questions over whether users of the right are actually using environmental information to engage with environmental decision-making procedures as intended by the right. Moreover, even if a user does engage with the right's participatory aims, it is also questionable whether the user holds the same understanding regarding the rationale for their participation as the public authority or as envisaged in the creation of the right itself. Further still, there is scope for debate as to how far users participating in environmental decision-making procedures are doing so with an altruistic environmental motive.

The presence of varying motives and expectations and the mismatch between underpinning assumptions and practice are significant. Differing expectations can lead to disagreements between different actors, in particular between users and public authorities, over whether the procedures are being properly observed or over the quality of the outcome. The resulting dissatisfaction with the experience of exercising the rights both to access environmental information and to participate in environmental decision-making procedures may even dissuade individuals from utilising their right to access and use environmental information. If the rights are seen as not delivering what is expected and lead to disengagement, then the environmental and participative aims behind their creation may be undermined.

4.1. RATIONALES OF PUBLIC PARTICIPATION: DO THEY INFLUENCE ACTORS' OPINIONS?

In terms of how the different actors engage with the participative aims of the rights established under the Aarhus Convention, there is generally a broad acceptance of the benefits of public participation in environmental decision-making procedures. This is true for both users of the right who are seeking to participate in environmental decisions and for public authorities that are obliged to assist with such participation. These positive views of public participation are based on a shared acceptance of the broad ideas behind the rationales underpinning such participative efforts. However, both users and public authorities emphasise different aspects of these rationales in their respective understandings of public participation.

4.1.1. Users

For most users of the right, their positive opinion of the right to participate in environmental decisions was primarily based on the substantive benefits of public participation and, specifically, the ability for users to improve the quality of the final decision taken:

> Councils don't like to get criticised, everybody knows that. But it's ... be[ing] more engaged with the public would actually help the Council in decisions they make.[411]

This view is based on the substantive benefits rationale discussed earlier: that by having the public participate in environmental decision-making procedures, the final decision taken will be improved through the provision of additional information or a better understanding of the needs and preferences of those affected. However, it should be noted that the substantive rationale does not necessarily have to have an environmental dimension – the same interest in improving decisions can apply in all areas of governmental activity. Again, there is an overlap between the environmental concerns that support the specific rights being examined here and more general concerns over good government that have inspired freedom of information laws and public participation procedures more widely, making it difficult at times to identify how strong the specifically environmental element of a user's motivation is.

However, this is not to imply that this is the only rationale accepted by users. Indeed, users often highlighted the validity of the normative and

---

[411] Interview with User No. 11.

instrumental rationales when discussing the transparency elements of public participation:

> There should probably be some sort of a citizen or non-government person who sits on some of their information council meetings, reviewing decisions and things like that. Yeah: it's got to be more transparency in how they're doing all this stuff to.[412]

It is important to note that these rationales are not exclusive to each other. Users would often refer to multiple rationales to justify public participation in environmental decision-making procedures and their desire to access environmental information – and, if pushed, it is likely that they might often struggle to disentangle the different strands that contribute to the overall idea that public participation is a "good thing". Thus, there is a multi-faceted basis for considering public participation and the associated need to access environmental information.

Notwithstanding this multi-faceted perspective on public participation, personal users broadly viewed such participation primarily as a means for them to provide information to the authority that would lead to them altering its decision or proposed decision. Under this conceptualisation, the user views themselves as correcting the authority's failure to consider all the relevant information and to reach a decision which reflects the user's preferred outcome. In this way, the user essentially takes on (or wishes to take on) the role of final decision-maker through their engagement with the participative process.

Such an approach is notable because it suggests that users are seeking the "decision-making clout"[413] which characterises the higher rungs of Arnstein's Ladder of Participation. This in turn creates a certain expectation for personal users: if public authorities do not ultimately take a decision that adheres to the wishes of the users, then their participation was not taken seriously and was worthless. This negative perception also extends to any preparatory efforts that the user undertook, such as accessing any relevant environmental information under the right to access environmental information.

Evidence of this can be identified in one interviewed user's perception of the outcomes of their engagement with the right to environmental

---

[412] Interview with User No. 7.
[413] ARNSTEIN, above n. 94, p. 217.

information and to participate in environmental decision-making procedures. The user noted that the majority of the information that they had accessed from the public authorities they had contacted "wasn't particularly useful".[414] This negative view could also be seen in their perception of the outcomes of their engagement with environmental decision-making processes:

> It was completely, predictably futile on engagement [chuckle] but these are the kind of statistics, I was trying to show ... that these figures were used to calculate ... what percentage of [REDACTED] was going where, you know? ... Well, I'm very, very cynical about this.[415]

However, while this interpretation of the right to public participation is one of those that can be seen as valid under the Aarhus Convention, it is not reflected in the provisions of the Aarhus Convention itself. The Convention requires public authorities only to enable the public to contribute to decision-making processes, not to give them the final decision-making power.[416] Indeed, such a perspective cannot work where two different users have different preferences for the outcome of a decision. If two users have separate (and non-complementary) desires for the decision's outcome, then they both cannot be satisfied with the outcome of the decision-making process.

The approach to the right focused on outcomes is not universal amongst users. In particular, professional users tend to view public participation as a means to provide their views and input into the decision-making process and not as a means of obtaining "decision-making clout". This is likely a consequence both of the professional users' greater understanding of how public decision-making processes work and of the fact that their motivations are different from those of personal users, leaving them likely to be more detached from the final outcomes of a decision than personal users. Nevertheless, because personal users make up the majority of users of the right, it is this "outcome-centric" perspective which dominates discussions on the right to access environmental information and to participate in environmental decision-making procedures.

---

[414] Interview with User No. 1.
[415] Ibid.
[416] Aarhus Convention, Preamble, para. 9, art. 6(8).

4.1.2. Public Authorities

Public authorities also held broadly positive views on public participation in environmental decision-making procedures.[417] Indeed, they also commonly referred to the normative, instrumental and substantive rationales when discussing their positive views of public participation in decision-making processes, but without emphasising any specifically environmental dimension:

> I mean the Council is a public body, it's public money, we're accountable.[418]

> But I think in terms of a wider, kind of, culture of openness, transparency, engagement, then it is important, you know, we ... we should welcome informed citizens who want to participate in decision-making processes, and raise their concerns and views to influence public debates, not, kind of, treat them like mushrooms and keep them in the dark.[419]

> But I think it also gives people the chance to disagree, and sometimes the public do have good points, and it is maybe something that we haven't been aware of, or maybe we haven't taken perhaps as much notice of as we should. And I think that that is a good thing.[420]

A divergence between users and public authorities is noticed here since the latter do not hold an "outcome-centric" view. Authorities tend to view public participation as conferring a more limited role to the public, as a means for individuals to convey their preferences as to the outcome of a decision, as well as ensure that the authority undertakes their duties in a transparent manner:

> And it allows them to potentially focus their arguments, either in support or as an objector to any particular application.[421]

> For us, and for all public authorities[, y]ou are always going to get that subsequent benefit from access to information that you need to get make sure your information can stand up to scrutiny, that is can lead to more robust decision making. Because as you know, any member of the public can have

---

[417] Differences within public authorities, in particular between the "information" teams and the "operational" departments, are discussed in Chapter 6, section 2.1.1.
[418] Interview with Public Authority No. 1.
[419] Interview with Public Authority No. 7.
[420] Interview with Public Authority No. 13.
[421] Interview with Public Authority No. 12.

their eyes on this at any given point in time, and we have to make sure that our decision making is justified.[422]

This greater focus on the use of participation to indicate preferences places less importance on the outcome of the decision alone and more emphasis on gathering inputs to make the best possible decision; the process is viewed as being as important as the outcome itself. Such a perspective does not go against the vision embedded in the legal obligations under the Aarhus Convention and the EI(S)R, but does not move beyond the "floor" that it provides. Further steps would be needed to fully satisfy the aspirational aims of states moving beyond simply guaranteeing the essentials recognised by the Aarhus Convention, or to achieve a "meaningful" empowerment of citizens in the way theorised by Arnstein.

However, this is not to suggest that public authorities are simply withholding decision-making powers from the public for no reason. Authorities are keenly aware that they should not act to reflect the interests merely of those individuals participating in environmental decision-making processes, but for the benefit of the public as a whole. In this way, public authorities can present a justification for retaining the power to make the final decision in order to ensure that the final decision reflects the wider public interest:

> But you will always get people, as I said before, that will disagree with some decisions that we make. It's … all we can do is explain as much as we can … but the bottom line is sometimes we're the bad guys. We have to make a decision and, you know, there's been a reason.[423]

Consequently, public authorities aim to strike a balance between empowering the public through participation in decision-making procedures and ensuring that the final decision is what is best for their conception of the public interest. Such a balance does not necessarily mean that the authority must retain final decision-making powers for every decision; authorities can design procedures which redistribute this power to interested members of the public, while still ensuring that the final decision does reflect the general public interest. However, in discussing this with Scottish public authorities, there was an identifiable trend in

---

[422] Interview with Public Authority No. 13.
[423] Interview with Public Authority No. 10.

merely being interested in the views of the public rather than granting them any final decision-making powers.

As a result, the primary distinction between how users and public authorities consider public participation is in the emphasis on the influence that users can exert on the final outcome. While these perceptions and associated expectations can be in stark opposition to each other, it is notable that they arise from the same underpinning rationales. This is significant because, as discussed above, these rationales are recognised and broadly adopted by the Aarhus Convention without any efforts to clarify the specifics of their implementation or the priorities between them. Consequently, both users and public authorities can claim that their differing views are legitimate and respecting the Convention, even when they do not align, a mismatch that can give rise to disputes and dissatisfaction as participation procedures are worked through.

4.2. IDENTIFIED USES OF ENVIRONMENTAL INFORMATION

There is a clear significance in identifying the impact that the Aarhus Convention and the EI(S)R have had on how the right of public participation is viewed by both users and public authorities. However, this impact is not the only aspect which needs to be considered. While the right of access to environmental information is viewed as a precursor to public participation in environmental decision-making procedures, this does not necessarily mean that it is being used in this way in practice. Indeed, while public participation may be viewed as the primary aim of the right, interviews with users who actually engaged with the right in practice identified five distinct uses of environmental information accessed under the right.

These five identified uses are not a comprehensive list of every use of environmental information accessed under the right. For example, professional users are generally excluded due to the lesser number of requests submitted by such users.[424] Moreover, there is no simple way of tracking the vast range of responses that may flow once people have come into contact with any of the vast array of information made available by authorities and that (although the user does not realise this) technically

---

[424] The ways in which professional users use environmental information accessed under the right are discussed in Chapter 3.

could be viewed as being provided in fulfilment of the obligation to proactively disclose environmental information. The uses of the right that are not discussed in this section are important; indeed, the existence of users responding differently further serves to highlight how much activity falls outwith the environmental vision of the right of access to environmental information. However, it is notable that even within the identified uses of the right considered here, only one of the five uses aligns with the vision of access to information being the precursor of participation in environmental decision-making procedures. While there are aspects of the other uses which can contribute towards the wider goal of environmental protection and enhancement, this deviation from the primary intended use further highlights the mismatch between the intended and actual use of the right.

The first use identified by the project is where users employ the information to participate in formal environmental decision-making processes and consultations. This use precisely fulfils the role envisaged in the Rio Declaration and the Aarhus Convention, although even here not necessarily driven by a strong environmental concern. Quite often these formal participatory processes are related to the granting of planning permissions, which vary in terms of their scale and scope.[425]

There is a general assumption that users seeking to influence the outcome of such decisions will be those who live in the area where the decision will impact. However, this is not entirely reflective of the experience of some public authorities, where public participation processes were engaged with by both locals and individuals who were further afield:

> As a result of technology, certainly, there's more opportunities for people all over the world, anybody, you know. Somebody that's the other side of the world can see this and decide, you know, I'm an ex-pat Scot and I don't like the sound of what you're doing there.[426]

A further notable point about the findings is that the interviewed users using environmental information to participate appear to do so primarily as a means of opposing a proposal put forward by the public authority. This was often done by using the participation opportunities to highlight new

---

[425] Examples of this can be identified in Interview with User No. 7 and Interview with User No. 1.
[426] Interview with Public Authority No. 10.

Chapter 5. Information and Participation

information or an argument which contradicted the original basis for the proposal:

> [Responding to a question about their participation in a consultation process] Yeah, I was able to point out errors, discrepancies or misinformation ... stuff that was clearly false information that they were ... acting upon.[427]
>
> So we used it [the accessed information] to, you know, make comparison with the previous census information which was then kind of 6–7 years out of date.[428]

While this contribution may not always be aimed at protecting and enhancing the environment, such contributions can result in decisions better reflecting various environmental concerns. This usage of environmental information aligns with the substantive rationale of public participation and on occasions with the aim of achieving better environmental protection.

The second use of information identified by this research is the use of environmental information to contribute to engagement with a public authority's actions, but where there are no formal public participation procedures to contribute to. This is generally characterised by users identifying an issue of concern, but one which is not arising directly from a recent decision or a current proposed decision. Examples include claims made regarding sustainable development[429] and cars idling outside of schools.[430] As with the first use, these issues were ones that were generally connected to the immediate local area and had some form of impact on the user or their interests.[431] However, unlike the first use, users who utilised environmental information in this way usually lived or worked in the area that the issue affected.

Such users are not merely using the accessed information as a means of opposing a specific proposal or decision taken by the authority. In contrast with the first use, they were often taking positive actions as well, proposing ways and means by which the relevant authority could remedy the issue identified by the user. As such issues often had an environmental

---

[427] Interview with User No. 10.
[428] Interview with User No. 14.
[429] Interview with User No. 12.
[430] Interview with User No. 10.
[431] This is true even where the issue was characterised as being an issue of national importance: see Interview with User No. 5 regarding waste management.

Intersentia 153

component to them, any actions taken often have, or seek, a positive impact on the environment:

> Yeah. I mean I wasn't challenging anything there ... I was just, yeah ... I was just looking at ... long-term ecosystem trends in the [REDACTED] region and compiling data on them and creating a timeline of significant events in the region.[432]

This results in this use aligning with the substantive rationale underpinning public participation, but in a way that differs from the first identified use of accessed environmental information where the connection with active proceedings more neatly fits the linear model of the provision of information being a precursor to more effective public participation in formal procedures. Here it is a broader sense of environmental citizenship that is being pursued, extending beyond taking advantage of the expressly created opportunities for public participation.

The third identified use of environmental information accessed under the right is using the information to further what the user sees as their own personal interests in ways that do not focus primarily on interactions with a public authority. This use of the right is very broad, including pursuing environmental interests such as seeking to avoid air pollution and protecting the habitats of bats, but also others, such as organising local events and festivals. This use differs from the first two identified uses in that it does not require the user to interact with the public authority once the environmental information is accessed. Users who engage with the right of access to environmental information and use the accessed information in this way are not driven by the substantive rationale, because they are not seeking to influence a decision taken by a public authority. Rather, their engagement with the right and its participatory aims is reflective of the normative rationale that access to environmental information allows for citizens to exercise active citizenship and take decisions that benefit both themselves and (potentially) the broader environment.[433]

An element here is that the user may decide not to do anything with the information; just being more informed about a matter may be sufficient for them. This does not go against the Aarhus Convention or the EI(S)R, which do not mandate that users of the right to environmental information must

---

[432] Interview with User No. 2.
[433] Depending on the interests and intended actions of the individual user, the use of the right can feed into, undermine or be separate from the environmental protection aims of the right.

use such information to participate in environmental decision-making procedures. Indeed, the promotion of environmental education and spreading of awareness are included as desirable outcomes.[434] Moreover, the role of transparency in the promotion of good governance[435] does not require any particular action to be taken on the basis of the information disclosed. However, it is questionable as to whether this "lack" of use really contributes to the aspirations of the Aarhus Convention in relation to environmental citizenship, which requires some degree of the citizen taking an active interest in environmental matters.[436]

This in turn highlights an awkward truth about the rights to access environmental information and to participate in environmental decision-making procedures which applies elsewhere as well. While the rights may have been created with the aim of helping to protect and enhance the environment, they are not designed in a way limited to or even intrinsically connected with achieving this goal. Rather, it is up to the motives of the user as to whether engagement with these rights has an environmental dimension at all and, if so, is directed to producing a better protected environment for future generations,[437] or one which suits the selfish interests of the user.

The fourth identified use is where the accessed information is used as the basis for engagement with other actors who are not the public authority that disclosed the environmental information. This use of accessed environmental information is broadly characterised by contributions to broader public discussions on the environment or decisions that impact on the environment, although information that is environmental may also be relevant and used in this way in relation to public conversations on other topics as well. Examples of such "contributions" include discussion within and between community groups via Facebook[438] or face-to-face discussions,[439] conversations between individuals on shared interests[440] and between the public and environmental NGOs.[441]

Discussions with public authorities are excluded here, falling more closely under the first or second uses identified. Community discussions

---

[434] Aarhus Convention, Preamble, para. 14.
[435] Ibid., paras 10–11.
[436] BARRITT, above n. 21, pp. 150–153.
[437] Aarhus Convention, Preamble, para. 7.
[438] Interview with User No. 3.
[439] Interview with User No. 8.
[440] Interview with User No. 4.
[441] The inclusion of environmental NGOs is particularly notable, considering the focus of the Aarhus Convention on such NGOs.

may, however, be the prelude to informal or formal engagement with public authorities and decision-making processes. The fact that information is being used not just in dialogue with public authorities highlights the range of actors involved in the overall network that arises concerning the right to access environmental information. The discussion and collaboration amongst users, even without engaging with the public authorities, and the diversity of motivation and expertise they display, serve to emphasise the inadequacy of any simple model that views the topic solely on the basis of a direct basis of users and authorities, each of which is treated as a single category.

This emphasis on the ability of environmental information to promote communication between different actors is significant because it suggests that the availability of such information is an important part of an active civil society.[442] Without this information, the different actors, individually or as groups, may lack the shared information and knowledge to communicate with each other. In turn, this broadly reflects the normative rationale for public participation: that by promoting discussion amongst actors, the right of access to environmental information is building a more active civil society that can better engage with environmental decision-making processes. This can be true even where the actors are not primarily driven by environmental motives, because the development of a more active civil society may lead to them becoming more interested in and engaged with all aspects of the world around them, including the environment.

The fifth and final identified use of environmental information accessed under the right is the use of such information for commercial purposes. Users seeking to use environmental information in this way may be engaged in general marketing research or looking to submit tenders to the public authority in question for a specific contract and will be seeking to act on the information obtained to improve and refine their tender.[443] This usage of environmental information is distinguishable from other uses because it does not engage, either directly or indirectly, with the environmental motives which underlie the Convention or the broader rationales behind public participation in general. Indeed, this usage of environmental information is purely concerned with a specific personal benefit, as it relates to the business interests of the user or their employer.

---

[442] Aarhus Convention, Preamble, para. 14.
[443] Some such users might be better classified as professional rather than personal users, but there is a variety in the level of expertise, the role of the individuals and the scale of the commercial organisation that defies simple categorisation.

Chapter 5. Information and Participation

The disconnect between this use of the right and the intended environmental aims of the Convention is noteworthy because, unlike the other uses, it explicitly eschews the right's environmental aims. While the other identified uses are not necessarily primarily driven by environmental concerns, there is at least the possibility that they will contribute, even indirectly, to the environmental aims of the right and the Aarhus Convention. However, commercial requests generally will not contribute to this environmental aim; they are further detached from the environmental rationales that underpin public participation.[444] Businesses who believe that their products or services will enable authorities or those they deal with to achieve a better environment more effectively or efficiently may be able to claim some environmental credit, but private, commercial interests are so dominant that this can be discounted. While there may on occasion still be environmental benefits (even if unintended) from such requests for information, they remain very much detached from environmental aims.

The detachment from the environmental goals, and even the wider rationales for public engagement, is significant in two ways. First, it emphasises the ability for the legal frameworks created to implement the right to be utilised in a way that ignores the environmental aims and ideals of engaged citizenship that lie behind them. This may be a price worth paying to avoid complexity and obstacles to those using rights for beneficial reasons that might not exactly fit any model on which a more restricted scheme might be based. Yet it shows how far removed practice can be from the ideals that led to the creation of legal frameworks. Second, the negative reaction to those using the right for purely commercial reasons demonstrates the strength of that environmental and participative vision in influencing expectations of what will be seen as a "proper" exercise of the legal rights, even though they do in fact allow for wider uses.[445]

---

[444] This is not to discount a possible positive environmental impact arising incidentally when "green" businesses engage with the right for their own commercial reasons. However, in the interviews, surveys and desk-based review of publicly available requests, no such "green" businesses were identified.

[445] E.g. the Society of Local Authority Lawyers and Administrators in Scotland and the Society of Local Authority Chief Executives and Senior Manages Scotland, *Submission to the Public Audit and Post-Legislative Scrutiny Committee for the Post-Legislative Scrutiny of the Freedom of Information (Scotland) Act 2002* (2019) <https://archive2021.parliament.scot/S5_Public_Audit/General%20Documents/24_Solar_-_Solace.pdf> accessed 20 April 2022.

4.3. TRANSLATING RATIONALES INTO REALITY: OPINIONS ON HOW ENVIRONMENTAL INFORMATION IS USED

The rationales which underpin public participation in environmental decisions, and which are connected to the right of access to environmental information, are valuable in that they reflect both rights' environmental aims and highlight the ambiguity that exists within the Aarhus Convention. This ambiguity is of particular importance, as it provides a basis under which competing interpretations of the intent behind the Convention's rights and its implementing measures such as the EI(S)R can be considered valid. As a consequence, different actors can hold different "valid" interpretations, leading to the possibility of mismatching expectations and rising tensions. In this way, it is important to ask and consider whether the outcomes of engaging with public participation through the right to environmental information are what users expect and if any tension arising from a mismatch of expectations leads to a detrimental impact on the environmental goals of both rights,

The users engaged in this research broadly did not feel that their use of the right lived up to their expectations.[446] This mismatch arises from the outcome-orientated approach that has been adopted by the majority of personal users who want their input to have a tangible impact on the decision that is to be (or has been) taken by the authority. Quite often, this impact is characterised in wanting a decision to be reversed or a proposed new development to be refused. The fact that such an outcome had not been realised was a common theme in many interviews:

> [Y]ou know, all they do is write down what you say or listen to what you say, but they never appear to change their, what was, you know that old thing what the number you first thought of?[447]

> Well the, hundreds if not thousands of hours I've spent on this, not a lot has changed. So there's your answer.[448]

> Well, it was a waste of time. I know – well I assume other people objected as well to this dredging and dumping. Ah ... elsewhere. But of course might as well not have bothered.[449]

---

[446] Although it should be noted that individuals who are dissatisfied are more likely to engage in follow-up surveys and research as an outlet for their dissatisfaction.
[447] Interview with User No. 1.
[448] Interview with User No. 5.
[449] Interview with User No. 3.

It should be noted that although this was the most common response, it was not universal. Other users of the right, who were often professional users, were satisfied with the outcomes of their participatory efforts:

> So mine was just like a trial and then I sent it to [advisory body] and they … they looked at it and decided that the … I think they decided that the baseline was useful and they did – did somewhat of a proper one themselves.[450]

It is also worth noting that users were generally satisfied when they sought to use any accessed environmental information to communicate with other non-authority actors:

> I share it with like-minded individuals; people who have either come to be associated via internet, social media, YouTube things like that. I'll share information, with maybe a handful of different people regarding these subjects, you know?[451]

In highlighting these positive examples of users utilising accessed environmental information, it is important to emphasise that these users were not seeking to oppose a specific decision taken or proposed by the public authority. Rather, these users placed a greater emphasis on the instrumental and normative rationales that underpin public participation in environmental decision-making procedures. As a consequence, there was less focus on the substantive rationale and, specifically, less focus on the outcome of any decision-making process and whether it reflected the desires of the user. This is important because the right of access to environmental information can be considered to be successfully implemented when viewed through this perspective.

Nevertheless, this positive perspective appears to be a minority view; the general trend in these interviews was that there is a dissatisfaction about how individuals influence (or fail to influence) the decisions of public authorities. As one interviewee phrased it:

> A lot of people are very cynical about these, these so-called opportunities to participate in decision-making.[452]

Such dissatisfaction can be viewed through Arnstein's theory of public participation. Many users engage with the rights both to access

---

[450] Interview with User No. 2.
[451] Interview with User No. 4.
[452] Interview with User No. 1.

environmental information and to participate in environmental decision-making procedures in order to have a direct influence on the final decision that is being taken. Specifically, they want to have the decision reflect their interests and beliefs, reflecting the highest rungs of Arnstein's Ladder of Participation.[453] In practice, however, these users feel that decisions are not influenced by their input, leaving them in the area of tokenism rather than citizen power in Arnstein's analysis.[454] This creates the impression that the right to participate in environmental decision-making procedures has little or no value, as it does not allow them to achieve their expected goals, goals encouraged by what they thought the right was intended to deliver. A similar view is taken of the right of access to environmental information for the same reason.

This gives rise to various questions regarding what these users may have read into the opportunities for accessing information and participating in decision-making that have been created by the Aarhus Convention and the EI(S)R. By seeing them as creating a means of achieving a preferred outcome, unrealistic expectations may arise. One clear issue is that where different users have different and non-complementary preferred outcomes, they cannot both achieve the outcome that they desire. As a result of this outcome-focused approach, where users have competing views on what is a "good" outcome, at least one will inevitably be dissatisfied with the result.

Moreover, the Aarhus Convention is quite clear that although it aims to empower individuals to participate in environmental decision-making procedures and support this through the provision of environmental information, it does not require that those participating will have the final say. The requirement is that "due account is taken of the outcome of the public participation"[455] and that such participation "should result in some increase in the correlation between the views of the participating public and the content of the decision".[456] While not entirely contradicting these users' outcome-centric view, it does not reflect the belief that users should be able to have the final say in the decisions taken by public authorities.

Disenchantment with public participation is far from unusual and not limited to environmental contexts,[457] often driven by the mismatch

---

[453] ARNSTEIN, above n. 94.
[454] See Figure 1 above.
[455] Aarhus Convention, art. 6(8).
[456] EBBESSON et al., above n. 119, p. 120.
[457] E.g. B. RICHARDSON and J. RAZZAQUE "Public Participation in Environmental Decision-Making" in B. RICHARDSON and S. WOOD, *Environmental Law for Sustainability*, Hart Publishing, Oxford 2006, pp. 191–194.

Chapter 5. Information and Participation

between the outcome-focused expectations of some members of the public in contrast to decision-makers' more limited view of the role for the public contribution. One risk of this is that if individuals feel that their contributions are not influencing the final outcomes, then they may stop engaging with public authorities and their decisions. This would affect their engagement with the process of accessing information as well, since there would be little point in obtaining information if there were nothing effective that could be done with it. Given the special focus placed by the Rio Declaration and the Aarhus Convention on public participation in environmental matters, this would be particularly undesirable in this context.

This risk of users disengaging from the process is real, but the impact in practice is hard to assess. On the one hand, it is impossible to know what role such disenchantment may play along with the many other factors that lead to people not taking the opportunity to participate in decision-making processes. On the other hand, many users seem to become more determined to make a difference and highlighted that they would like to see specific reforms to decision-making procedures that allowed for a greater degree of citizen involvement:

> There should maybe be a body that is ... public-run, just a public body that can organise and go speak to them. As in the Scottish Government is going to set up people councils round about the country; that kind of idea.[458]

> I think [the council] would benefit greatly, that I, you know maybe like an elders' council or something like that.[459]

Further, many interviewees answered positively when asked "would you like to become more involved in how Scottish public authorities make decisions around the environment?":

> Yes, definitely, 100%.[460]

> I guess if it was something relevant and it was something we felt could be improved on a local level then yes.[461]

---

[458] Interview with User No. 11.
[459] Interview with User No. 4.
[460] Interview with User No. 11.
[461] Interview with User No. 13.

However, it is important to highlight that this positive response does always reflect a desire to be involved in every issue. Responding to the same question, one interviewee responded:

> Not really, no. I think I'll be passive in this case and respond where necessary when it affects the environment round about me.[462]

From these responses, it can be suggested that, despite the dissatisfaction arising from the mismatch of expectations, a broad range of users are still interested in engaging with the right to participate in environmental decision-making procedures. This finding reflects only members of the public who access environmental information and seek to participate in environmental decision-making procedures, and not the wider population as a whole.[463] Nevertheless, both these responses and the satisfaction of users who use accessed environmental information for other purposes indicate that the Aarhus Convention's participative aims are, to some extent, being achieved.

In contrast to the degree of negativity shown by many users, public authorities appear to have adopted broadly similar, positive views on the impacts of users exercising their right to access and use environmental information. In the context of users participating in environmental decision-making processes, supported by environmental information accessed under the right, many authorities held positive views on enabling and empowering the public to participate:

> And I think it is good to be able to have that dialogue, because it actually does lead to better policy making.[464]

> I think in terms of a wider, kind of, culture of openness, transparency, engagement, then it is important, you know, we ... we should welcome informed citizens who want to participate in decision-making processes, and raise their concerns and views to influence public debates, not, kind of, treat them like mushrooms and keep them in the dark.[465]

These views are notable not just for their positive perception of public participation and the connections between such participation and the right

---

[462] Interview with User No. 8.
[463] HAZELL et al., above n. 5, chap. 15.
[464] Interview with Public Authority No. 13, although they also note that this does not happen very often.
[465] Interview with Public Authority No. 7.

of access to environmental information. They are also notable because the authorities' views are generally based not on one particular rationale, but reflect all three of the instrumental, normative and substantive rationales that underpin efforts to promote public participation in environmental decision-making processes. Unlike the users who stressed the substantive rationale and focused on the final outcome, the authorities interviewed mentioned all three rationales equally.

This contrast is further reflected in how authorities viewed the role of the public in contributing to environmental decision-making processes. Public authorities tended to focus more on the value of creating opportunities for the public to *contribute to* the decision-making processes rather than redistributing the final decision-making power to the general public. Such a position rejects Arnstein's view of public participation, which emphasises the redistributive nature of public participation, but it does align with the approach adopted by the Aarhus Convention and the EI(S)R. Under these instruments, public authorities are not required to create decision-making procedures that cede decision-making powers, but rather to allow the public to express their views in a way that will be taken seriously and contribute to the decision-making process, but will not determine the outcome.[466]

In adopting this position, both Scottish public authorities and the relevant environmental information regimes are conceptualising public authorities as bodies that act on behalf of the public interest. However, the term "public interest" is more nuanced than it may at first appear. The "public" whose interest is to be considered includes not just the individuals engaging with the participatory processes but also the remaining members of the public.[467] Consequently, in fulfilling their legal obligations, public authorities seek to balance the need to encourage interested individuals to participate in decision-making procedures while still keeping hold of the final, decision-making power in order (it is hoped) to ensure the final decision best reflects the wide array of interests held across the whole of the general public.[468] Public authorities themselves adhere to this approach:

> But you will always get people, as I said before, that will disagree with some decisions that we make. It's ... all we can do is explain as much as we can ...

---

[466] Aarhus Convention, arts 6 and 7.
[467] See generally Aarhus Convention, Preamble, paras 17 and 21; and EBBESSON et al., above n. 119, p. 36.
[468] Such an approach does assume at least the potential for the two goals to be in opposition with each other, an assumption which may not be the case in practice where there is a strong consensus.

But the bottom line is sometimes we're the bad guys. We have to make a decision and, you know, there's been a reason.[469]

However, this conceptualisation of the role of public participation may disappoint some members of the public and can lead to the mismatch between user expectations and the reality of participating in environmental decision-making procedures.

Notwithstanding this, it is important to emphasise that the Aarhus Convention does not reduce the role of actors participating in decision-making processes to simply being a source of input. There is an implicit requirement, made explicit in subsequent guidance, that users must have a real opportunity to influence the final decision adopted by the authority.[470] This is also reflected in the views and experiences of some public authorities, who are willing to alter decisions on the basis of contributions to decision-making processes:

> Other people have a mission in terms of a campaigning or challenge and sometimes what they ask and what we find makes things change because they've picked up on something. It's not a given ever, that what they're asking for is bad, at all. Because sometimes they have really highlighted things we could challenge, change and publish.[471]

> But I think it also gives people the chance to disagree, and sometimes the public do have good points, and it is maybe something that we haven't been aware of, or maybe we haven't taken perhaps as much notice of as we should.[472]

In this way, users can have an impact on the final decision taken, shaping the decision to reflect their preferences or interpretation of the facts. Yet especially when the outcome is still a disappointing one (even though possibly less so than if they had not intervened), this positive impact is not appreciated, and dissatisfaction arises from the mismatch between users' expectations and reality.

Central to this is the lack of confidence on the part of those participating in decision-making procedures that their views have been listened to as one aspect of a wider lack of trust in the authorities concerned.[473] Unless

---

[469] Interview with Public Authority No. 10.
[470] Aarhus Convention, art. 6(8); EBBESSON et al., above n. 119, p. 120.
[471] Interview with Public Authority No. 15.
[472] Interview with Public Authority No. 13.
[473] See Chapter 4, section 2.2.

Chapter 5. Information and Participation

the outcome matches their own preference, it may seem that they have been ignored. One way of trying to offer reassurance is through a further procedural obligation that has been introduced. The Aarhus Convention imposes an overarching obligation on public authorities to give reasons for their decision and to list the various facts and arguments they considered in reaching their decision.[474] In line with this, although there is not a general statutory duty for public authorities to provide reasons for all decisions in Scotland or the rest of the UK, such a duty can be and often is imposed through statute[475] and case law.[476]

Yet this may not be sufficient for some users who are focused on the outcome of the decision-making process. Where a final decision does not align with what the user perceives as a "good outcome", it may be hard to persuade them that their legitimate views were taken into account and may even have moved the outcome closer to their desired position, but were outweighed by other, equally legitimate views. In these circumstances, creating a more transparent decision-making process does not by itself guarantee an increase in trust in the public authorities concerned. Indeed, the provision of access to information, as well as of opportunities to participate, may be seen as an empty gesture.

The dissatisfaction arising from a mismatch between what users might expect and what is delivered under the rights to access information and to participate in environmental decision-making is thus a consequence of their conceptualisation within the right itself, not solely of public authorities failing to implement it properly. Framed through Arnstein's Ladder of Participation, the right to participate as envisioned by the Aarhus Convention and the EI(S)R is merely "tokenism"[477] rather than meaningful participation. There may be a desire among some people to go further in empowering the public, but that is not what the Convention calls for, nor what the rights it creates are designed to achieve. The dissatisfaction and frustration that results may create a risk of disengagement that undermines

---

[474] Aarhus Convention, art. 6(9).
[475] An example of this in the planning context can be identified in s. 43(1A) of the Town and Country Planning (Scotland) Act 1997.
[476] A clear example of this in English planning law (likely to be followed in Scotland) is *Dover District Council v. Campaign to Protect Rural England (Kent)* [2017] UKSC 79. In a non-environmental context, an example of this duty to give reasons can be seen in *United Co-operative Ltd v. National Appeal Panel for Entry to the Pharmaceutical Lists* [2007] CSOH 125. See M. ELLIOTT, "Has the Common Law Duty to Give Reasons Come of Age Yet?" [2011] *Public Law* 56.
[477] ARNSTEIN, above n. 94, p. 220; see also Figure 1, above.

the participative goals being sought, but resolving it would require addressing the wider issues of the distribution of power, with ramifications well beyond the environmental sector.

5. CONCLUSION

The link between the right of access to environmental information and the right to participate in environmental decision-making process is clear, both in terms of the structure of the Aarhus Convention itself and how the two rights support each other. Yet while the Aarhus Convention portrays this right to participate as simply the next step following the exercise of the right to information, it is instead a broad and wide-ranging concept. The Aarhus Convention itself recognises the validity of three separate rationales to justify the promotion of public participation, each with subtly different interpretations of what public participation should entail and its overall goals. Moreover, rather than just following the ideal of the Aarhus Convention, users can and do access environmental information to use it in a variety of ways, ways that can contribute to or deviate from the environmental and participative aims that lie beneath the creation of the right to such access.

This is all significant because the model of accessing information in order to use it in participative processes is an oversimplification of a complex position which has created the mismatch in expectations between users of the right, public authorities and the Aarhus Convention itself. Generally, users and public authorities emphasise different rationales for promoting public participation. Personal users primarily adopt a substantive, outcome-focused rationale, whereas public authorities value public participation on the basis of a wider range of benefits and the normative and instrumental rationales, as well as the substantive rationale. These expectations also extend to perceptions regarding the usage of environmental information accessed under the right. Users generally expect their contributions to influence a decision towards their preferred outcome, with other outcomes being perceived as a failure of the process. Conversely, public authorities view these contributions as matters to be considered along with many others in their role as the final decision-maker. This overview is, of course, itself an oversimplification that does not represent the position of every user or public authority. In particular, users who utilise environmental information for purposes other than formally engaging with environmental decision-making processes are less focused on the substantive rationale and in obtaining the decision-making power held by authorities. Nevertheless, and noting that Actor-Network Theory warns against homogenising wide and diverse groups, such views do represent a common enough pattern to characterise the expectations of each broad group of actors.

Refined down to their core, these expectations can be characterised as users wanting to hold the decision-making power and public authorities wanting to retain this power. Phrased in this way, the mismatch between the expectations of the different actors who engage with the right of access to environmental information is clear and is not directly related to any specifically environmental objectives. On a practical level, this creates tension between them, which will lead to frustrations and in extreme cases may lead users to abandon the right, which they see as failing to deliver what it has promised. Users are undoubtedly better off by virtue of the right than they would be without it, and for some the opportunity to have their say may be sufficient, but the fact that expectations built on the existence of the rights to information and participation are unfulfilled is not ideal.

Although the expectations of authorities and users may differ significantly, each can be seen as being linked to the Aarhus Convention. The Convention is specific in the procedures it requires of public authorities, but its rationale for promoting access to environmental information and participation in environmental decisions is ambiguous. The instrumental, normative and substantive rationales are all accepted as valid by the Convention. As a result, actors looking to the Convention can derive different valid expectations from the Convention, leading to mismatches and conflicts when it is considered that others are not implementing the Convention properly. This is also true of the Convention's wider empowerment aims, with the increased role envisioned for citizens capable of being viewed as leading to them becoming decision-makers alongside (or independent of) public authorities. Yet this is not reflected in the Convention itself, which only goes so far as to empower citizens to participate in environmental decision-making procedures and to encourage authorities to move beyond the minimum legal requirements.

Therefore, it appears that tensions between the different actors, whether they are users or public authorities, are not wholly due to the actions and views of these actors. The Aarhus Convention itself contributes to and validates mismatching expectations through its ambiguity over the underpinning rationales for the rights it guarantees and its implementation of these through procedures that are not restricted to those using them in line with any particular objective, nor even with any environmental purpose at all. In this way, while the Aarhus Convention has a positive effect through establishing the minimum legal requirements for guaranteeing the rights to access information and participate in decision-making processes in environmental matters, it also has a negative effect on how these rights are used in practice.

However, beyond this lies another finding, which has so far been only implicitly engaged with here. In analysing the right of access to environmental information, the overarching narrative has been based on a simple relationship between users and public authorities. The work here shows that there is a need to pay more heed to the individual humans involved, acting either as users driven by a range of motivations or as the means through which public authorities fulfil their obligations. The variety of the human actors involved shows the value of an approach drawing on Actor-Network Theory to understand the many different relationships involved. Yet there is a need to look beyond the assumption that the only actors who interact with each other under the right's actor-network are human. As demonstrated here, the Aarhus Convention itself exerts an influence over these human actors and can thus itself be defined as an actor. This is important not just for identifying the source of the tensions which can inhibit how the right is guaranteed and how environmental information is used; it also points to the need to identify other non-human actors which either exert an invisible influence over other actors or have been lost through the right's implementation in practice.

CHAPTER 6
NON-HUMAN ACTORS

The starting point for the creation of a right to environmental information is "the need to protect, preserve and improve the state of the environment and to ensure sustainable and environmentally sound development".[478] This need has become all the more pressing at a time of significant anthropogenic environmental change. However, the right of access to environmental information is framed in a way that primarily emphasises the concerns and needs of humanity.[479] While this anthropocentric framing influences the interpretation of the right's environmental aims, it also emphasises the role of human actors, particularly users of the right, in the operation of the right itself. Yet human actors are not the only actors that exert influence over how the right is guaranteed, implemented and utilised in practice; non-human actors influence how the right to environmental information is guaranteed. Notable examples of such actors include technology and the law, which influence the interactions between other actors, and the environment itself, an actor given limited attention both by the right itself and its implementing legal instruments. The role and impact of these actors remains unexplored, to the detriment both of how the right is implemented in practice and of how it seeks to achieve and understand its own environmental and participative aims. This chapter will discuss how to give better consideration to these actors and, in particular, will argue for the need to give more attention to the environment as an actor.

1. INTRODUCTION

Actor-Network Theory is concerned with the "the tracing of associations" between different actors in order to understand how they each engage

---

[478] Aarhus Convention, Preamble, para. 5.
[479] PETERSMANN, above n. 42, p. 247.

with and interact with each other within society.[480] It is these associations between the different actors which construct the "actor-network", a network which is built up through the connections made between different actors. Through the construction of the actor-network, Actor-Network Theory provides a useful perspective to analyse and understand the operation of various aspects of society, including the right of access to environmental information.

Part of the value of Actor-Network Theory is how it defines the term "actor" as "something which acts or to which activity is granted".[481] There are various aspects to this definition which lead to Actor-Network Theory providing a valuable framework for analysing the operation of the right in practice. One particular aspect of note is that Actor-Network Theory implicitly resists the categorisation of actors within general categories; instead, it places greater emphasis on the influence exerted by individual actors upon each other in constructing the actor-network. This allows the theory to not be "trapped" within patterns based on artificial categories of actors, but instead to identify and consider each unique actor on the basis of their influence that they exert within the actor-network. A second, and perhaps more important, aspect of how the theory defines actors is that whether or not an entity constitutes an actor is not dependent on whether it has human-like agency or capacity for intentionality. Through not limiting what entities can or cannot become an actor based on their capacity for agency, Actor-Network Theory allows for non-human entities to be considered as actors: actors with the capacity to influence how other actors engage with each other within the actor-network.

Combining these two aspects together under Actor-Network Theory is invaluable in broadening discussions of social and legal processes – to move beyond thinking about human actors and instead to consider how interactions between human and non-human actors together create the legal and social relationships that shape the right to environmental information and how it is implemented in practice. While this may initially sound quite abstract, the role of non-human actors in this area of law has grown to become intrinsically intermeshed with the operation of the right in practice. Technological changes, such as the increased use of computers, electronic files and the internet as a means of communication, have led to a radical shift in how people access information and engage with public authorities under the right. The law that governs the right

---

[480] LATOUR, above n. 58, p. 373.
[481] DOOLIN and LOWE, above n. 59, p. 72.

of access to environmental information, and the way in which the state has responded to this obligation also influence the way in which actors engage with each other under the right. Finally, the environment itself also acts to influence how, and indeed why, actors engage with each other through the right to environmental information. In this way, the initially abstract concept of "non-human actors" becomes more concrete, allowing discussions on the right to shift from the more visible human actors and to examine the real impact that non-human actors have on the right and its implementation.

Drawing on the evidence gathered through the surveys and interviews with users and public authorities, this chapter examines the significance of non-human actors and their impact on how the right is implemented and engaged with in practice. It first examines non-human actors which are largely or entirely constructed by humans, but go beyond any individuals. Examples of such actors include public authorities, the Aarhus Convention and the Environmental Information (Scotland) Regulations (EI(S)R), and technologies. The chapter then moves on to discussing a non-human actor which was not created by, but both was and is currently being influenced by humans – the environment itself.

Encapsulating both "natural" and "urban" environments,[482] the environment as an entity is overlooked in discussions on the right to environmental information and its implementation. This low profile risks the environmental ambitions of the right being set aside: reducing the right to little more than a minor variation of the wider general right to information. A core reason for this is that the environment itself is not viewed as an independent actor within the context of the right to environmental information – rather, it is viewed through the anthropocentric lens of the human actors which engage with each other under the right. Using Actor-Network Theory, it is possible to redress this imbalance and provide a better appreciation for the role of the environment in the right of access environmental information.

2. NON-HUMAN ACTORS CONSTRUCTED BY HUMANS

The first category of non-human actors to be considered in this chapter is the non-human actors that have been constructed by humans – for

---

[482] Woods, above n. 140.

example, the state and its emanations, the law itself and technologies. Such non-human actors are significant within the context of the right of access to environmental information because they exert substantial influence over how human actors, such as users and freedom of information officers, engage with and guarantee the right of access to environmental information.

It is valuable to highlight two key points in relation to these non-human actors and their relationship with the right to environmental information. First, it is important to understand that while these non-human actors independently exert influence within the right's actor-network, they are not wholly independent of human actors. Public authorities constitute the clearest example of this. While the right, embodied in the Aarhus Convention and the EI(S)R, conceptualises public authorities as entities in and of themselves, they only exert influence on the basis of individual humans employed within the authority making decisions on behalf of the authority. In this way, it is important to dissect the connections between human and non-human actors to understand their impact on the operation of the right.

Second, it is also important to emphasise that non-human actors are not immune to influence from human actors. Users tend to discuss public authorities as singular entities that are resistant to change, and both users and freedom of information officers spoke about the law, the regulators and technology in similar ways. Yet these non-human actors are not immune to change. Indeed, the humans that animate these non-human actors, such as those that maintain the relevant technologies, design the relevant legal regimes or work for the state, can take different decisions to alter how non-human actors interact and engage with the right of access to environmental information. Nevertheless, non-human actors have a considerable effect on the operation of the right, yet the extent of this impact and the influence exerted on other actors is not adequately considered in the existing work on this topic. By using Actor-Network Theory to highlight these non-human actors, it is possible to examine the extent of their impact and the nature of their relationship to other actors within the right's actor-network.

2.1. ORGANISATIONS

2.1.1. Public Authorities

In the context of the right of access to environmental information and the legal instruments that guarantee it, public authorities are viewed primarily as information holders – singular entities which are responsible

Chapter 6. Non-Human Actors

for proactively publishing environmental information and for disclosing environmental information on request. This can be evidenced in the obligations imposed on "public authorities" under the Aarhus Convention (and the EI(S)R):

> Each Party shall ensure that, subject to the following paragraphs of this article, public authorities, in response to a request for environmental information, make such information available to the public, within the framework of national legislation.[483]

In this, and other, obligations imposed on public authorities, the public authority is conceptualised as a monolithic entity - a singular body where there is no delay or conflict in receiving the information and preparing it for disclosure. There is also an implicit assumption that each public authority engages with the right in the same way, and that they are equally able to fulfil the obligations enshrined within legal instruments such as the Aarhus Convention and the EI(S)R. Such an approach is notable because while it makes sense from a theoretical perspective, it does not reflect the reality in which public authorities operate.[484]

An obvious yet often overlooked reason for this is that public authorities are not a singular entity, but instead are made up of multiple individuals working across different departments, each with a unique relationship with the right of access to environmental information. A general trend within the interviewed authorities was that they had a specific position or office which worked on processing requests for information, environmental or otherwise, as well as general data protection issues. Commonly referred to as the "FOI Officer", it is these individuals which constitute the frontline of how public authorities engage with the right to environmental information and the obligations which arise from it.

This structuring of the internal operations of the public authority gives rise to a few important points. First, by designating someone specifically to respond to requests for environmental information, it means that the remainder of the authority's staff does not need to engage with the right unless asked to provide environmental information by the FOI Officer for disclosure. Such requests by the Officer could lead to tensions arising between the Officer and the relevant member of staff asked to pass the

---

[483] Aarhus Convention, art. 4(1).
[484] Such a divergence also includes instances where public authorities are users of the right, as discussed in Chapter 3, section 2.5.

requested information over. Specifically, this exercise could be viewed by the other member of staff as a burden or a non-priority:

> I think that the impact [of receiving an EI(S)R request] would be … it would be … essentially, it would be treated by the department virtually the same as an FOI request and they would go oh, God, got another one of these to do, sort of thing, you know.[485]

These tensions are significant because the different prioritisation granted to environmental information issues by different actors within an authority can impact on how users experience and engage with their right to environmental information. Some of the delays involved in getting things done between different departments meant that, from the point of view of some members of the public, the public authority as an actor might be slow, frustrating and obstructive to deal with, even if they found, for example, the FOI Officer as an individual more helpful and responsive. This is particularly true in the context of requests for environmental information, where the staff who process such requests often work within their own department, but have to obtain a response from other separate departments that deal with the substantive matters, but where staff members rarely encounter such requests.

The distinction between different actors within public authorities does not merely impact the right to have environmental information disclosed on request; it also has an impact on the right to have environmental information proactively disclosed. Specifically, it is notable that the staff members who are aware of the specific obligations in relation to proactive disclosure, the FOI Officers, are often not the staff members who are proactively disclosing the relevant environmental information. Rather, it is the other staff members of the public authority, who are less engaged with the right to environmental information, who take the lead in disseminating this information:

> [W]hilst we take the lead on maintaining the publication scheme, it is for … the responsibility to publish lies with the departments or teams that are responsible for the particular piece of information. So, we support as a process, but the publication scheme links towards those other teams' websites, where the information is published, if that makes sense.[486]

---

[485] Interview with Public Authority No. 8.
[486] Interview with Public Authority No. 9.

Chapter 6. Non-Human Actors

This has a practical impact on how environmental information is proactively disclosed, in that the disclosure is guided not by the principles underpinning the right to environmental information, but by the norms relating to the environmental information – norms which can differ depending on the topic that the environmental information relates to. To quote one of the interviewed public authorities:

> [W]e have a centralised access to information team and have had since day one, so it's always been centralised ... It meant we could build the expertise in one place. We have looked and had looked at what needed to be done, similar to what the Scottish Government used to do which is having everybody do their own thing. And what we have here, we have a lot of people who regulate. We have scientists who see data in a very pure data terms. Regulators whose whole job is to regulate.[487]

In this way, there is a clear distinction drawn between those who work in guaranteeing the right to environmental information and those who do not. While this is beyond the scope of this book, further unpicking of how these differences manifest in terms of how the right is guaranteed, and thus unpicking of the perceptions and working practices across all parts of public authorities is required in order to get a fuller sense of experience of and attitudes towards the right to access environmental information.[488]

What is most notable about the differentiation of different actors within the authority is that different users will perceive the authority in different ways. Some users, primarily professional users, drew a distinction between individuals in an information-holding public authority and the authority itself:

> It's easy to see the organisation as an anonymous large organisation, and a bit of a faceless thing. And then once you have, once you get to know people and, you know, and specific contacts and phone numbers and emails ... it becomes a lot more ... a lot more, you feel like you ... like you're being listened to and heard. But also understand that these individuals are working ... for a massive Council ... that isn't the best coordinated and their internal communication leaves quite a lot to be desired.[489]

---

[487] Interview with Public Authority No. 15.
[488] Hazell et al. offer interesting data and analysis about the impact of the Freedom of Information Act on the civil service in the UK's central government; HAZELL et al., above n. 5, chaps 6 and 9.
[489] Interview with User No. 12.

This differed from personal users, who would swap between discussing the authority as a monolithic entity and identifying specific individuals working within the authority:

> [T]hey had just stuck to their guns basically. It was, it was always the letter would come from [anonymised] who's the man in charge.[490]

A common element shared between both categories of users is that while they can identify (and perhaps sympathise with) the individuals who work within public authorities, they see the authority itself as having an agency. Viewed through Actor-Network Theory, this perception makes sense: while an authority may not hold human-like intentionality, the values that it represents and its management goals do influence the way in which the staff that work within it operate. It can also explain the mismatch that occurs between how users and public authorities perceive their interactions under the right to environmental information. While the individual staff members discuss processing requests for individual users, the same users may perceive themselves as engaging with an actor larger than the individual FOI Officer: a public authority which is not necessarily aligned with the goals of the right to environmental information or the (potentially separate) goals of the user. Through unpicking these interactions via Actor-Network Theory, the negative perceptions of users and their engagement with the right, despite the high rate of disclosure by public authorities, can make more sense.

2.1.2. Regulators of the Right to Environmental Information

Actor-Network Theory can also help to dissect the bodies which are tasked with regulating and enforcing the right of access to environmental information, as well as their influence within the right's actor-network. In Scotland, there are various actors which merit further discussion: the Scottish Information Commissioner, the judiciary and the Aarhus Convention Compliance Committee (ACCC).

The position of the Scottish Information Commissioner was established by the Freedom of Information (Scotland) Act 2002.[491] In the context of the right to environmental information, the Commissioner is tasked with

---

[490] Interview with User No. 6.
[491] Freedom of Information (Scotland) Act 2002, Part 3.

Chapter 6. Non-Human Actors

ensuring that public authorities comply with their obligations under the EI(S)R and hearing challenges regarding decisions taken under the EI(S)R.[492] The Commissioner is supported by the Office of the Scottish Information Commissioner (OSIC); a "small team" of staff members that support the Commissioner in exercising their functions.[493] In the same way as public authorities are seen as acting as unitary and distinct bodies, there is a tendency to discuss the Scottish Information Commissioner or the OSIC as singular actors that operate by themselves. Yet not only are they interlinked, but the OSIC itself is a body which is made up of various different members of staff. While this is less impactful than the distinction between different member of staff within public authorities, as all OSIC staff members are unified by a shared goal of guaranteeing information rights, differences in opinion regarding interpretations of the EI(S)R can still lead to divergences in terms of how the powers held by the OSIC and the Scottish Information Commissioner are exercised.

In undertaking their responsibilities under the EI(S)R, both the Scottish Information Commissioner and the OSIC exert significant influence over how users and public authorities engage with the right. For users of the right, the Scottish Information Commissioner and the OSIC are viewed as the primary method of appealing a decision made by a public authority, in line with their role established in the EI(S)R:

> [A]nd if she [the FOI Officer employed by the public authority] didn't answer properly I would refer her to the Information Commissioner.[494]

For public authorities, the role of the Scottish Information Commissioner and the OSIC was more nuanced. In view of its role as a regulator, some public authorities felt that they did not hold power under the EI(S)R because requests were:

> [A]n adjudicated process because obviously the Scottish Information Commissioner's in the background.[495]

In this context, the Scottish Information Commissioner was perceived as a potentially opposing force, providing oversight over the way in which

---

[492] EI(S)R, regs 17–18.
[493] Scottish Information Commissioner, "About the Scottish Information Commissioner" <https://www.itspublicknowledge.info/home/AboutSIC/AboutCommissioner.aspx> accessed 21 April 2022.
[494] Interview with User No. 1.
[495] Interview with Public Authority No. 2.

Intersentia 177

public authorities guaranteed the right to environmental information and (potentially) issuing decision notices to alter the decision taken by these authorities. Yet the Scottish Information Commissioner was also viewed as a positive force for navigating the complex relationships between different departments within the authority itself. One public authority interviewee discussed how the Commissioner's letter to the authority's chief executive gave impetus to the authority to speed up the handling of requests, and this was also linked in with training offered by the Office.[496]

The Scottish Information Commissioner and the OSIC thus exert agency in a variety of ways. Through providing guidance and hearing complaints submitted by users, they both support and challenge how public authorities guarantee the right to environmental information, acting to influence and shape the behaviour of public authorities and the members of staff who work within them. Both actors seek to steer practice in a way that helps to secure the goals behind the right of access to environmental information – environmental goals which both actors consider to be separate from (though closely related to) the general transparency aims of the general right to information:

> This was because as I say there were two different drivers for the two different pieces of legislation and because of the international agreements which had been entered into, or in the case of the directive issued, it was necessary to ensure that the better relationship to environmental legislation complied fully with all of those boxes.[497]

The second regulator that can be discussed as an actor is the judiciary, which acts as a route of appeal from the Scottish Information Commissioner.[498] Initially, the judiciary may seem to be an actor with the potential to exert substantial influence over how the right of access to environmental information is guaranteed. Yet, in practice, this influence appears to be limited. Despite recourse to the Court of Session being the next appeal procedure available to users from the Scottish Information Commissioner, users did not really highlight the court's role within the EI(S)R regime at all. This low profile suggests that although the Scottish judiciary do act as the more "senior" and authoritative enforcement mechanism available to users under the EI(S)R, this level of authority does not make up for

---

[496] Interview with Public Authority No. 1.
[497] Interview with the Office of the Scottish Information Commissioner.
[498] Freedom of Information (Scotland) Act 2002, s.56.

Chapter 6. Non-Human Actors

the difficulties of making use of this possibility. Cases can reach the court only where there is a legal issue involved and only after both the internal review procedures and the right of appeal to the Scottish Information Commissioner have been used without a satisfactory result.[499] Moreover, legal action is notoriously expensive[500] and stressful, and with very few cases on access to information (environmental or more general) reaching the courts, there is no publicity to draw attention to their role. The Scottish Information Commissioner is therefore the primary place that users look to when seeking to enforce their right to environmental information, with the Court of Session acting as an actor of limited influence, despite its formal power.

Similarly, public authorities also did not really mention the judiciary in the context of the right to environmental information. Where the judiciary was mentioned, it was done in two ways. The first of these is that court actions provide a motivation for users to seek out environmental information – in essence, using the right as a way of gathering information to present their case:

> [I]f they're having a dispute. And so to support their case they're looking for information from us, that they're going to use. Whether it's in a court case or whether it's just to take it to [anonymised], and say, "Look, I do own this share".[501]

The second way is in relation to the courts acting to enforce the law, although this was rarely discussed and when it was, it was framed as a way for the authority to challenge a decision of the Scottish Information Commissioner:

> Now, we were going to go to the Court of Session to challenge the decision of the Commissioner on a number of points of law.[502]

The Scottish Information Commissioner and the OSIC were also aware of the judiciary, specifically the Court of Session, acting as an appeal

---

[499] See Chapter 2, section 3.5.
[500] This has been the subject of negative findings by the Aarhus Convention Compliance Committee; B. CHRISTMAN, "Aarhus Convention Compliance Committee: 2020 Findings about Protective Expenses Orders in Scotland" (2020) 198 *Scottish Planning and Environmental Law* 33.
[501] Interview with Public Authority No. 11.
[502] Interview with Public Authority No. 3.

mechanism against decisions that they made.[503] In this way, the Court of Session does become an actor that exerts greater influence over public authorities and the Scottish Information Commissioner than over users. In terms of the traditional hierarchical lens of ordering actors based on significance, this fits with actors focusing on the levels immediately above them rather than considering the full hierarchy, elements of which are likely to be remote from their own experiences.

The last actor to discuss in the context of regulating and enforcing the right of access to environmental information is the Aarhus Convention Compliance Committee (ACCC). The ACCC is an international body which oversees compliance with the Convention, both by monitoring the general level of implementation by parties and considering specific applications by individuals or groups that their rights under the Convention have been breached.[504] Established under the remit of the Aarhus Convention, the ACCC acts as a regulator which is fully cognisant of the right's environmental aims and which does not need to consider any parallel general right to information.

Given its relevance to Scotland,[505] it might be expected that the ACCC is a significant actor within the context of the right to environmental information in Scotland. However, in practice, this is broadly not borne out. Neither users of the right nor public authorities tasked with guaranteeing the right under the EI(S)R mentioned the ACCC when discussing the right, suggesting that the ACCC is of little relevance in the day-to-day use of the right.

What this suggests is that the ACCC is of limited direct relevance to actors that are engaging with the right to environmental information in Scotland. Yet such a finding does not consider the indirect impact that the ACCC can have. For example, the Scottish Information Commissioner often references the Aarhus Convention Implementation Guide in its decisions – a guide designed to assist public authorities and policymakers in implementing the Convention[506] and which heavily cites and references decisions of the ACCC. Further still, the Scottish Government has implemented revised laws in light of the decisions of the ACCC – the most

---

[503] Interview with the Office of the Scottish Information Commissioner.
[504] Aarhus Convention, art. 15.
[505] The ACCC has heard cases from Scotland in relation to access to information; e.g. *Aarhus Convention Compliance Committee Communication 2010/53* (United Kingdom) ECE/MP.PP/C.1/2013/3, 28 September 2012 and *Aarhus Convention Compliance Committee Communication 2012/68* (European Union and the United Kingdom) ECE/MP.PP/C.1/2014/5, 24 September 2013.
[506] EBBESSON et al., above n. 119, p. 9.

Chapter 6. Non-Human Actors

direct influences of these reforms being the revisions made to the Court of Session rules on protective expenses orders[507] following the finding by the ACCC that the costs of bringing a case to court was prohibitively expensive.[508]

Ultimately, despite a lack of explicit recognition, the ACCC does have a substantial impact on how actors engage with the right to environmental information in Scotland. This lack of recognition is reflective of a broader lack of awareness of how bodies such as public authorities and those regulating them engage with the right and affect other actors. This is significant since how actors, in particular users, engage with the right, and also how they experience the right when seeking to access environmental information, are influenced by these bodies. A similar lack of understanding can also be identified in terms of how the law itself serves to shape how actors engage with and experience the right to environmental information.

2.2. LAW

Labelling the law as an under-recognised actor within the context of the right to environmental information may initially appear to be an unusual approach in light of the legal writing[509] on the Aarhus Convention[510] and its domestic implementation in the UK.[511] Both the Aarhus Convention

---

[507] Court of Session Rules, Chapter 58A – Protective Expenses Orders in Environmental Appeals and Judicial Reviews.
[508] Aarhus Convention Meeting of the Parties, "Decision VI/8k, Compliance by United Kingdom with its obligations under the Convention" (ECE/MP.PP/2017/2/Add.1). For more on this, see B. CHRISTMAN, "New Rules, Old Problems: The 2018 Protective Expenses Order Regime and the Aarhus Convention" (2019) 195 *Scottish Planning and Environmental Law* 106.
[509] Beyond the more practical works such as C. BANNER (ed.), *The Aarhus Convention: A Guide for UK Lawyers*, Hart Publishing, Oxford 2015; DUNION, above n. 138.
[510] E.g. L. KRÄMER, "Citizens' Rights and Administration Duties in Environmental Matters: 20 Years of the Aarhus Convention" (2018) 9(1) *Revista Catalana De Dret Ambienta* 1; U. ETEMIRE, "Insight on the UNEP Bali Guidelines and the Development of Environmental Democratic Rights" (2016) 28(3) *Journal of Environmental Law* 393 and M. PALLEMAERTS (ed), *The Aarhus Convention at Ten: Interactions and Tension Between Conventional International Law and EU Environmental Law*, Europa Law Publishing, Amsterdam 2011.
[511] E.g. K. DUNION, *Troublemakers: The Struggle for Environmental Justice in Scotland*, Edinburgh University Press, Edinburgh 2003; P. COPPEL, *Information Rights*, 5th ed, Hart Publishing, Oxford 2020, vol. I part III and E. FISHER, "Exploring the Legal Architecture of Transparency" in P. ALA'I and R. VAUGHN, *Research Handbook on Transparency*, Edward Elgar, Cheltenham 2014, pp. 63–73.

and its domestic instruments are commonly referred to when the topic of environmental information is discussed, even where the focus of these discussions is on emphasising the importance of other actors such as the environment.[512] Such discussions often relate to the requirements set out by these specific laws, and the sanctions that can follow if they are not complied with.

This perspective is reflected in both how users and public authorities view the role of "the law" in ensuring that the right of access to environmental information is guaranteed:

> Well, the law exists … as I say it's not my problem if the council have to employ one, two, three people to [fulfil their legal obligations].[513]

> The law allows for information to be released. Equally it allows for information to be withheld.[514]

> But [the] public authority has to … has to comply with the law, and I know that this [authority] does its very best to comply with the legislation, and to support applicants, and … with their rights, as we should.[515]

In this way, the desire (or, indeed, the necessity) to comply with the law was the primary way in which the law was viewed as exercising influence over actors that engaged with the right to environmental information. This is particularly notable because the law has taken on an agency that is independent of the human actors which drafted and implemented the Aarhus Convention and the EI(S)R – it has become an actor that has taken on a kind of agency that may outlive, or exist apart from, those humans who were involved in its development.

However, there is a benefit in examining the role and nature of the law as an actor independent of its ability to guide (or coerce) the behaviour of public authorities, and instead seeing the law as an actor in the broader sense of the word. The law here does not simply forbid, allow or mandate particular things, but also acts to help constitute the broader social reality in which the right operates. For example, despite users and public authorities making references to "the law" as an actor, in reality their interactions with the law were often experienced through the actions of a relevant body, either a public authority or the Scottish Information Commissioner

---

[512] PETERSMANN, above n. 42, p. 247.
[513] Interview with User No. 3.
[514] Interview with Public Authority No. 3.
[515] Ibid.

and the OSIC. This is relevant because the Aarhus Convention and the EI(S)R contain provisions which allow for a degree of discretion in the implementation of their legal requirements. Such discretion allows users, public authorities and the Scottish Information Commissioner some flexibility in interpreting what the law "requires", in turn granting greater agency in terms of how they engage with the right to environmental information and other actors under the right.

Another connected way in which the law exerts influence beyond its coercive abilities or any likelihood of enforcement is in how it establishes the expectations regarding the disclosure of environmental information. Both the Aarhus Convention and the EI(S)R establish that the "default" position of public authorities is that they should disclose environmental information – a position further emphasised by the limitations placed on the ability of authorities to withhold environmental information upon receiving a request for disclosure.[516] Yet emphasising only these two instruments, which contain a specific conceptualisation of the right, implies that "the law" is a singular actor. This is not the case in practice, where various legal instruments impact on how the different actors interact in the context of the right to environmental information.

Before continuing on this point, it is important to emphasise that while the Aarhus Convention and the EI(S)R can be considered in tandem, they operate as separate actors when guaranteeing the right of access to environmental information. For example, despite the right to access environmental information originating from the Aarhus Convention, many users are unaware of the Convention or its environmental aims. This is significant in terms of how users understand and engage with the right of access to environmental information, and feeds into subsequent discussions on the role of the environment as an actor.

For actors with a greater awareness of the law, such as public authorities and the Scottish Information Commissioner, the law encapsulates not just the Aarhus Convention and the EI(S)R, but also other instruments that relate, directly or indirectly, to environmental information:

> [W]e're required to either make information publicly available and, or there's a requirement to exercise information rights on individuals. So that covers Freedom of Information (Scotland) Act, Environmental Information (Scotland) Regulations, ... the Data Protection Act, the General Data Protection Regulations as well.[517]

---

[516] Aarhus Convention, art. 4(4); EI(S)R, reg. 10.
[517] Interview with Public Authority No. 3.

Other laws, such as the Water Framework Directive[518] and the Contaminated Land (Scotland) Regulations 2000, are also relevant here[519] in that they also shape how information is gathered, held and disseminated. A clear example of this is the establishment of the contaminated land register:[520] the law here not only imposes a legal obligation that public authorities must follow, but it also creates a source of information independent from, and more specific than, the obligations contained in the right to environmental information. Consequently, the influence that "the law" exerts over the right is not singular and uniform; it can be sourced from different legal instruments and can result from different laws interacting with each other.

In detailing how "the law" is not a singular entity, it is imperative that the Freedom of Information (Scotland) Act 2002 (FOI(S)A) and the general right to information are discussed. Like the EI(S)R, FOI(S)A establishes a regime that guarantees the right to information held by public authorities, but more broadly. In the context of the right of access to environmental information, FOI(S)A's only legal relevance is that public authorities cannot respond to requests for environmental information under FOI(S)A, but must do so under the EI(S)R.[521] Yet, despite this division between the two regimes, for many users of the right, there is no distinction to be drawn. For these users, these separate information rights and regimes run into each other:

> [T]o be honest I don't fully understand the difference between the Freedom of Information and [the Environmental Information Regulations].[522]

To an extent this is understandable, as both regimes do share a range of procedural similarities. Yet this misunderstanding is important, both from a practical perspective and for the environmental aims of the right to environmental information. From a practical perspective, while the two regimes are similar, they are not identical; one obvious example of this is the price cap (or lack thereof) imposed on charges for responding to

---

[518] Directive 2000/60/EC of the European Parliament and of the Council of 23 October 2000 establishing a framework for Community action in the field of water policy [2000] OJ L327/1.
[519] Interview with Public Authority No. 14.
[520] Environmental Protection Act 1990, s. 78R; Contaminated Land (Scotland) Regulations 2000 SSI 2000/178, reg. 14.
[521] Freedom of Information (Scotland) Act 2002, ss 39 and 62.
[522] Interview with User No. 3.

requests for information under both regimes.[523] A possible result of this intermingling of the two rights by actors using the right is that they may misunderstand their legal rights under each regime, potentially leading to tensions where their expectations are broken.

From the perspective of the environmental goals that underpin the right to access environmental information, this intermingling of the two regimes is problematic. A key assumption of the right to environmental information is that those using the right are doing so in order to fulfil their moral duty to "protect and enhance the environment".[524] In contrast, the general right to information under FOI(S)A does not contain this environmental motive, nor does it attribute a particular motive to users who are seeking information under FOI(S)A. The merging of the two rights from a user perspective is significant, because as FOI(S)A is the more well-known instrument, the environmental aspects of the right to environmental information are significantly diluted. The distinctive environmental goals are obscured by the focus on transparency and accountability that lie behind the wider right, reducing the prompt for users to pursue the environmental motives attributed to them by the right.[525] This suggests that the relationship between the two sets of law has a degree of influence over the perceptions of users in a way that is not currently accounted for in examining how the right is implemented in practice.

What this perspective suggests is that there is a need to move beyond a straightforwardly hierarchical view where the law sits above other actors, prescribing clear ways of acting. Instead, the law, in its various emanations, exerts influence within the right's actor-network in a variety of ways. The law acts to inform, guide and coerce behaviours, but it exerts influence only through the human actors that are interpreting and enforcing the law – most commonly information officers within public authorities and regulators such as the Office of the Scottish Information Commissioner, but also members of the public seeking to exercise their right to environmental information. In this way, the law is not just a multi-faceted actor in terms of what laws affect actors seeking out and disclosing environmental information. It is also multi-faceted in how it exerts this influence through human actors, reflecting a depth and complexity with regard to how the right is guaranteed and conceptualised.

---

[523] See the Freedom of Information and Data Protection (Appropriate Limit and Fees) Regulations 2004 (2004/3244), reg. 3, which sets an upper limit of £600 for central authorities and £450 for other authorities, and EI(S)R, reg. 8, which does not set an upper limit of fees.
[524] See Chapter 2, section 2.
[525] See generally Chapter 4.

2.3. TECHNOLOGIES

The final non-human actor to be discussed in this section is the technologies and the technological platforms that are significant here. Viewed through Actor-Network Theory, technologies such as email both act as a conduit for the human actors to engage with each other and operate as independent actors in and of themselves. This is further emphasised by the uptake of technology and the greater availability of information, both in terms of how workplaces, such as public authorities, operate[526] and in society more generally.[527] In the specific context of the right to access environmental information, the influence that technologies exert can be seen in how information is recorded and how they act as a communication channel for different human actors.

At the core of the right of access to environmental information is the information itself. Whether proactively disclosed or disclosed upon request, the information has to be created and stored in some form before being subject to the right to access environmental information. It is in this creation and storage process that developments in information technology exert substantial influence. Information and data that used to take a lot of time and effort to sort, arrange and present can be combined and compiled quickly and (setting aside the benefits of providing metadata and further contextual information) the product is in a form where instant online distribution is an option.[528] Public authorities are well aware of this, utilising a wide range of different online dissemination methods to reach the greatest proportion of the general public:

> People will sign up to our page, Twitter account because they're interested in what's going on. If we're promoting events and things, then hopefully they will use that to then go along to the event ... some of the information that we post online, for example we have a whole area of the website devoted to landscape data.[529]

---

[526] See generally K. BYSTRÖM, J. HEINSTRÖM and I. RUTHVEN, *Information at Work: Information Management in the Workplace*, Facet Publishing, London 2019.

[527] L. SHCHERBAKOVA et al., "Features of Information Technologies Influence on Social Development" (2018) 198 *Advances in Social Science, Education and Humanities Research* 70.

[528] Nevertheless, the way in which data is organised for its primary use may not make it convenient for presentation in response to a specific request.

[529] Interview with Public Authority No. 6.

Chapter 6. Non-Human Actors

The shift to using technology to store and disseminate environmental information reflects an improvement in terms of how the right to have environmental information proactively disclosed is implemented. The active right to environmental information is characterised by the aim of accessibility: that environmental information can be accessed at any time without having to submit a request.[530] Through significantly reducing barriers to access, technology, as a non-human actor, exerts a positive influence on how human actors engage with the right and secures some of the right's intended aims.

This increased ease of accessing information electronically has normalised seeking information online, to the extent that being asked to visit a paper register would be seen as a jarring, strange or obstructive request in a way that was not previously the case.[531] Yet the role of technology is not wholly reflected in instruments such as the Aarhus Convention. While the role of technology is accepted as key within the Convention,[532] it only obliges states to make environmental information "progressively available" through electronic databases[533] – an obligation which appears antiquated in light of the expectations of contemporary users that information will be made available online. In this way, technology as an actor has far exceeded the expected rate of progress seen within the Convention and its domestic implementations.

Yet even describing technology as exceeding the expectations of the Aarhus Convention may undersell its impact. Technology, and in particular email technology, has fundamentally influenced the interpretation and use of the right to environmental information. The almost universal shift towards using emails as a method of communication has changed how users interact with public authorities, with some approaches (for example, speaking face to face with a public authority staff member for advice) being less common. This shift towards email communication has an impact on how human actors, specifically users and public authorities, communicate with each other, with studies evidencing a greater use of "hard" negotiating tactics[534] and a lesser

---

[530] EBBESSON et al., above n. 119, p. 95.
[531] Contrast the early experience shown in studies such as T. BURTON, "Access to Environmental Information: The UK Experience of Water Registers" (1989) 1 *Journal of Environmental Law* 192; E. JOHN, "Access to Environmental Information: Limitations of the UK Radioactive Substances Registers" (1995) 7 *Journal of Environmental Law* 11.
[532] Aarhus Convention, Preamble, para. 15.
[533] Ibid., art. 5(3).
[534] A. GALIN, M. GROSS and G. GOSALKER, "E-Negotiation versus Face-to-Face Negotiation: What Has Changed – If Anything?" (2007) 23(1) *Computers in Human Behaviour* 787.

development of rapport between the actors.[535] Such a perspective is reflected in the views of public authorities, with one interviewee noting that there was a "lot of nervousness" about emails within and between authorities, alongside concerns about the ease of which email communication can be shared:

> [T]here [is] a legitimate reason why certain things should be kept private, confidential. If so, people should be told what will be private and confidential.[536]

In this way, email goes beyond being a simple tool or platform for communication, and comes to influence what is shared and what the shared information can do. Emails act to shape how those communicating via email perceive the motives of others and interpret the messages themselves. The medium of communication itself alters how human actors perceive each other, which in turn influences how they interact when engaging in the context of the right of access to environmental information. This further emphasises the invisible role that technology plays in terms of how the right to environmental information is guaranteed, but it does not set out the outer limits of how technology exerts influence as an actor within the context of the right.

Another significant way in which technology has shaped interactions under the right of access to environmental information is through facilitating the creation and operation of the WhatDoTheyKnow website.[537] WhatDoTheyKnow is a website through which individuals can submit requests for the disclosure of information from public authorities. The site then tracks any responses (or lack of response) by the authority, making it easier to follow up on any requests for environmental information made through the website. A key feature of the website is that the requests submitted by users, and the responses to those requests, are publicly available for anyone to read and comment on – a service which is possible due to the use of emails rather than paper-based mail as a communication method.

The significance of WhatDoTheyKnow as an actor can be evidenced in terms of how it exerts influence over how users of the right interpret,

---

[535] J. PARLAMIS, "Face-to-Face and Email Negotiations: A Comparison of Emotions, Perceptions and Outcomes" (2010) *Organization, Leadership, and Communications*, Paper 5.
[536] Interview with Public Authority No. 14.
[537] <https://www.whatdotheyknow.com> accessed 21 April 2022.

Chapter 6. Non-Human Actors

conceptualise and engage with the right of access to environmental information itself. The site simplifies the submission of requests in various ways: users can search for the authority they want to send a request to and send it to the relevant member of staff, rather than having to negotiate the process of finding the right person to contact; the site keeps track of and updates users on any response (or lack of timely response) from the authority rather than the user themselves having to organise communication and follow-ups.

WhatDoTheyKnow also provides templates for some of the messages that users might want to send to authorities and helps to set some norms of good practice – for example, not sending "ALL CAPS" emails to authorities. These norms are enforced through various informal and formal means, with the final method of enforcement being the potential suspension of accounts that break their "house rules".[538] Through setting templates for what makes a "good" request for information, the site helps to shape norms for how a request might be phrased or structured. WhatDoTheyKnow's process for guiding people through options to follow up or appeal responses also helps to set norms for how users chase up requests (and to encourage them to do so).

The normative impact of this has some clear positive effects – providing well-written templates for non-experts to use is likely to improve the quality of requests sent and answers received, improving the process of requesting environmental information for both users and public authorities. However, some of the ways in which the platform shapes and frames requests can be more problematic. Particularly relevant to this text is the way that WhatDoTheyKnow links requests for environmental information with Freedom of Information Act requests and (in common with much discussion on access to information) emphasises freedom of information broadly speaking over the specific right of access to environmental information. As a consequence of this focus, WhatDoTheyKnow acts to further reinforce the dominance of the general right to information in the perception of the general public.

This continued dominance of the general right to information can be evidenced by the views of some users who sought access to environmental information through WhatDoTheyKnow. These users were under the impression that they were submitting freedom of information requests,

---

[538] WhatDoTheyKnow, "House Rules" <https://www.whatdotheyknow.com/help/house_rules> accessed 21 April 2022.

unaware of the separate right to environmental information guaranteed under the environmental information legislation:

> I already had a freedom of information account.[539]

This impression continued to persist even after the user received environmental information that was expressed by the authority to be disclosed under the EI(S)R. As a result, WhatDoTheyKnow appears to shape how users engage with and consider the right of access to environmental information in a way that diminishes its distinctiveness and environmental aims.

In saying this, it is important to note that it may not be the case just that WhatDoTheyKnow exerts a unidirectional influence on users of the right, shaping their conceptualisation of the right to exclude the distinctive right to environmental information. The design of the WhatDoTheyKnow website has been influenced by the views of users and public authorities, who often do not identify the specifically environmental dimension to the rights conferred under the EI(S)R and their equivalents elsewhere in the UK. Nevertheless, the fact that WhatDoTheyKnow contributes to the erasure of the right to environmental information is important because it has the potential to become the primary way in which users consciously engage with their environmental information rights. For many interviewed users who had used WhatDoTheyKnow, they considered the site to be the default way to engage with their right to environmental information:[540]

> I might not have made ... these requests if I had not come across this site, because they make it so easy ... and they ... they extended my knowledge about ... you know, who is obliged to reply ... and under what circumstances and so on and so forth.[541]

> There's an easy alternative in WhatDoTheyKnow. If it didn't exist, or it didn't work very well then I probably would go down the other route.[542]

This route was often perceived as the standard approach even where other options might seem to serve users' interests better. For example,

---

[539] Interview with User No. 2, who is referring to the account they have with WhatDoTheyKnow from which they submitted a request for data on river pollution.
[540] As noted previously, such users may also be taking advantage of information that has been proactively disseminated, but this is not perceived as a manifestation of the right to access information.
[541] Interview with User No. 1.
[542] Interview with User No. 3.

it was striking to note that WhatDoTheyKnow was used for some requests for environmental information with what appeared to be the goal of private commercial benefit. In the context of these requests, putting the information in the public domain, as happens automatically with requests on WhatDoTheyKnow's free service, was likely to be against the commercial interests of the requester due to the risk of competitors also benefitting from the information. However, as the public availability of requests is the default option on the WhatDoTheyKnow site, users default to making their requests public, despite the risks to their goals.[543] In this way, WhatDoTheyKnow's role goes beyond being "just" a well-designed platform; instead, it acts to shape the type of requests made and to set the context for many members of the public making requests.

Ultimately, the role of technology within the context of the right of access to environmental information is multi-faceted. It influences how human actors interact with each other, it shapes how information is created, stored and provided to the public, and it also shapes how the right itself is viewed and conceptualised within society. In turn, the shapes that technologies take and the purposes they are used for are designed through the lens of what human actors, such as users and those working in public authorities, desire. Viewed in this way, technologies are a critical actor within the right's actor-network, both exerting influence over and being influenced by other actors within the network. Yet the role of technologies is often overlooked, despite their significance and impact on how the right of access to environmental information is guaranteed. By explicitly recognising technologies as actors through Actor-Network Theory, and analysing how they sit alongside other actors, it is possible to better understand the right and its implementation.

3. THE ENVIRONMENT

The second category of non-human actors is those that have not been created by humans. Such actors do not have to remain independent from humanity to be placed within this category; indeed, even the "natural" environment in Scotland has been extensively influenced by humans. Rather, the only criterion for this category is that such actors must not have

---

[543] It should be noted that there is a "Pro" version of the site, which does allow users to make requests private for a set period of time: WhatDoTheyKnow, "Pricing" <https://www.whatdotheyknow.com/pro/pricing> accessed 21 April 2022.

been created by or originated from humanity. In the context of the right of access to environmental information, the key actor which belongs to this category of actors is the environment itself.

The environment is fundamental to the right of access to environmental information. It is the subject that the disclosed information is about, it provides the basis for the (presumed) motives of those seeking to use the right and it lies at the heart of the right's environmental aims. In this way, the environment provides the focal point around which the right of access to environmental information is built. However, notwithstanding the significance of the environment, the extent to which the environment is recognised as an actor may not be as clear as is implied by its importance.

This is partly due to how "the environment" is defined in relation to humanity. Anthropocentrism is a perspective which has been heavily critiqued as ethically problematic.[544] Through adopting this perspective, the agency of the environment as an actor is diminished in order to emphasise the agency of human and human-created actors. Such a view does more than alter how the environment itself is defined. The dual role of the environment here, exerting pervasive influence as an actor but also having its role as a distinct actor minimised, also shapes the efforts of humanity to protect the environment – efforts that include creating and exercising the right of access to environmental information, and the legal regimes designed to implement and guarantee the right.

3.1. THE ENVIRONMENT AS AN ACTOR

"The environment", particularly in a UK context, is often seen as referring particularly to rural areas – to "socially constructed ideas of landscape and nature as expressions of the rural idyll" which can be "prioritized over economic and global environmental arguments".[545] Such an approach seeks to contrast "the environment" with urban settings such as cities, and the associated environmental risks of such a setting, including pollution.[546]

---

[544] PETERSMANN, above n. 42; H. KOPNINA, H. WASHINGTON, B. TAYLOR and J. PICCOLO, "Anthropocentrism: More Than Just a Misunderstood Problem" (2018) 31 *Journal of Agricultural and Environmental Ethics* 109; S. ADELMAN, "The Sustainable Development Goals Anthropocentrism and Neoliberalism" in D. FRENCH and L. KOTZÉ (eds), *Sustainable Development Goals: Law Theory and Implementation*, Edward Elgar, Cheltenham 2018.
[545] WOODS, above n. 140.
[546] BELL, above n. 140, pp. 150–151.

Chapter 6. Non-Human Actors

Yet in practice this divide is not sustainable. Rural settings are influenced and often shaped by human actions through everything from agriculture to housing to pollution, and have the associated needs for governance and regulation from public authorities. Emphasising "natural" landscapes as the embodiment of the environment does not adequately consider how alterations made by humanity are part of the environment or how humans are ourselves part of the Earth's environment. The concept of the environment should incorporate not just the types of landscapes and spaces that are conventionally seen as "the natural environment", but also urban and industrial environments.

To the credit of the right of access to environmental information, this is reflected in how "environmental information" is defined. The Aarhus Convention defines "environmental information" as follows:

"Environmental information" means any information in written, visual, aural, electronic or any other material form on:

(a) The state of elements of the environment, such as air and atmosphere, water, soil, land, landscape and natural sites, biological diversity and its components, including genetically modified organisms, and the interaction among these elements;

(b) Factors, such as substances, energy, noise and radiation, and activities or measures, including administrative measures, environmental agreements, policies, legislation, plans and programmes, affecting or likely to affect the elements of the environment within the scope of subparagraph (a) above, and cost-benefit and other economic analyses and assumptions used in environmental decision-making;

(c) The state of human health and safety, conditions of human life, cultural sites and built structures, inasmuch as they are or may be affected by the state of the elements of the environment.[547]

This broad definition and the similar definition provided in the EI(S)R[548] clearly go well beyond the idea of the environment as rural. Such a shift is required, as many issues which act as the driver for individuals to become concerned about the environment originate from urban environments: concerns about littering,[549] air pollution[550] and planned construction

---

[547] Aarhus Convention, art. 2(3).
[548] EI(S)R, reg. 2(1).
[549] Interview with User No. 5.
[550] Interview with Public Authority No. 2.

projects.[551] In this way, the practical usage of the right to environmental information deviates from traditional rural characteristics which can dominate perceptions about "the environment".

The wide range of interactions between humanity and the environment encapsulated by the definition in the Aarhus Convention has been hailed as "modern", creating both an "enumerative" and adaptable definition for future interactions between humanity and the environment.[552] Linking this to Actor-Network Theory, one strength of this definition is that it recognises the environment as an actor – one that is present in the right's actor-network and is both exerting influence and being influenced by other actors within the network. Such an approach is notable because it is one of the specific points where the actor-status of the environment is embedded and recognised within the right of access to environmental information.

A similar recognition of the environment as a specific actor can be identified in how these information regimes treat the environment within their exceptions. Both the Aarhus Convention and the EI(S)R justify the withholding of environmental information where public authorities believe that disclosure would substantially prejudice "the protection of the environment to which the information relates".[553] This exception can be viewed as an embodiment of the right's environmental aims,[554] but it is arguably more than this. By explicitly recognising the environment as a thing that needs protecting, this exception is conferring upon the environment the status of an actor. On a similar (but distinct) point, the duty to disclose environmental information relating to emissions is significant as it recognises the vulnerability of the environment to such impacts and places its interests at the core of consideration.[555] Singling out the role of emissions reflects the integral and embedded nature of the environment as an actor within the context of the right to environmental information.

It should be noted that while not every provision explicitly recognises the environment as an actor that merits emphasis, this is not to suggest that explicit consideration is always required. Some provisions within the legal instruments that guarantee the right involve implicit recognition

---

[551] Interview with User No. 1.
[552] ETEMIRE, above n. 510, 399.
[553] Aarhus Convention, art. 4(4)(h); EI(S)R, reg. 10(5)(g).
[554] WHITTAKER, above n. 24, p. 86.
[555] Aarhus Convention, art. 4(4)(d); EI(S)R, reg. 10(6).

of the environment as an actor. One example of the environment being embedded in the legal provisions guaranteeing the right is in how both instruments define public authorities. Both the Aarhus Convention and the EI(S)R do not explicitly identify the environment as a relevant consideration when defining what constitutes a public authority,[556] but this is because every authority is considered to have a link to, and an effect on, the environment.[557] In this way, despite not explicitly mentioning the environment, the environment's status as an actor is embedded within the regime.

From these specific elements of both regimes guaranteeing the right of access to environmental information, it could be argued that the environment is already fully considered as an actor within the right and its legal emanations. However, such provisions within both environmental information regimes are the exception to the rule: no other provision recognises the environment as an actor that merits particular emphasis. Indeed, within the operational provisions of both instruments in terms of processing and disclosing environmental information, there is a greater focus on the procedural aspects of guaranteeing the right. To an extent, this is by design: the procedural rights enshrined within the Aarhus Convention, such as the right to have requests responded to "as soon as possible", are viewed as an essential element of achieving its environmental aims.[558] Yet these procedural rights are not inherently environmental; they need to be contextualised as such in order to be viewed as contributing to the right's environmental aims.

Inherent to this is the idea that the procedural rights within the Aarhus Convention and the EI(S)R are environmental in nature because they allow users to hold authorities to account in environmental matters and to participate in environmental decision-making procedures. It is the environmental aims of the right and the assumed environmental motives of those using the right that provide the reason why the procedural rights are considered to be procedural *environmental* rights, rather than the substantive content of these procedural rights themselves. This contextualisation is required because these rights, which constitute the largest number of provisions within both environmental information regimes, do not explicitly engage with the environment itself as an actor;

---

[556] Ibid., art. 2(2); ibid., reg. 2(1).
[557] EBBESSON et al., above n. 119, p. 46.
[558] B. PETERS, "Unpacking the Diversity of Procedural Environmental Rights: The European Convention on Human Rights and the Aarhus Convention" (2018) 30(1) *Journal of Environmental Law* 1.

yet, without such engagement, there is nothing to differentiate the right to environmental information from that under wider freedom of information regimes.

In the context of this text, this is important because in practice it means that people will view these procedural rights as environmental only if they are already aware of the environmental aims that underpin the right to environmental information. While the right, and its implementing instruments, assume that this is the case, in practice users (and quite often public authorities) are not aware of either the distinct right of access to environmental information or the specifically environmental aims of the right. This can be partially attributed to the lack of explicit engagement that these provisions show with the environment as an actor; because the environment is not emphasised throughout the entirety of the regime, and thus minimised as an actor exerting agency within the context of the right, the right's environmental aims are equally diminished and overshadowed by other concerns. This overshadowing can be evidenced in terms of how the right is used in practice by both professional and personal users, as well as in terms of how the right continues to embody an anthropocentric relationship with the environment.

3.2. ANTHROPOCENTRISM AND THE "ENVIRONMENT" IN ENVIRONMENTAL INFORMATION

The focus on "environmental" information within the right of access to environmental information might lead one to imagine that this right is an area that stands apart from the criticism of anthropocentrism that is levelled against so much environmental law and policy, and might offer a way of looking beyond the human elements in human-environment relations. However, this is not the case here. To an extent, this is understandable; both the rural and urban environments in Scotland have been, and continue to be, shaped by humans, so the relationship between human actors and the environment plays a prominent role in viewing the environment. Yet the right of access to environmental information and many of the people engaging with the right are unashamedly anthropocentric in terms of how they conceptualise the view the environment as an actor.

In the Aarhus Convention, the environment is acknowledged as an actor, with an affirmation of the need to "protect, preserve and improve the state of the environment and to ensure sustainable and environmentally sound development".[559] It is also acknowledged as an actor in the exemption against releasing information that will harm the environment. In the foreground is the recognition that "adequate protection of the environment is essential to human well-being and the enjoyment of basic human rights, including the right to life itself".[560] The Convention aims "to contribute to the protection of the right of every person of present and future generations to live in an environment adequate to his or her health and well-being".[561] While these synergies between human rights, well-being and environmental protection are important, it is also worth noting here that running them together can be problematic. As Petersmann argues, there are potential "conflicts between environmental protection laws and human rights".[562]

As discussed above, in the UK, including Scotland, there is a tendency for the right of access to environmental information to be obscured by the greater volume of activity which is carried out in the context of freedom of information more broadly. The environment continues to have an impact – for example, the members of the public interviewed were often motivated by changes to or issues with their local environment – but this role of the environment risks being obscured through excess emphasis on (human and organisational) procedures.

This can lead to problems. The broad objectives of the Aarhus Convention and its domestic implementation, in terms of intergenerational environmental protection,[563] can be lost behind a focus on the procedures to be applied and on making specific information available. The role of the environment in the right of access to environmental information thus risks being obscured by an emphasis on procedure and information. While current practice tends to run together the right of access to environmental information with the freedom of information regime (with its important, but narrower, objectives),[564] it is important to retain the broader environmental objectives underlying the right of access to environmental information. A greater emphasis on the environment in the right of access to environmental information – and on the Aarhus Convention's objective of intergenerational environmental protection – is needed here to ensure

---

[559] Aarhus Convention, Preamble, para. 5.
[560] Ibid, Preamble, para. 6.
[561] Ibid., art 1.
[562] PETERSMANN, above n. 42, pp. 235–236. See also C. REID, "Pitfalls in Promoting Environmental Rights" in S. BOGOJEVIĆ and R. RAYFUSE (eds), *Environmental Rights in Europe and Beyond*, Hart Publishing, Oxford 2018.
[563] Aarhus Convention, Preamble, para. 7.
[564] See Chapter 1, section 2.

that the overriding purpose is kept in mind as the detailed rules are interpreted and applied.

Yet such an environment-centric approach is merely aspirational, an objective which does not fully match with the concrete procedural obligations contained within the Aarhus Convention and the EI(S)R's neutrality on the environment in the majority of its provisions. Defenders of the Convention may suggest that it is unnecessary that its provisions, and those of domestic environmental information regimes, explicitly engage with the environment as an actor because the right itself is immersed in an implicit understanding of the importance of the environment. However, this understanding is contextualised through the environment's relationship with humanity, which in turn leads to the same issues regarding the "invisibility" of the environment within the right of access to environmental information.

This invisibility is reflected in how both professional and personal users of the right actually engage with and utilise the right of access to environmental information. While the right to environmental information envisages users acting to fulfil their duty to protect and enhance the environment,[565] in practice users are motivated by personal, and human-centric, concerns. As one public authority put it:

> [W]e don't get environmental questions, as in, climate change. We don't get those kind of questions. It's very personal. It's people looking for particular information.[566]

Such a mismatch between the expectations of user motivation and the actual use of the right (and information disclosed under it) reflect a fundamental truth about the right – that despite its environmental aspirations, the right is ultimately anthropocentric and prioritises the needs of humanity. This focus is problematic, both in the sense that it artificially structures the right's actor-network by placing humanity at the "top" and because such a focus will lead to further sacrifices of the environment for the benefit of humanity.[567] This would also explain why many users fail to distinguish between the general right to information and the specific right to environmental information; because the procedural elements of both rights are broadly similar, and the right to environmental information

---

[565] Aarhus Convention, Preamble para. 7.
[566] Interview with Public Authority No. 11.
[567] PETERSMANN, above n. 42, pp. 235–236.

Chapter 6. Non-Human Actors

does not contain many explicit references to the environment, from the perception of the public the two rights are interchangeable.

The anthropocentric approach of the right and environmental information regimes does not wholly excise the environment as an actor that exerts influence. Notwithstanding the motives of users engaging with the right, the information being sought is still *environmental* in nature. As a result, the state of the environment will influence what information users seek to access – for example, information relating to red squirrels in Scotland and the amounts of money spent with the goal of protecting them[568] or the destruction of herring gull nests and eggs.[569] In this way, the "environment" does exert agency through its impacts on the requests that are made. However, such an influence further highlights that the environment, as an actor, merely exists as a part of – rather than separate from – the way in which "the social" and humanity's self-interest are assembled. Wherever one looks, there seems no straightforward escape from anthropocentrism.

The irony of this anthropocentric approach adopted within the right, and by instruments such as the Aarhus Convention, is that while this approach centres humanity, it does so in a way that does not match how individuals actually act and behave. Embedded within the right is an idealised version of humanity: one which is driven by an impersonal altruism to engage with its moral duty to "protect and enhance the environment", but which is not reflected by the majority of individuals, who either choose not to engage with the right or do so for broadly personal reasons. It is helpful to return to Petersmann's critique of anthropocentrism in environmental law here. Petersmann uses the metaphor of Narcissus gazing at his reflection in the lake as part of this critique, arguing that environmental law is like "Narcissus losing the sight of the nature surrounding him when staring at his reflection in the lake".[570] However, in discussing the right of access to environmental information, this metaphor can be taken further. The reflection of the human in nature which drives the anthropocentrism of much environmental law is also a reflection which distorts one's view of the human – Narcissus is left transfixed by a reflection that does not give an adequate view of the humanity it is reflecting. As a result, the right risks losing sight of both the human and the environmental.

---

[568] Interview with User No. 2.
[569] Interview with User No. 3.
[570] PETERSMANN, above n. 42, p. 258.

The consequences of losing sight of both the human and the environment is significant. To further develop Petersmann's metaphor, rather than staring into the lake and seeing just our own reflections, current environmental change means that the water level is climbing ever higher, risking our safety as a species. Yet it is important not to focus solely, or even predominantly, on humanity, human actors or non-human actors created by humans. Appreciating the environment, and the influence it exerts, necessitates a deeper understanding of its role in the actor-network through which the right to environmental information operates. In this way, there is an increasing need to move away from an anthropocentric approach in environmental law and politics, and to better engage with the environment in regimes such as those which guarantee the right of access to environmental information.

3.3. PUTTING THE "ENVIRONMENT" IN THE RIGHT OF ACCESS TO ENVIRONMENTAL INFORMATION

Drawing on Actor-Network Theory,[571] this text has identified both a mismatch between expectations and reality regarding how users engage with the right, and the need to move beyond anthropocentrism and emphasise the actor-status of the environment. Petersmann offers a powerful challenge to law's focus on human interests as mirrored in environmental protection, comparing humans' excessive focus on "their own interests when thinking about environmental protection" with the myth of Narcissus.[572] Such arguments are compelling and, alongside Actor-Network Theory, might seem to enable a move away from the anthropocentrism which characterises the right to environmental information.

However, it is not easy to escape the anthropocentrism which characterises the right of access to environmental information. One reason why people focus on the environment, and seek to build an account of the right of access to environmental information, is due to the self-interested desire to find ways to protect human well-being and to limit or respond to potentially catastrophic environmental change. This creates the somewhat paradoxical situation where it is anthropocentric concerns, created in part by the damage done by anthropocentric politics and economics, which are

---

[571] See Chapter 2, section 1.
[572] PETERSMANN, above n. 42, p. 235.

the motivation to seek ways out of anthropocentrism. The anthropocentric view can lead to a focus on the procedural rights associated with the right to access environmental information, but it is important to broaden this view to also consider how the right may substantively have an impact on the environment and vice versa. In this way, giving more serious attention to the role of the environment as an actor can either be part of attempts to move away from anthropocentrism or can be driven by anthropocentric interests in environmental protection.

Two potential responses to this bind come to mind, both drawing from different jurisprudential traditions: rethinking what it means to understand actors intergenerationally and giving legal personhood to non-human parts of the environment. The first of these approaches, the intergenerational approach, remains anthropocentric to start with through the focus on human generations. This fits into a long tradition of considering intergenerational aspects of environmental law and justice:

> [A]ll generations are partners caring for and using the earth. Every generation needs to pass the earth and our natural and cultural resources on in at least as good a condition as we received them.[573]

However, there might also be ways to take fuller account of responsibilities to non-human actors. For Berry, in the example of water and irrigation in Hawaii, Actor-Network Theory can allow a fuller appreciation of how both intergenerational knowledge of a place alongside understandings of how "natural" features can themselves act across generations (for example, impacting on how people can or cannot live well in a place, and how the environment in a place is maintained).[574] Actor-Network Theory can thus help challenge ideas of land and water sources as "objective, recordable, institutionalised property" and instead allow understandings of them as part of "long-term, intergenerational" spaces.

This leads to a second potential response to this anthropocentrism: granting rights and legal personhood to non-humans such as rivers, and potentially drawing on traditions of jurisprudence that may include non-human actors in different ways. From Stone's seminal article "Should Trees

---

[573] E.B. WEISS, "Climate Change, Intergenerational Equity, and International Law" (2008) 9(3) *Vermont Journal of Environmental Law* 615, 616.

[574] K.A. BERRY, "Actor-Network Theory and Traditional Cultural Properties: Exploring Irrigation as a Hybrid Network in 19th Century Hawai'i" (2014) 7(2) *Human Geography* 73.

Have Standing?"[575] to more recent recognition of constitutional rights for Mother Earth (Pacha Mama)[576] and legal rights for rivers,[577] there has been a move to bring the environment, or features of it, within the legal frameworks which have traditionally failed to take account of it, except through the lens of property and other human-based concepts.[578]

New Zealand is a prominent example here, building on the decision to grant legal personhood to the Whanganui River.[579] For Charpleix, this decision is notable not only because of its potential for protecting the environment, but also due to its drawing on Māori traditions, where the river and the human occupants of the land are seen to share a common genealogy and where the river is seen to have personality in ways that render it non-tradeable.[580] A trustee arrangement has been put in place in order to give the river a "human face".[581] Rodgers suggests that this might offer insights to English law (and it might also make similar contributions to Scottish law):

> This provides a marked contrast to the legal framework for protecting the natural environment in English law, where the focus on individual property rights remains problematic, and is – in particular – unhelpful to attempts to establish a broader system of environmental protection focused at a landscape level and based on protecting ecosystems and their constituent elements.[582]

Drawing on other traditions of jurisprudence to think about the legal personhood of non-human actors in some different ways might offer a useful way forward. This could open up two forms of trustee-type arrangements. First, as in the New Zealand example, trustees might represent non-human actors such as rivers which are part of the environment. Second, though,

---

[575] STONE, above n. 123.
[576] Constitution of Ecuador, 2008, art. 71.
[577] C. AGNEW and I. JAHAN, "A Critical Analysis of the Development of the Concept of Giving Rivers a Personality: Does it in Fact Help to Protect the River?" (2021) 21 *Journal of Water Law* 77.
[578] D. CORRIGAN and M. OKSANEN, *Rights of Nature: A Re-examination*, Routledge, Abingdon 2021.
[579] K. SANDERS, "'Beyond Human Ownership'? Property, Power and Legal Personality for Nature in Aotearoa New Zealand" (2018) 30 *Journal of Environmental Law* 207.
[580] C. CHARPLEIX, "The Whanganui River as Te Awa Tupua: Place-Based Law in a Legally Pluralistic Society" (2017) 184(1) *Geographical Journal* 19.
[581] C. RODGERS, "A New Approach to Protecting Ecosystems: The Te Awa Tupua (Whanganui River Claims Settlement) Act 2017" (2017) 19(4) *Environmental Law Review* 266.
[582] Ibid., p. 274.

Chapter 6. Non-Human Actors

one might build on the above example of intergenerational thinking from Hawaii to think about authorities as holding environmental information in trust for past and future generations. While a focus on past and future generations of humans would clearly be anthropocentric, one could also broaden this out to include past and future non-human actors; for example, information about a river might be held in trust in part for past and future iterations of the river.

While this approach might seem abstract, it does have policy implications. First, considering the environment as an actor might give more meaning and utility to the existence of a separate regime for the right to access environmental information. This research found that many members of the public were unaware that they were using a regime separate from freedom of information rights to access environmental information, and they were also sometimes even annoyed when authorities handled a request under the EI(S)R:

> [The] majority of the time yes. I know that the – you've the differences between a straightforward freedom of information request and an environmental information request ... I don't sit down and analyse it to the nth degree, so I get which side [it] is on. So I'll just ask under freedom of information.[583]
>
> I put an FOI in to [REDACTED] and it's gone to their environmental department: environment and transport I think. But it's not [an] environment issue.[584]

Public authorities sometimes saw the separate regimes as an unjustified complication:

> Well I think the customer doesn't care [about a separate regime for environmental information]. And they must get these letters sometimes, we're not doing this but we're doing this. Do we do this, does that matter? I imagine that the only thing that [it] does is probably confuse some people. And they maybe think, is that better than, I wanted it under Freedom of Information.[585]

By giving fuller consideration to the environment as an actor, the right of access to environmental information could become part of a broader picture where information is held in trust for the environment and for past

---

[583] Interview with User No. 5.
[584] Interview with User No. 8.
[585] Interview with Public Authority No. 11.

Intersentia 203

and future generations. This might offer a revitalisation of – and clearer meaning and purpose for – the EI(S)R, meriting a distinction between the two regimes.[586]

Second, a fuller consideration of the environment as an actor might justify giving more attention to the environmental benefits and motives of requests made under the EI(S)R. A stronger version of this argument would see the EI(S)R being administered on behalf of the environment – so the potential benefits (or harms) of a request are something to be given crucial weight as part of acknowledging the interests or well-being of the wider environment. A weaker version of this argument would see the environment as one of the actors in the broader system of which the EI(S)R are part, but would still seek to use an increased consideration of both the motives for a request and any potential environmental benefits in order to consider how the requester and request will interact with the wider environment. Both of these arguments could be used to support modifications to the EI(S)R that add weight to the consideration given to the potential benefits of and motives for requests – so that, for example, requests driven by environmental motives and with likely benefits could be prioritised.

These proposals are intended to provide a basis for giving more emphasis to the environment as an actor when discussing the right of access to environmental information. This is needed because the environment can sometimes be lost amongst the procedural rights which characterise the right of access to environmental information – a characterisation exacerbated by the dominance of, and similarities to, the general right to information and its narrower focus on procedure and governance. By pivoting away from the current anthropocentric approach and explicitly engaging with the environment as an actor within environmental information regimes, it is possible to better reflect the importance of the environment and better secure the right's environmental protection aims. While this, and the general shift away from anthropocentrism, will be hard to accomplish, current environmental crises mean that radical measures are necessary.

4. CONCLUSIONS

This chapter has drawn on Actor-Network Theory and on broader critiques of anthropocentric approaches to environmental law and politics in order

---

[586] See Chapter 7.

Chapter 6. Non-Human Actors

to do two things. First, it has offered an account of the right of access to environmental information which emphasises the role of non-human actors. Building on previous chapters' accounts of the role of human actors in the actor-network, this chapter has demonstrated that (alongside compelling theoretical reasons to give more account of the role of non-human actors) the recognition of the significant role of non-human actors enables a richer picture to be drawn of the uses and impacts of the right to environmental information. For example, this approach allows a better account of the influence of technology and of the environment in the right of access to environmental information.

Second, the chapter has acknowledged the anthropocentric focus embedded in the approach to environmental issues here and an unavoidable tension in seeking a more holistic approach. While this tension can hinder how the role of the environment as an actor is considered within the right of access to environmental information, anthropocentrism does not act only as an obstacle to this goal. Humanity's self-interest, and knowledge of the current degradation of the environment, can also drive this critique of and interest in ways to move beyond anthropocentrism. Caring for the well-being of humanity also results in caring for the environment, since humanity depends on a well-functioning environment. As a result, anthropocentrism can act as both a point of tension and a driver for expanding on the role and centrality of the environment.

This duality of anthropocentrism is the source of tension that arises when discussing the necessary expansion of the role of the environment as an actor, and shapes how the law, such as the EI(S)R, characterises and minimises the role of the environment as an actor within the respective actor-networks. While this chapter does not offer a solution to the tension, by exploring this and the challenges to anthropocentrism, it can open up new ways to think about where the environment sits in relation to the right of access to environmental information and about wider questions of environmental law, governance and politics. By critiquing how the right of access to environmental information combines an anthropocentric approach with an inadequate understanding of how people might use the right, new policy options for enhancing the right and new avenues for research open up.

CHAPTER 7
REFLECTIONS AND LESSONS

This book has shown that the reality of the exercise of the right of public access to environmental information is rather different from and more complicated than much of the discussion of the topic suggests. From the Rio Declaration through the Aarhus Convention to the Environmental Information (Scotland) Regulations 2004 (EI(S)R), the provision of information is seen as a means of promoting the development of environmentally engaged citizens and enabling them to participate effectively in decision-making procedures with a view to protecting and enhancing the environment. Only a few of the uses fit well with this vision and, even when they do, users are left frustrated that they are not able to exercise more influence over decision-making procedures. As such, there is a gap between the aspirations of the right and the reality of its use that needs to be considered.

The most basic point perhaps is the low level of awareness of the existence of the particular right to environmental information that is distinct from any entitlements under more general laws on freedom of information and that lies behind information being accessible. Whether or not the use of the right is recognised as such by those involved, the practice does not always match the aspirations that lie behind it. The parties involved are more diverse than can be encapsulated in a single category of "users" or "holders" of information, and their relationships are shaped by their engagement not only with each other but also with a range of non-human actors. In addition, their motivations are often very different from the environmental objectives that providing access to environmental information was designed to serve. The overall result is a system where mismatches arise as a result of different motives and expectations, leading to frustrations and getting in the way of the right always being smoothly and successfully implemented. That different actors will define success in relation to the right differently, particularly in terms of focusing on procedural or substantive outcomes of engaging with the right, adds to the complexity. Since none of the features identified seem to depend on any peculiarity of the Scottish rules or context, the lessons are of wider relevance. The overall picture is not of a system that is broken, but of one where efficacy and efficiency could be increased and the environmental aims of the right better served with a greater understanding of the different elements involved.

1. AWARENESS

The low awareness of the right of access to environmental information has two elements. One is the confusion with the separate and more general rules on freedom of information. As noted in Chapter 1, these two regimes have separate origins and objectives. Given their wider reach, it is perhaps inevitable that the broader freedom of information legislation will have a higher profile, but this is exacerbated by four factors.

The first is that general information regimes will often overshadow regimes dedicated to guaranteeing the specific right to environmental information. This can be evidenced in Scotland with the creation of the EI(S)R. This was done in order to implement the revised EU Directive based on the Aarhus Convention, but happened very much in the shadow of the activity surrounding the making and bringing into force of the Freedom of Information Act 2000 and the Freedom of Information (Scotland) Act 2002. A second factor is that in handling requests for information, the much greater volume of requests under the more general rules inevitably colours the perception of how the two sets of legislation are viewed, a position reinforced by the fact that the task of handling matters under both sets is normally allocated to the same team within a public authority. Indeed, the initial guidance made by the Scottish Government had wrongly suggested that authorities could simply choose whether to deal with requests under the environmental or general rules, as opposed to recognising the priority of the former.[587] Third, the fact that the procedures for handling requests for environmental information, reviews and appeals mirror those under the wider freedom of information rules blurs the distinction between the two. The adoption of consistent procedures has many advantages in terms of simplicity, coherence and efficiency, but does mean that the distinct aims of creating a right to environmental

---

[587] Freedom of Information (Scotland) Act 2002, s. 39(2)(a). See Scottish Information Commissioner, Decision 218/2007, *Professor AD Hawkins and Transport Scotland*, paras 53–58.

information get overlooked. Finally, other elements within the actor-network, notably the electronic platform WhatDoTheyKnow used by many people requesting information, encourage the public's use of information rights without clearly distinguishing between the two rights.

At a more basic level, many people benefiting from the right to access information are unaware of the fact that they are doing so, and that their access to information, environmental or more general, is in fulfilment of a legal obligation imposed on public authorities. In some ways this is a sign of success. The broad trend across governance towards greater transparency, both reflected in and driven by the laws on access to information, coupled with the technological revolution that has transformed how information can be disseminated mean that the public's expectations have changed. It is simply expected that a lot of information held by public authorities will be routinely accessible. Obtaining such information is therefore seen as a matter of "business as usual" as opposed to an exercise of a specific right that arises from the legal obligation on an authority to be proactive in making environmental information available. It simply does not cross most people's mind that when they are looking at official websites with information on environmental or planning issues or at the noticeboard on a bathing beach giving details of the water quality, they are the beneficiaries of legal duties placed on the authorities concerned. Indeed, it may not always be appreciated by those making the information available that they are not just following good practice but are also fulfilling legal obligations.

The fact that the law is delivering positive results without even being noticed is a mark of success which should be celebrated. However, greater recognition of the right to access environmental information acting as the legal basis of current practice may serve as a bulwark against the possible erosion, whether deliberate or accidental, of the benefits that have been achieved. This might be achieved by a simple label on relevant published material noting that it is being provided in accordance with the duty under the Aarhus Convention and/or EI(S)R, bringing these provisions into the public consciousness.

2. ASPIRATIONS AND PRACTICE

Turning to the gap between aspirations and practice, the biggest mismatch is probably between the ideal that shapes the Aarhus Convention, and the EI(S)R that implement it, and how these provisions are being used in practice. The rights created in the Convention, including the right of access to environmental information, are expressly provided:

> In order to contribute to the protection of the right of every person of present and future generations to live in an environment adequate to his or her health and well-being.[588]

Yet when the right is operationalised and above all when the motives and uses in actual practice are examined, this purpose is far from dominant.

The Convention does not limit the exercise of the rights to those using them for the desired objective. Although it sets out the purpose of the rights, this is not carried through in the drafting so as to be closely reflected in its own operational provisions. The right of access to information is provided without any restriction on the reason for the seeking the information or the purposes for which it is used.[589] This ensures that the right is widely available and avoids the need for any procedures to separate those requests for information which are legitimate from the others, avoiding a burden on both users and public authorities that would obstruct the use of the right. Furthermore, where information is being sought on issues that may lead to conflict with the authority that is subject to the request, the adoption of this open and applicant-blind approach protects those seeking information from premature revelation of their intentions and from being subject to discrimination or reprisal. Yet this approach also divorces the use and operation of the system from the underlying environmental aspiration. Access to information is a right provided to everyone, whatever their motive, not only those keen to ensure a healthy environment for current and future generations.

Experience shows that there is indeed a wide range of motivations behind the use of the right. Altruistic environmental concern does feature, but is far from being a dominant driver behind seeking information. Even where environmental issues feature, it is the state of the local environment today that is of much more of a concern than the wider picture for future generations. Protecting private interests are more likely to feature, including pursuing a grudge against another individual or authority as well as pursuing commercial or business goals. Moreover, in many cases there are mixed motives, so that although some desire to safeguard the environment may be present, it is lagging behind, or may even be just a

---

[588] Aarhus Convention, art. 1.
[589] Ibid., art. 4.

Chapter 7. Reflections and Lessons

(not unwelcome) side-effect of, other more immediate concerns that have prompted action in seeking information. The right may have been created with a view to environmental well-being, but that is far from the only, or even the main, reason why it is being exercised.

This diversity of motives is part of a second big mismatch between the messy reality and the simpler model envisaged under the Aarhus Convention and the EI(S)R. The provisions in these are built on a neat view of the right operating as a simple, direct relationship between the one homogeneous category of "users" seeking information and the other monolithic category of "holders" who have control of the information. However, both groups are much more varied in practice.

The "users" are far from homogeneous and vary greatly in terms of their motives and expertise, so cannot be treated as a single group. At the most general of levels, this research has illustrated the big difference between professional and personal users, both in the reasons why they are seeking information and in their likely level of expertise and experience in navigating the material held and provided by authorities. But there is great diversity within each of these broad groups too.

Professional users may be driven by purely commercial motives (as in the case of those seeking information to enable them to sell goods or services) or by the need to further their clients' interests (for example, lawyers), in effect adopting their motives. They may also be driven by concern over how the environment has been treated, in turn based either on personal sentiment (for example, environmental campaigners) or by the demands of their job (for example, journalists) or both. Some professional users will be acting mainly in pursuit of the short-term goal of doing the job they are paid for, whereas others will be following longer-term personal or public interests. For many such users, a further point is that the use of the legal right to access information is likely to be only one of several means of gathering the information needed to pursue their goals within their wider relationship with a public authority. The intermediary nature of many professional users is also noteworthy, as these professional users may be acting to access and re-present information for their employer or a specific client, or as a conduit to the wider public, as is the case for journalists and campaigners.

Personal users also vary greatly in terms of their expertise, motives and what they intend to do with the information they access, with few acting purely for the altruistic environmental objectives that the Aarhus Convention proclaims. Yet all users, whether personal or professional, are encompassed by the single phrase "the public" in the Convention and are treated the same way in the more detailed procedural rules. Any assumption that users form a single group with homogeneous shared needs quickly falls apart when the range of people making use of the right to access environmental information is appreciated. Especially when combined with the applicant-blind approach, this can cause difficulties for authorities, which are unable to tailor their responses to the needs and capacities of those they are dealing with, a clear source of potential frustration on both sides when the availability of published data is not appreciated or poorly focused requests are made.

The public authorities who hold information must also be viewed in a more nuanced manner. Here the differences are not so much between authorities (although the scale of authorities and the range and diversity of information they hold will result in major differences in practice) as within them. In relation to requests for information, there tends to be a difference between those whose responsibility it is to handle the requests and ensure that they are processed in accordance with the legal rules and those involved with the substantive content of the information. The former, who are usually handling these matters alongside a workload dominated by the broadly parallel task under general freedom of information laws, will have their focus on the procedural aspects of ensuring that requests are answered in a timely manner and any information is provided or denied in line with the legal tests for what must be disclosed or can be withheld.

In such circumstances it is easy for the explicitly environmental goals of laws based on the Aarhus Convention to get lost where much work is being done in the fulfilment of the simpler transparency goal of the wider freedom of information law. By contrast, for those whose work engages with the subject matter of the request, not only are they likely to face the task of gathering and presenting the information requested, but their future work may also be affected by what information is disclosed and how it is used. Their perspective and what they view as positive or negative outcomes of the exercise of the right are likely to differ from those whose focus is on ensuring that an appropriate response is provided in a timely manner. In relation to proactively published material, the difference may be less stark, but the team responsible for processing requests is unlikely to be so heavily involved, if at all. Other staff such as those in public relations may play a part, but across the wide range of information made available, the onus will fall on those involved in creating the information (often just as a side-product of their main functions).

One consequence of this differentiation within both the users and the holders of information is that there will be differences in how the successful operation of access to environmental information is judged. A commercial user interested in selling services would consider their use of the right a success if the details needed to target their activities are obtained. For other professional users, success will depend on how well the information obtained works, when combined with information acquired from other sources, to enable them to further their own or their clients' goals. For personal users, success is more likely to be coupled with substantive outcomes and how far the information obtained leads to their desired changes in the authority's actions or decisions.[590] Significantly, it will be in only a few instances that success will be judged in terms of the "contribut[ion] to the protection of the right of every person of present and future generations to live in an environment adequate to his or her health and well-being".[591] Moreover, with different parties looking for success in different places, there is the chance of friction and misunderstandings as each works through their role in the process.

3. THE RANGE OF ACTORS

The previous comments show that in analysing the operation of the right of access to environmental information, it is not adequate to view this on the basis of a simple relationship between users and holders of information. Actor-Network Theory is used to draw attention to the much richer set of relationships and actors which are in play here. As well as the need to disaggregate the broad categories of users and holders, further relationships must be considered. These include the roles of external oversight bodies such as the Aarhus Convention Compliance Committee and the Office of the Scottish Information Commissioner – the former perhaps unexpectedly absent, except through very indirect routes and the latter a constant presence, both in playing a direct part when individual cases are referred for decision and in influencing the operation of the whole system through its guidance and monitoring.

Also of fundamental significance is the interplay with non-human actors. The ways in which individuals act cannot be properly understood without an appreciation of how their relationships with a range of non-human actors shape their conduct. The most influential of these is

---

[590] See Chapter 5, section 4.3.
[591] Aarhus Convention, art. 1.

probably the law, since it is the legal provisions that secure an enforceable right to access information and set down its scope and the procedures to be followed. The need to comply with the law is the overriding factor in determining how public authorities deal with access to information issues. Yet the law as it applies in Scotland is itself the product of a relationship between domestic law, the EU provisions applying and refining the terms of the Aarhus Convention, and the Convention itself. Although having a low profile, court decisions and more prominently the determinations of the Scottish Information Commissioner also have considerable weight in terms of moulding what happens in practice.

Whereas the law proves to be a significant actor, the environment turns out to feature surprisingly little in practice. Given that the right, and the Aarhus Convention, expressly attach access to information to the purpose of safeguarding the environment, it might be expected that regard for the environment would be a constant thread affecting all other actors, human and non-human. Yet the EI(S)R and their operation focus on securing procedural compliance rather than substantive environmental gains, and the environment does not feature strongly, if at all, in many of the motivations leading to information being sought. As discussed later, one consequence of this is that the distinct aspirations which distinguish the more specific regime for access to environmental information from the broader regime for freedom of information are lost from sight, creating a vicious circle which may ultimately undermine the support for having a separate regime at all.

Also significant is the role played by technology. Information nowadays is created, presented, manipulated and above all shared on a scale and in ways undreamt of not so many years ago. Moreover, communication between the various actors by electronic means transforms how they can interact. In the light of this, it is remarkable that the terms of the Aarhus Convention, which were being conceived in the early 1990s when post, (fixed-line) telephones and paper files were dominant,[592] continue to provide a sound framework even though they are now operating in markedly different circumstances. WhatDoTheyKnow, as a very widely used platform for making requests for information and publicly sharing responses, has had a major impact on the use of the right today.

---

[592] See the research on the operation of the earliest laws providing public access to environmental information, e.g. BURTON and JOHN, both above n. 531.

Such technological change has perhaps had most impact on the element of access to environmental information that is often overlooked or overshadowed: proactive publication. Those seeking information in the digital age may find it hard to imagine how little was available when providing access meant either physically printing and distributing copies of reports or enabling visitors to inspect records or files in the office where they were held. Expectations have changed so much that the vast majority of people benefiting from access to information have no concept that they are exercising a specific legal right as opposed to just going along with "business as usual". The fact that information is created in a way that enables easy sharing and that there is little additional cost in making it widely available has transformed the landscape. Such technological advances, coinciding with a political move towards greater openness as shown by the embrace of freedom of information, mean that disclosure rather than secrecy has become almost the default position. Whereas the cost and effort of publication in the past meant that it was a big step when something was to be published, now it is probably a bigger step to decide that information that is being held should be withheld from disclosure. The scale of this culture change should not be underestimated.

However, this transformation in potential and expectation can give rise to its own problems. Because expectations are so high, there can be frustration when they are not easily satisfied. This can arise because of a mismatch between what a person seeking information thinks an authority is doing, and how it does it, and the reality. In the first place, the authority may not gather or hold information that the user thinks it should have. Authorities are driven by their legal functions, not general curiosity about the world around them, but are also constrained by the limits on their legal powers and resource considerations. They gather the information that is required for them to carry out their functions and this may not extend to everything that a member of the public thinks it would be useful for them to know. Accordingly, a member of the public, accustomed to the vast amount of data gathered by all sorts of bodies on all aspects of life, may be disappointed when a public authority says that it does not hold the specific information being sought.

Moreover, the information will be gathered and stored in the way that suits the operations of the authority. This may not fit with the way in which an individual seeking information views the position. A request about the state of the environment in a single location may seem simple from the outside, whereas from within an authority it may involve interrogating various files and databases of various ages that have been structured to provide information in ways that serve the authority's distinct functions, potentially organised on different geographical scales. The apparent ease with which modern search engines can access material on the internet may lead to the expectation that all information held electronically by an authority can be easily retrieved and packaged to answer any question, but that may not match the reality of how an authority's information systems operate. The requester may think they have asked a simple question, but answering it may require a lot of effort to extract and draw together data from many sources. Again, disappointment and frustration at delays and possible gaps in the information are likely results. In all these ways, the clash of users' expectations in engaging with the right and the reality of this use can become a source of frustration, potentially dissuading individuals from using the right and undermining the right's intended use as a way of protecting and enhancing the environment.

4. LESSONS

As was noted at the start of this chapter, by revealing a number of mismatches between practice and the aspirations and expectations that helped to form the legal right, a more realistic understanding can be reached of what the right is and might be achieving. The aspirations behind providing the rights to access information and participate in decision-making in order to enhance the well-being of the environment are to be lauded.[593] Yet analysis should be tempered by consideration of what is happening in practice and how far this differs from the idealised picture that those responsible for the establishment of these rights were seeking to create. Greater transparency and accountability bring benefits in themselves and actions driven by selfish reasons may bring about wider environmental gains. Falling short of high ambitions – which may not themselves have been realistic or helpful – does not mean that the enterprise has not been worthwhile. However, the reality of how the right operates in practice must be acknowledged, and lessons can be drawn from this mismatch of reality and practice to improve how the right contributes to environmental protection and environmental governance.

---

[593] BARRITT, above n. 21.

4.1. REFINING THE RULES

A greater appreciation of the variety in the users and their motives and of the challenges faced within public authorities would enable all concerned to understand why other parties are acting as they are, as opposed to becoming frustrated when they do not act in line with the expectations created by the ideal. A lot of this is simply a matter of good practice, trying to spot and address mismatches before they become a problem and endeavouring to communicate in ways that reflect the different positions of the different parties. The lack of trust that some users feel towards public authorities may remain an obstacle to building a better relationship in some cases, but even appreciating that genuine attempts to be helpful may be misinterpreted may help to improve the position.

However, reflecting on practice does raise questions about refining the formal procedural rules in a way that better fits the reality. The rules in Scotland must meet the requirements of the Aarhus Convention, but following the UK's withdrawal from the EU, there is no longer a need to follow the precise ways in which they have been elaborated and implemented under the EU Directive.[594] There is scope for change. Does it make sense for there to be a single procedure that treats all users of information the same? Could distinctions be drawn between different categories on issues such as timing, assistance, costs and revelation of motives to make things better for either authorities or those seeking information?

There are real benefits in having a simple and open approach that does not require users to identify themselves or the reasons why they are seeking information, even at the cost of "undeserving" users gaining private benefits.[595] Trying to provide a more differentiated response to requests would carry burdens and risks that might undermine the objective of encouraging wider access to and use of information. Such a revised regime would require users to provide their identity,[596] but would users need to go further and provide both their reason for wanting the information and their level of expertise? Requiring disclosure of the reason for requesting information opens up the risks of prejudice that the applicant-blind approach consciously tries to avoid, and opens the

---

[594] See Chapter 2, section 2.3.
[595] Editorial, "The Price of Knowledge" (1994) 44 *Scottish Planning and Environmental Law* 55.
[596] As is already required under the Freedom of Information (Scotland) Act 2002.

door to authorities unduly altering how they process a request due to the identity of the individual or their motives.[597] To limit this risk, perhaps it would be sufficient to grant public authorities the power to ask for (but not be entitled to receive) this information on the basis that it would help them fulfil the request. Yet, even that might lead to some users being less favourably treated.

Changes that enable public authorities to consider the individual characteristics of users and tailor how they guarantee the right to these users more effectively are beneficial when all parties are happy to work together, but become problematic when there is tension or conflict. There is a careful balancing act between maintaining the procedural safeguards that enable any user to seek information for any reason without fear and a more intrusive procedure that may enable authorities to respond better in view of the diversity of people and purposes that have to be dealt with. Moreover, there would be formidable difficulties in establishing clear and appropriate boundaries that could not be easily bypassed (e.g. by a "professional" user getting a lay friend to make a request, or vice versa, to avoid any special rules that were unwelcome). Nevertheless, now that Scotland has the freedom to refine its rules to some extent (while still complying with the obligations under the Aarhus Convention), there may be issues that are worth exploring.

4.2. IS A DISTINCT RIGHT TO ENVIRONMENTAL INFORMATION NEEDED?

More significantly than contemplating a refinement to the procedural rules, the findings here raise the question of the need for a right of access to environmental information distinct from what might be provided under wider freedom of information laws. The research found that many members of the public were unaware that in accessing environmental information, they were using a legal structure separate from freedom of information rights and were even sometimes annoyed when authorities handled what they saw as a freedom of information request under this different, unfamiliar regime. Public authorities sometimes saw the separate regimes as an unjustified complication, making life difficult for what

---

[597] A practice already seen in some instances in relation to the handling of requests from journalists; see Chapter 3, section 2.1.

Chapter 7. Reflections and Lessons

is almost invariably the one team responsible for dealing with matters arising under both regimes. The much greater volume of work under the freedom of information scheme, with its emphasis on transparency and accountability alone, leads to the environmental information regime and its substantive goal of enhancing the environment being overshadowed. On the other hand, it has been shown that few of those using the right to environmental information are actually doing so to fulfil the aspiration of there being an environmentally aware public seeking to engage in public processes primarily in order to achieve a better environment for themselves and future generations.

This suggests that the environmental information regime is not fully delivering what its creators hoped for. However, simply because a regime is not operating exactly as its creators may have intended does not mean that it should be abandoned. The fact that many parties are not using the right to pursue predominantly environmental goals does not mean that its existence is not a benefit to the environment – many seminal legal cases about controlling state power have begun with much narrower, and indeed selfish, goals,[598] but still play a part in establishing the landscape for the benefit of the public as a whole. That actual practice does not always live up to the aspirations of the Aarhus Convention may disappoint idealists, but does not mean that we are left with a failure.

If we are not satisfied with the status quo, there appear to be two possible responses. One is to consider how the environmental dimension that justifies a separate regime can be enhanced and made more prominent. The other is to abandon a distinct regime and allow environmental information to be treated like any other under the wider freedom of information laws. The challenge of the first response has been explored in the previous chapter, and rests as much on culture and attitudes as on formal legal rules.

Exploring the notion of moving away from a separate environmental information regime does raise more technical, legal questions. It would call for a detailed comparison at two levels: between the current freedom of information and environmental information regimes, and between

---

[598] In relation to the limits of police powers in Scotland, the leading case on the admissibility of unlawfully obtained evidence arose not from a constitutional concern to set the limits of state power, but from protecting a dairy owner from a charge of using other dairies' bottles to supply milk when many of her own had not been returned promptly: *Lawrie v. Muir* 1950 JC 19.

the freedom of information regime and the requirements of the Aarhus Convention. The outcome of the former task will depend on the position in the jurisdiction in question. Some countries, including some parties to the Aarhus Convention,[599] already have a unified system, and where separate systems exist, the extent of difference will vary. In Scotland, this comparison will show up a range of differences – some trivial, some substantial – on issues such as the definition of "public authority", time limits, costs, the format of requests, the scope of exceptions and the existence of the general obligation to disseminate material proactively.[600]

Comparison between the freedom of information laws and the Aarhus Convention would then show how far any distinct provisions in the environmental regime are there in order to fulfil the requirements of the Aarhus Convention. Where this is the case, moving to a unified scheme would entail changes to the wider freedom of information laws so as to ensure continuing compliance with the Convention.[601] For Scotland, the language of the Convention itself may allow more leeway on some issues than the provisions in the EU Directive which the EI(SR) had to follow – for example, in relation to exceptions, the Convention refers simply to "taking account" of the public interest and the status of emissions,[602] as opposed to the much more definite language in the EI(S)R.[603] Some of these may not be controversial, but others may be seen as involving a significant shift in the balance between competing interests, which would be unwelcome when applied across the board. However, reopening debate on such issues would be inevitable if a unified system that was compliant with the Aarhus Convention were to be proposed.

---

[599] For example, in Sweden the Public Access to Information and Secrecy Act 2009 is a freedom of information regime which is considered to be capable to meeting the obligations set out in the Aarhus Convention, despite not being an explicitly environmental information regime.
[600] Scottish Information Commissioner, *Differences between FOISA and the EIRs* (EIRs Guidance Series) (2020).
[601] The half-way house of having a single freedom of information regime but with some adjustments for environmental information to ensure compliance with the Aarhus Convention seems only to make the position more confusing and less satisfactory.
[602] Aarhus Convention, art. 4(4).
[603] EI(S)R, reg. 10(1) and (6), allowing information to be withheld only when the interest in disclosure is "outweighed" and denying the application of certain grounds for non-disclosure when emissions are involved.

5. CONCLUSION

The detailed study of one jurisdiction, Scotland, in this volume has shown that the ideals behind creating a right of access to environmental information are not always realised in practice. Those actually making use of the right often do not fit with the vision of active citizens using information in a disinterested way, primarily to engage with public processes in order to secure the long-term health of the environment. Instead, a varied set of personal and professional users seek information for a variety of reasons, often serving their own narrow interests rather than the greater good, with the environmental aim behind the right sometimes all but disappearing. Differing expectations between and among those seeking information and those holding it lead to frustrations on all sides. Moreover, many of those who benefit from the right are not aware of its existence, either at all (especially in relation to proactively published information) or as something distinct from the rights established under the wider laws on freedom of information, which have developed over the same period and enjoy a higher profile.

Therefore, the efforts to create and implement the right may not be delivering all that those involved might hope for, but the achievements are nonetheless real, and may continue to grow as environmental awareness spreads in a society becoming increasingly conscious of the climate and biodiversity crises it faces. Yet the mismatch between aspirations and reality, between the users envisioned in the founding documents and actual practice, does spark further thought. Can the environmental objectives that lie behind the distinct right to environmental information be restored to prominence? Or should a simplification be achieved by merging this right with the entitlements under wider freedom of information laws?

Any such consideration should proceed on the sound basis of appreciating both the vision and the practice. Without knowledge of how the right is actually being used, discussion of what the right might achieve remains detached from the world in which it must operate. A pragmatic assessment of the benefits of where things stand and of different options for strengthening the present position will serve better than chasing a model of human motivation and behaviour that does not exist in real life. This book has sought to provide a basis for starting such an assessment.

INDEX

A

Aarhus Convention 2, 5–7, 9–10, 14, 23, 32, 36–42, 44–54, 57–60, 63, 72–74, 77–89, 94–100, 112–114, 119, 124–128, 132–134, 141–145, 150–156, 160, 163, 167–169, 173, 181–185, 194–197, 207, 210–212, 216–221; *see also* right of access to environmental information
   access to information 217; *see also* requests for environmental information
   access to justice 38–39, 54
   aspirations 2, 24–25, 27, 30–31, 37, 44, 50, 55, 74, 99, 119, 128, 144, 150–151, 154–156, 194–196
   assumptions 2, 10, 25, 32–33, 37, 40–41, 59, 74, 77, 81, 84–89, 94, 96–97, 100, 112–114, 124, 127, 137, 141–145, 152–155, 173, 207, 212, 216–221
   disclosure of environmental information on request, *see* passive right to environmental information *and* requests for environmental information
   duty to protect and enhance the environment, *see* environmental citizenship
   environmental citizenship, *see* environmental citizenship
   history 5, 37
   participative aims 2, 5–7, 9–10, 14, 38–41, 50, 60, 63, 72, 83, 132, 141–145, 155–156, 160, 163, 167, 207
   proactive disclosure of environmental information, *see* proactive disclosure
   procedural rights and obligations, *see* requests for environmental information
   public participation, *see* public participation
   scope 6–7, 37, 58
   three pillar structure 38–39
Aarhus Convention Compliance Committee 39, 54, 176, 180–181, 213
academics 77–81
accountability, *see* transparency and accountability
active right to environmental information, *see* proactive disclosure

Actor-Network Theory 3, 17–18, 24–30, 40, 47, 59, 62, 73, 79, 86, 95, 129, 168–172, 176, 186, 191, 207, 213; *see also* human actors, non-human actors *and* environment as actor
   concept of actor 17, 26–28, 86, 95, 129, 168, 170, 213
   concept of network 17, 26–28, 40, 55, 170, 207, 213
   hierarchy 18, 29–30
   influence 17, 62
   the social 25–32, 199
actors, *see* non-human actors, personal users *and* professional users
advice and assistance 50, 109–118, 126; *see also* personal users
   public authorities 109–110, 112–115, 118, 126
   user-generated 112, 115–118
   WhatDoTheyKnow 116, 118, 188–190
anthropocentrism 10, 30–31, 35, 40, 169, 192–200, 203–204
appeals 54; *see also* Aarhus Convention Compliance Committee *and* requests for environmental information, internal reviews
applicant-blind approach 49, 58, 69, 71, 81, 90, 96, 113–114, 122, 128, 210, 212
Arnstein 139–143, 147, 159, 163
   homogenisation 140
   Ladder of Participation 137–140, 143, 147, 159, 163

B

Barritt 5, 23, 37, 48, 57, 94, 96, 155, 216
Brundtland 34

C

courts 54, 122, 178–179

D

Dunion 44, 46, 117, 181
duty to protect and enhance the environment, *see* environmental citizenship

Index

E

Ebbesson   34–36, 39, 45–50, 54, 111, 125, 134, 143–144, 160, 163–164, 180, 187, 195
environmental citizenship   1–2, 5, 31, 37, 57, 68, 81, 84, 89, 134, 141, 146, 152–155, 161, 167, 207, 219
   aspirational aims of the right   1, 38–39, 57, 68, 84, 134, 162, 167, 207
   ideal users   57, 81, 89, 199
Environmental Information (Scotland) Regulations 2004 (EI(S)R)   7, 9, 25, 33, 42–54, 181–185, 214, 220
   as actor   40–41, 72, 90–91, 127, 143–144, 170, 191
   divergence from Aarhus Convention   43, 220
   proactive disclosure   9, 43, 49, 57, 60, 104–108, 174
   relationship with Freedom of Information (Scotland) Act 2002, *see* freedom of information
   requests for environmental information, *see* requests for environmental information
   scope and definitions   58
environmental information definition   45, 193
environment as actor   3, 10, 13, 30, 53, 55–56, 171, 190–205, 214
   connections to humanity, *see* anthropocentrism
   granting legal personhood   31, 201–202
   intergenerational approach   201–203
   omission of   3, 10, 13, 35, 40, 190, 195, 204, 214
   recognition of   27, 30, 47, 52, 192–196, 201–203, 214
European Union   42, 208, 220
   Directive 90/313   42
   Directive 2003/4   42, 208, 220
exceptions to disclosing environmental information, *see* requests for environmental information
expertise and knowledge, *see* personal users *and* professional users

F

freedom of information   4–11, 65–67, 98, 100, 108, 129, 133–134, 137, 184–185, 189–190, 196–198, 203–204, 207–209, 212–214, 220–221
   aims   4, 7–9, 65, 129
   distinguishing from access to environmental information   6–11, 28, 31, 43, 53–55, 66–67, 98, 100, 108, 129, 133–134, 137, 184–185, 189–190, 196–198, 203–204, 207, 212, 214, 220–221

Freedom of Information (Scotland) Act 2002   4, 9, 43, 184–185, 208
Freedom of Information Act 2000   4, 9, 208
freedom of information officers   173–174, 208, 212

H

Hazell   1, 4, 8–9, 162, 175
homogenisation
   public authorities   18, 36, 41, 46, 86–87, 90, 111, 156, 168, 173, 207, 213
   users   2, 11–13, 18, 36, 41, 47, 58–59, 73, 76–77, 79, 81–85, 90, 96–97, 102, 111, 127, 140, 156, 168, 207, 212–213
human actors, *see* personal users *and* professional users

I

intermediaries, *see* professional users

J

journalists   41, 61–71
   accuracy of published information   64
   mistreatment by public authorities   65, 68, 70
   role in society   62–65, 68–69

L

Latour   17–18, 25–31, 170

M

motive-blind approach, *see* applicant-blind approach
motives   2, 12, 30, 58–60, 65–67, 71–89, 94–102, 145–148, 156–157, 191, 198–199, 207, 210–211, 214, 221
   assumed   2, 81, 94
   commercial benefit   73–75, 156, 191, 210
   deviation from intended environmental motives   12, 24–25, 58, 61, 74–79, 82–85, 89, 94–99, 127–128, 145, 157, 198–199, 207, 211, 214
   employment   60, 67, 71–79, 86
   environmental altruism   74–75, 79, 83, 94, 98–99, 146, 198, 210, 221
   overlapping   66–67, 79, 83, 99, 146, 210
   personal motive   75–79, 83, 97–99, 210
   transparency and accountability   65–67, 98

N

non-governmental organisations (NGOs)   36–37, 58, 81–85, 155
   Aarhus Convention   81
   international environmental interest groups   82, 85

Index

local environmental interest groups 82–84, 155
mySociety, *see* WhatDoTheyKnow
non-environmental non-governmental organisations 81–83
 resources 82–85
non-human actors 3, 11–13, 27–28, 40, 62, 98, 154–155, 168–205, 213–214
 animals 98, 154, 199
 courts 178–179
 environment, *see* environment as actor
 law 13, 170, 181–185, 214; *see also* Aarhus Convention *and* Environmental Information (Scotland) Regulations 2004 (EI(S)R)
 Office of the Scottish Information Commissioner 29, 176–178
 public authorities, *see* public authorities as users
 technology, *see* technology

P

parliamentary researchers 85–86, 88
passive right to environmental information, *see* requests for environmental information
personal users 11–12, 57–59, 62, 77, 81, 89–103, 106–127, 145, 160, 164–165, 174–176, 211–215
 assumed characteristics 11, 57–58, 81, 89, 94; *see also* environmental citizenship
 definition 12, 47, 59, 62, 91–93
 environmental aims 97–100, 127–130
 expectations 160, 165, 213, 215
 expertise and knowledge 12, 58, 90–91, 94, 103–109, 119, 124–127, 211
 interaction with public authorities 94–96, 98, 100, 102, 107, 109–112, 117, 121, 123, 126, 174, 176, 212, 215
 motive, *see* motives
 proactively disclosed environmental information, *see* proactive disclosure
 receiving advice and assistance 94–96, 103, 111–118, 126
 trust, *see* trust
Petersmann 10, 40, 169, 192, 197–200
proactive disclosure 2, 9, 11, 35, 38, 40, 48–49, 62, 66, 69, 76, 80, 83, 95, 103–108, 124–127, 174, 187, 209, 212, 215
 accessibility 76, 80, 106, 209, 212, 215
professionals representing clients 41, 71–77
 consultants 71
 instructions 71–74
 lawyers 71
 pro bono work 75

professional users 12, 58–90, 145, 148, 174–175, 211–213
 definition 12, 47, 59–60, 62
 environmental aims 65–67, 71
 expertise and knowledge 12, 60, 63, 68, 72, 76, 80–84, 88, 148, 211
 interactions between public authorities 86–88
 interactions with public authorities 61, 65, 69–70, 73–77, 174–175
 intermediaries 41, 59–60, 63–65, 68–73, 78, 82, 86, 89, 211
 motive, *see* motives
 proactively disclosed environmental information, *see* proactive disclosure
public authorities 104, 172–176, 183, 208, 212, 215
 definition 36, 45–48
 internal structure 104, 173–175, 208, 212
public authorities as users 85–88, 142, 172–176, 212
 connection with the state 85
 holding information relevant to functions 87
 internal division of responsibilities 87, 212
public participation 2–3, 5–6, 13–14, 38–40, 60–61, 72, 79, 94, 126–127, 131–167, 207; *see also* Arnstein's Ladder of Participation *and* uses of environmental information
 alignment with intended environmental aims 152–153, 219
 dissatisfaction with right to participate in environmental decision-making procedures 14, 126, 133, 138, 142, 145, 147–148, 151, 160–162, 166
 dissatisfaction with right to environmental information 133, 142–147, 161
 expectations 40, 132, 135, 141–143, 160–161, 165
 homogenisation of views 138–141, 145, 151, 158
 instrumental benefits 5, 136, 147–150, 159, 163
 mismatch of expectations and reality 3, 11–13, 24–25, 28, 40, 55–59, 64, 81, 89–90, 94, 97, 102, 111–114, 121, 126–129, 132, 137, 141–143, 146–152, 155–161, 164–167, 207, 210, 216, 219
 non-environmental considerations 56, 58, 89–90, 132–134, 137, 146–147, 149–157, 166–167, 207, 210, 216, 219
 normative rationale 5, 136, 146, 149, 154–156, 159, 162–163
 outcome focus 14, 132, 139–144, 147–152, 158–161, 163–166, 207
 personal user perceptions 132, 142, 148, 158–159, 162, 166

Index

professional user perceptions 72, 132, 142, 148, 158–159
public authority perceptions 133, 142, 151, 158, 164, 166
satisfaction with right to environmental information 159, 161–162
substantive rationale 5, 61, 137, 140, 146–149, 153–154, 162–163, 166
tokenism 143, 160, 165
wider public interest 150, 163–164
purpose, *see* motives

R
requests for environmental information 2, 9, 13, 16, 28, 35, 38, 49–54, 62, 65, 68–69, 73, 76–77, 80, 84, 93–96, 101–105, 108–111, 114, 117–124, 128, 173–174, 177–180, 184, 188–190, 194–195, 208, 217
advice and assistance, *see* advice and assistance *and* personal users
appeals 53, 101, 177–180, 208
deviation from intended environmental aims, *see* motives, deviation from intended environmental motives
fees 51, 54
impact on public authorities 51, 109, 118, 123
internal reviews 53–54, 101, 208
manifestly unreasonable requests 119–122
refusal to disclose 51–53, 69, 119–124, 194
submission of request 50, 68, 77, 108, 189–190, 208
timescale 51, 54, 65, 73, 195
transfer of request 50
right of access to environmental information 2–12, 57–68, 72, 79–82, 89–91, 94, 97–99, 102–104, 111–114, 121–134, 137, 141–145, 151, 155–157, 163, 166, 196, 207, 209, 210, 216, 219–221; *see also* Aarhus Convention
awareness of 9–14, 67, 104, 134–137, 196, 207–209, 221; *see also* freedom of information, distinguishing from access to environmental information
connection to public participation, *see* Aarhus Convention, participative aims
disengagement 133, 145
domestic implementation, *see* Environmental Information (Scotland) Regulations 2004 (EI(S)R)
environmental aims 2, 6–8, 39–40, 43, 57–58, 97–99, 127, 210, 216–219
history 5, 124, 133, 207
treatment of intermediaries 61–68, 72, 79, 82, 89–91

Rio Declaration 5, 23, 32–37, 40–44, 58, 89, 97, 124, 131–132, 207
assumptions 32, 58, 89, 132
Principle 10 5, 32–35, 131, 207

S
Scottish Information Commissioner 54, 75, 176–178, 180, 183, 213–214
Office of the Scottish Information Commissioner 176–178, 213
Stockholm Declaration 5, 23, 32–33
students 78, 81
sustainable development 6, 34, 153

T
technology 11–13, 40, 62, 107–108, 116–117, 155, 159, 170, 186–191, 209, 214–215
accessibility 187, 209, 215
collection and storage of information 27, 62, 107, 186, 214
e-mail 62, 76, 110, 187–188
impact 187, 209, 214–215
social media 155, 159
WhatDoTheyKnow, *see* WhatDoTheyKnow
transparency and accountability 1–2, 5, 8–9, 65, 121, 136, 149, 155, 209, 215
trust 53, 94, 97, 100–102, 110–114, 121–123, 164, 217

U
uses of environmental information 61–67, 72–86, 97–100, 124, 129, 140–142, 147–148, 152–159, 188
challenging decisions made by public authority 72, 79, 82, 97–98, 147–148, 158
commercial 67, 72–74, 156
disconnect from environmental aims 61, 67, 74–75, 78, 82–83, 100, 129, 152–157
dissemination to the public 63, 66, 78, 82, 188
engaging with public authority 72, 124, 153
environmental aims 67, 74, 82–83, 97–98, 152–155
litigation 83
not used 154
personal purposes 97–100, 154
professional purposes 65–67, 72, 78, 86
wider engagement 155, 159
users, *see* personal users *and* professional users

W
Whanganui River 31, 202
WhatDoTheyKnow 109, 116–117, 188–191, 209, 214
Whittaker 6, 9, 11, 32, 37–40, 43, 48–51, 105, 194

ABOUT THE AUTHORS

Sean Whittaker is Lecturer in Law at the University of Dundee, having been appointed to this post in 2020. Specialising in public law, information law and comparative law, his doctoral work focused on the right of access to environmental information and its implementation in various jurisdictions.

Colin T. Reid is Professor of Environmental Law at the University of Dundee where he has worked since 1991. He has taught and written on various environmental law and public law themes, notably biodiversity law and the implications for environmental law of the UK's withdrawal from the European Union, especially in the context of devolution. He is a founding member and Patron of the UK Environmental Law Association and founded the Environmental Law section of the Society of Legal Scholars.

Jonathan Mendel is Senior Lecturer in Human Geography at the University of Dundee. He has researched and taught on topics related to policy, networks and technology, notably around: access to environmental information; data, information and surveillance policy and technology and anti-trafficking.

Printed in the USA
CPSIA information can be obtained
at www.ICGtesting.com
LVHW011206281223
767285LV00011B/80